THE
DELMORE BROTHERS
TRUTH IS STRANGER THAN PUBLICITY

THE DELMORE BROTHERS
TRUTH IS STRANGER
THAN PUBLICITY

BY ALTON DELMORE

Edited, with introduction and discography, by Charles K. Wolfe

Country Music Foundation Press

Nashville, Tennessee

Distributed by University of Illinois Press

Country Music Foundation Press

222 Rep. John Lewis Way S.

Nashville, Tennessee 37203

First edition published in 1977 as

Truth Is Stranger than Publicity: Alton Delmore's Autobiography

Library of Congress Control Number: 2023941458

ISBN 978-0-915608-42-3

CONTENTS

Introduction vii

One: Boyhood Days 1

Two: Adolescent Days.. 11

Three: High School Days 24

Four: The Cafe, the Printing Office 29

Five: The Brown's Ferry Country 34

Six: The Old Fiddlers' Conventions 41

Seven: Our First Record.. 51

Eight: We Audition for the Grand Ole Opry 69

Nine: Trials and Tribulations... 81

Ten: The Way the Opry Was in the Early Thirties 94

Eleven: Personal Appearances—Uncle Dave Macon, Sam & Kirk McGee........ 103

Twelve: Personalities at WSM 118

Thirteen: The Places We Lived in Nashville............................. 131

Fourteen: Behind the Scenes—No. 1 143

Fifteen: We Meet the Jimmie Rodgers Kinfolks in Meridian;
The Trip to New Orleans—Making Records, A Hard Task 152

Sixteen: Behind the Scenes—No. 2 172

Seventeen: Joe Frank, Pee Wee King, Trouble Stalks 182

Eighteen: Roy Acuff Comes to Nashville 194

Nineteen: Leaving the Opry 208

Twenty: On Tour in North Carolina 219

Twenty-One: The Greenville Days 232

Twenty-Two: Roaming 236

Twenty-Three: Washington Days 246

Twenty-Four: Back to Birmingham 260

Twenty-Five: Our Days at WLW 272

Editor's Postscript: The Delmores' Last Years, 1945–1964 285

Discography 297

Index 321

INTRODUCTION

The 1980s and 1990s have seen a virtual explosion of books by and about country music figures: autobiographies, memoirs, biographies, journalistic portraits, as-told-to accounts, collections of interviews, and even works of fiction. While some of these are superficial or self-serving accounts intended for fan consumption, many can qualify as serious source documents—first-person accounts that offer real insight into the workings of country music as a commercial art form. Future historians will not lack for material when they seek to understand the development of post–World War II country music culture. This is not the case, unfortunately, for earlier country music. Unlike motion pictures, pop music, jazz, or even blues, very few of the defining figures of this art form have left us any substantial first-hand accounts. We have no interviews, much less autobiographies, of figures like Fiddlin' John Carson, Jimmie Rodgers, A. P. Carter, Uncle Dave Macon, Charlie Poole, Vernon Dalhart. We have few detailed accounts of the music's first two decades, that all-important era when it suddenly and mysteriously transformed itself from a rural folk music into an urban commercial music. This is one of the reasons why the discovery and original publication of *Truth Is Stranger Than Publicity: The Autobiography of Alton Delmore* (as it was then titled) in 1977 was a major event. It is an immensely rich and readable book, and it gives us our most authentic and detailed look yet at the formative years of country music. It is a Rosetta Stone of sorts, an account which links the modern world of country music in the 1950s with the dim, shadowy world of the 1920s and 1930s. And best of all, it is an account by someone who was there, and who was a key player in the dramatic events he describes.

INTRODUCTION

Truth Is Stranger Than Publicity stands as the final contribution to country music by one of its most creative artists, Alton Delmore. For many years Alton was known to fans and historians as one half of the Delmore Brothers, and as the composer of hundreds of songs, including classics like "Brown's Ferry Blues," "Gonna Lay Down My Old Guitar," and "Blues Stay Away from Me." In the 1930s, the Delmores won national fame over WSM's Grand Ole Opry, setting new standards for close-harmony singing and intricate gui tar work. It was an age which was dominated by close-harmony duet singing, and by acts like the Monroe Brothers, the Callahan Brothers, the Blue Sky Boys (the Bolick Brothers), and the Shelton Brothers. But the Delmores were far more than just another duet act. They were one of the first of these groups, and they retained their popularity longer than any of the others. They sang highly original songs and performed them in such a unique style that they influenced generations of later country and bluegrass stars. Grandpa Jones, the Louvin Brothers, Merle Travis, Johnny Bond, Doc Watson, Jim & Jesse, Ricky Skaggs, Tony Rice, and Bob Dylan are only a few of the artists who have admitted their debts to the Delmores, and who have kept alive their music. Historians now see the Delmores as a vital transitional act in country music, one linking the blues, ragtime, parlor songs, and shape note gospel singing of the rural nineteenth-century South with the polished, complex, media-oriented styles of more modern times.

As a result, they became one of the first true country acts of the 1930s to appeal to a wider audience and enjoyed some of the first crossover hits with pieces like "Beautiful Brown Eyes'.' and "There's More Pretty Girls Than One." In the 1940s, when the older close-harmony acts were fading fast, the Delmores discov ered rhythm & blues, country boogie, and Black gospel quartet styles, and used them to revitalize their music. The result was a second career and a series of brilliant records for the influential King Record Company.

INTRODUCTION

Though much of the Delmores' success came from their own innate skill and drive, part of it also came from their being in the right place at the right time. Whitney Balliett has written of how the development of the hand-held microphone helped change the style of American pop singers, how it helped singers move away from the loud piercing style of the acoustic era to the subtle phrasings of a Mel Tormé or Ella Fitzgerald. An argument could be offered for the development of radio having a similar effect on country music styles. In the 1920s it was necessary for the Carter Family or Riley Puckett to generate enough volume to be heard under primitive staging conditions; but by 1930 radio had made it possible to sing softly and still be heard, and by the mid-1930s sound systems had developed to the point where in-person concerts could accomplish the same end. The first generation of country music stars—Jimmie Rodgers, the Carters, the Skillet Lickers—could not depend on radio to establish their reputations; in many cases their artistic style was simply not suited to the new radio medium. But the second generation of country performers sensed the absolute need to fit their art to the medium, and the Delmores were wonderful at this. Their carefully crafted harmonies were appreciated, their strikingly effective lyrics understood.

Both Delmore brothers were born in Elkmont, in north Alabama: Alton on Christmas Day 1908, Rabon on December 3, 1916. Their parents were tenant farmers who struggled to eke out a living on the rocky red clay of north Alabama, and much of their lives the brothers saw little but hard times. Musical talent ran in the family; the boys' mother and uncle were skilled gospel singers who could read and write music. Uncle Will was a well-known gospel music teacher who had composed and published several sacred songs.

The gospel tradition was very much a part of Alton Delmore's life and values, and it remained so throughout the years. As late as the 1940s, when the Delmores were well established as major country songwriters and performers, Alton continued

INTRODUCTION

to publish gospel songs in the small paperback shape note songbooks issued by companies like that of R. E. Winsett in Dayton, Tennessee. While the Delmores were enjoying nationwide hits on the King label in the late 1940s, they insisted on recording gospel songs under the pseudonym the Brown's Ferry Four for the same label. The convictions and values of Southern Protestantism represented in gospel music are present at every turn in Alton's autobiography.

By the time Rabon was barely ten years old, in 1926, the brothers were playing together and singing the close, soft harmony they later became famous for. Their struggle to gain entry into professional country music is well documented in the early chapters of Alton's book: how they began by winning local fiddling contests, their first recordings for Columbia, their early years on the Grand Ole Opry, their attempts to set up tours. What makes their struggle especially interesting to music historians is the brothers' determination to become fully professional musicians. Country music was hardly a profession in 1930. Most of the first generation of country music pioneers had seen music as, at best, a part-time vocation; most of the recording artists in the 1920s made their music as a hobby. There was little money to be made from radio (the Delmores started out playing on WSM for $5 a week) and even less in records (royalties usually ran from 1/2¢ to 1¢ per record). Full-time professionals were necessary to improve the quality of the music, and to make it develop, but support for professionalism in 1930 was token at best. To complicate matters, the movement toward professionalism came at the time of the country's worst economic depression in history; even those rural Southerners who were willing to pay for the entertainment found that by 1930 they could hardly afford to do so. Exactly how country music overcame these obstacles and professionalized itself in the early 1930s has always been a rather murky chapter in the music's history. We can thus be very grateful that Alton spends well over half his memoir detailing these important years.

INTRODUCTION

Alton's book is historically important from another aspect. It contains a wealth of information, anecdote, and insight into important early musicians like Uncle Dave Macon, Arthur Smith, Goebel Reeves, Jimmie Rodgers, John Carson, the Allen Brothers, and Roy Acuff. These legendary figures come alive through Alton's fine narrative style and unusual recall of detail. The chapter on Uncle Dave Macon, one of the seminal figures in folk and country music, is as insightful as anything in print about him.

Scattered throughout the book, too, are brief portraits of non country entertainers, including the roster of stars then at WSM, which included Dinah Shore, Snooky Lanson, Francis Craig, and Fred Rose. The hectic and at times unethical world of professional music in the thirties comes alive through Alton's descriptions of dealings with various managers, promoters, and agents. Inevitably, perhaps, these descriptions often cast the musicians as the Good Guys, the businessmen as the Villains. If some bitterness can be detected, one might remember that as Alton was writing the book he was working at a variety of part-time jobs, from delivering papers to teaching guitar, to keep his head above water.

But aside from its value as history, Alton's book is a moving human document as well, interesting in its own right even to those not interested in or knowledgeable about country music. When the Delmores first began making a career in music they were, in Alton's own words, "divinely innocent." Their story chronicles the brothers' growth as men as well as their development as musicians, and Alton is remarkably candid and frank about their mistakes and shortcomings. A great deal of the book deals with personal problems and personal relationships, sometimes at the expense of topics that a fan or historian might be more curious about. For example, we now know from independent research that during their stay on the Opry, the Delmores were far more popular than Alton suggests. In 1936 they were the single most popular act on the show, they were featured in WSM's press releases, and they were selling more records than any other star on the Opry. Nor do we have specific comments about how the brothers wrote songs, about their many recording sessions, about which records sold best, about why they selected certain songs to record. We now know, too, that Alton's gospel music background was more complex than he suggests here; he wrote numerous songs for the Athens Music Company, the gospel publisher located in his hometown, and his mother Mollie wrote a number of songs independent of Alton. We do not learn much about the very rich gospel music scene around Athens, one that produced the Speer Family, Statesmen singer Jake Hess, pianist Dwight Brock, and dozens of other figures—figures Alton must have known and worked with.

On the other hand, Alton seemed very much aware of other aspects of the north Alabama folk culture that nourished them and their music, and he describes both the bright and tarnished facets of that culture. Descriptions of folk customs and beliefs fill the early part of the book, but the sense of harsh, grinding poverty is also there. Alton also confronts the odd prejudice against country music held by many middle-class Southerners; there are too many "Southern aristocrats" in the region, he notes. Some Southerners eagerly embraced mainstream pop culture imported from New York or Hollywood, but dismissed native talent as "hillbilly."

Alton would have smiled with understanding at the song "I Was Country When Country Wasn't Cool." This cultural attitude, coupled with the class consciousness both Delmores felt, had a great deal to do with their ambition to succeed, to earn respect for themselves and their music.

What possessed Alton Delmore to do what so very few of his fellow musicians did, to write a full-scale autobiography, and further more to write it without any ghostwriter, and apparently without any encouragement from a publisher? Probably the same kind of creative urge that led him to compose hundreds of songs under

INTRODUCTION

four different names. Alton was basically a writer whose energies had been channeled into the very limited literary form of the country song, and Alton himself felt frustrated by his role. He writes at one point: "I had always wanted to write novels and short stories but I didn't get much encouragement from the folks at home. Sometimes people just don't understand a fellow when he is trying to be something; they think he is away off in the stars. I would steal away to some room in the house and write for hours, and about time I really got started writing some of my brothers or my dad would come around to warn me I was off my rocker. . . . You never lose the urge to write once you have the yen for it. But my songwriting helped me to stand the push you get for being creative. The songs satisfy partially, but not wholly, my desire to do something lastingly worthwhile." At another point, Alton reports that fellow country star Ernest Tubb said "he would never die happy unless he could write a story and have it published. . . ." For years before his retirement from music Alton had been writing short stories and sending them to markets like the *Saturday Evening Post* and *Colliers*. As far as we know, none were ever published, though he wrote dozens. Manuscripts for a few of these stories survived in Alton's papers, and they show him to be a competent local-color writer with a good eye for detail and dialogue. Curiously, few of these stories dealt with music or musicians.

We don't know exactly when Alton decided to forego short stories and start the major writing project represented by his autobiography, nor do we know his precise motive. Internal evidence in the manuscript suggests that the work was started between 1958 and 1960, and that the last finished portions were written in 1963, barely a year before Alton's death. At the time he was writing the manuscript, Alton was living in Huntsville; he mentioned the project to several of his friends there, including writer Bill Harrison. "I didn't think he was all that serious," Harrison later recalled. Nor did any of his friends take seriously Alton's ability as a writer of prose. Alton died without completing the manuscript, and apparently

INTRODUCTION

without any real prospects of publication. The story of the manuscript's history since then sounds like something out of the history of the famous Boswell papers. The first public mention of the work was by Bill Harrison in his liner notes to County Records' reissue of some of the early Delmore records; Harrison, however, had never seen the manuscript and was reporting only what Alton had told him. In 1974 I began to do research on the Delmore Brothers' career for another reissue album and used as my starting point Bill Harrison's notes. By this time Alton's son Lionel was living near Nashville and embarking on his own successful career as a songwriter. In an interview with Lionel, I mentioned the autobiography manuscript, and after some rummaging around we found it in one of his father's filing cabinets. Lionel agreed to loan me the manuscript to use for my liner notes, but after reading it over I felt the entire work deserved publication. Not only was it historically important, but it was rather well-written; it had a remarkable oral quality about it, a delightful honesty and informality.

Large segments of the manuscript were missing, however. In the following weeks Lionel turned up two long sections and later found that an aunt in Missouri had taken a third section for typing; soon this too was recovered. Revisions of several chapters were found. Apparently Alton had turned over part of the manuscript to a newspaper writer he knew, but efforts to locate this writer and what sections he might have had have been futile. It is quite possible, therefore, that Alton in fact completed his story beyond the 1945 point at which it ends here; someday, perhaps, more chapters will be found. (It is doubly frustrating that the manuscript cuts off just before the Delmores' success on King Records; the story of their "second career" would have been perhaps the most historically significant in the book.) As for now, though, the manuscript ends about two-thirds of the way through Alton?s outline. I have attempted to sketch the outline of the last decade of the Delmores' career in a final chapter.

INTRODUCTION

The original edition of this book was published in the summer of 1977 by the fledgling Country Music Foundation Press in Nashville. I recall the day Lionel first showed me the manuscript, and that I literally stayed up all that night reading it with absolute fascination. The next day I took it into Doug Green at the Country Music Foundation offices. Though now known to millions as "Ranger Doug" in Riders in the Sky, Doug in 1977 was the oral historian at the CMF, the editor of its *Journal*, and the director of its press. (In his spare time he also played music and wrote his own books.) Doug looked over the Delmore manuscript and immediately understood my enthusiasm. "We have to publish this," he said, and at once set about seeking funding. What resulted was a handsome paperback edition, but both Doug and I were disappointed at the response; there were too few reviews, and too little attention. We had thought of the book as a major historical find, but not many others shared our enthusiasm. Fans of old-time music certainly found the book, and distributors like Dave Freeman's County Sales continued to promote and sell it; in the two decades since then, I have had dozens of old-time and bluegrass musicians tell me how much the book meant to them.

But too many fans of American music never got the word about the book. On the other hand, the music and songs of the Delmore tradition have continued to grow in the years since this book first came out. There was a well-publicized drive to get the brothers into the Hall of Fame; renewed recognition of their work by their native state and by scholars around the country; the reissue of almost all their old 78s; the success of Lionel's own songwriting career with hits like "Swingin'. The time seems right, therefore, to bring Alton's book back before the public.

A final note is in order regarding the editing of the manuscript. In the original edition, Doug Green and I simply photocopied Alton's manuscript and let it stand pretty much as it was. There were obvious typos, which we corrected, and some

INTRODUCTION

names that were spelled oddly, but our general principle was to let Alton speak for himself. Where Alton mentioned a person or incident that might puzzle a modern reader, I simply added an explanatory footnote at the bottom of the page. In a few cases, there were two versions of a passage, and in those cases I tried to determine which version Alton wrote last. For this revised edition, we have made additional copy edits—nearly all having to do with basic punctuation and spelling—to enhance readability without compromising Alton Delmore's prose. As with the first edition, the absolute editorial priority has been to preserve the voice, language, and integrity of the original manuscript.

Certainly Alton was telling his history from his own perspective, but where we have been able to check his dates and places, his memory has proved to be remarkably accurate. In sum, everything about the book seems to confirm its title: truth is here, and it is stranger than publicity.

Acknowledgments:

A prime debt here to Lionel Delmore, who for years kept his father's manuscript intact and provided most of the information about the manuscript's history and for the material in the final chapter. Bill Harrison generously made available his notes about Alton and Rabon, and shared his memories of Alton with us. A special thanks to Bill is due for first calling the attention of historians to the existence of the manuscript. Frank Driggs of RCA Victor made available the original Delmore session sheets for their 1930s recordings, and Bob Pinson and Tony Russell assisted in the compilation-of the discography. Special thanks to Doug Green, formerly of the Country Music Foundation Press, for encouraging the project from the very first day I described the manuscript to him. The officers of the Faculty Research Committee at Middle Tennessee State University, as well as the officers of

INTRODUCTION

the National Endowment for the Arts in Washington, made possible the editing and publication of the original, 1977 edition of the book. Finally, thanks to the editorial and design staff of the Country Music Foundation Press for their efforts in producing this handsome new edition.

Charles K. Wolfe
Middle Tennessee State University
Murfreesboro, Tennessee
April 1995

CHAPTER ONE

BOYHOOD DAYS

The very first thing I remember is that we were a big family and my father worked hard. That is, when he could get any work to do. He was not a ditch digger, but a skilled worker. And the only thing a skilled worker could get to do around Elkmont, Alabama, in the early 1900s was running a cotton gin. My father had been a foreman with construction companies around Birmingham and other big cities before he came to Elkmont.

I remember my mother telling how my dad came into Elkmont on a freight train. He took a job as a farm hand with her uncle and that is how she met him. They were married about two years after they got acquainted. Their first two children died before they were very old. So one can see that my parents had a very tragic beginning. There were three older boys and three younger boys and two sisters in between. Rabon and I were of the younger three boys. I was the oldest of the younger set and consequently sort of a lone wolf. I tried to tag along after my two older brothers Ed and Leonard when they went exploring into the woods, and learned by watching them ply their various arts of woodcraft, trapping, and fishing.

We were farmers. Sharecroppers. That means the landlord gets 50 percent of what corn, cotton, sorghum and any other things the tenant makes.

It seemed we never got a good place and we moved nearly every fall or winter. Seldom did we ever stay in one house more than a year. I don't believe I have ever seen so many rocks on top of the ground. We lived out in the country west of

BOYHOOD DAYS

Elkmont and cotton was the biggest crop. Plowing the cotton was a bad job, but when the hoeing began you had it. The little cotton plants would fall down if you moved the rocks, and you had to move the rocks to cut the crab grass. So there you were with a "heads I win, tails you lose" deal.

My brother Max was a fiddle player. He learned to be the first musician in the family and people would come to our house to hear him play. That is why I took an interest. They would brag on him and he would swell up with pride and play some more.

I had an aunt who could beat the strings on a fiddle, and after I saw her doing it, I learned the trick myself and then I was in the act. I guess some of you never heard of beating the strings, so I will explain how it is done. You take two little switches, each about a foot long, strip the bark off, and let them dry. Then you have the "beaters" or some say "fiddlesticks." A fiddle has to be tuned in the old "A" position or you can't beat the strings. It will be a discord or out of key. The old "A" tuning is EAEA, each letter correspondingly an octave apart. That was my first effort in music. Sometimes when Max was in a good mood he would let me saw on the fiddle. I learned to strike a few tunes out but never learned too well.

Back in those days we used to visit our kinfolks in Elkmont frequently. My mother's family, they were. She had several uncles and aunts there and lots of cousins. I always loved to visit them because they all treated us good and I could see the trains go by. Merritt Compton, our cousin, lived right by the L&N Railway, a line that stretched north and south. A train had the most awesome force about it I had ever experienced. It would come chugging down the tracks like a gigantic dragon, belching out smoke and steam and keeping a steady, rhythmic roar that was fascinating to a small boy like me.

BOYHOOD DAYS

That all happened before Rabon was big enough to be noticed; he was the baby of the family and so he had the status of that situation.

Those people, my kinfolks, had their stories, legends, and superstitions that were handed down, partially from fact and partially from fabrication. There were some tall tales and some of them could muster up a super thrill. Tales of the graveyard down below Aunt Lillie's were rife and accepted. One of the family had met a woman late in the night and she was dressed in ballroom attire, everything in perfect order, except she didn't have a head—hence the headless woman. It seemed the wind always had a peculiar moan, and the moon was always a half hidden accomplice to the shadows that stalked the trails of the late wanderer. And the low lying hills always added a somber, sinister atmosphere to the tales of the people.

Of course, every people have their own legends and stories, and you will find that all through this book, because they seem to give stimulus and stamina to a fellow like me, who is honestly trying to put down his history in writing.

My daddy would get up very early in the morning and walk about four miles to the gin where he ginned cotton all day and into the night. He walked, going and coming on the lonely roads that were said to be haunted, and he never saw or heard many things that he couldn't explain. One time, he told us, he thought he surely saw a genuine ghost. He had to pass the cemetery on his way home and that particular day a person had been buried. It was well after dark and the solemn wind whipped at the underbrush and sang a lonesome wail in the trees as he went by the graveyard. There was a fence around the cemetery, and it bounded the road. Suddenly, he saw a drifting, shifting, wraith-like movement rolling toward him on the ground. He was startled and he thought this, now, was the real thing. He wanted to run, he told us, but he waited, just to see what would happen when he met a real ghost. As he waited, scared stiff, he finally saw what the monster was. The undertakers had left some of the paper they had used in the boxes. It had rolled up, and, with the wind, had drifted and tumbled over to the fence and stopped there, flapping in the darkness. My dad said he began humming an old church song and thought no more about it as he headed for home and mother and us kids.

It seemed I never could get enough to eat in those embryo days. Kind of like a young cicada or some other kind of insect when it is first introduced to the world.

I recall that Easter Sunday we always ate eggs and lots of them. Mother would buy them and boil them and scramble them and it really was a big feast for all of us. That was one time of the year that I really got filled up on eggs and had the exhilaration of contented fullness. I will never forget those Easter Sundays, for the eggs really had the leading place in the Delmore domicile.

We lived in and around Elk River and never so far away from it that we couldn't prowl up and down its banks, exploring and hunting and fishing. My two brothers Leonard and Ed were the main ones in this sort of adventure, and my problem was to keep thinking up ways to persuade my mother to let me accompany them when they started out with the dogs and guns and traps and other hunting and fishing paraphernalia. Lots of times my methods of persuasion were not convincing enough for mother and she wouldn't let me go with them. When that happened, it was really a jolt. I can still see them tramping off through the woods, the dogs whining and barking with joy, and me, left behind, a forlorn and helpless pilgrim of sorrow.

But my mother was so right, as you will agree, after reading the following incident:

One hot and dry afternoon in summer, Ed carried me down to the river with him. He had learned the trick of catching the mammoth-sized catfish as they lurked under the rocks at the bottom of the river, near the banks. He picked this knowledge up from watching old experienced rivermen come out with captured prizes, the fish flapping and whipping them till they were black and blue. But the fisherman always held on, in spite of the beating he took, and the big catfish always lost the battle. I have known some of these fish to weigh well over a hundred pounds. The lucky man, after getting a prize like this, would immediately head for Athens and proudly exhibit his reward to the complimentary crowd that gathered around him. That is the way of all fishermen: to catch the big one. Ed was no different.

On this particular afternoon Ed waded and swam, exploring across the river, leaving me behind on the bank. I was only about six years old and couldn't swim.

Suddenly he called out to me to bring the rope across to him so he could tie the fish and hold it when it started trying to get away. There was a lot of excitement in his voice so I grabbed the rope up and started wading across the river. It was dry weather and the river was low but there were sink holes along its banks and also in the middle. So there I was, a crazy kid, who couldn't swim, taking a chance on my life for a catfish!

My brother, in his excitement, forgot about the whirlpools and sink holes. I made it across to him alright. But just as I got dose enough to hand the rope, the big fish took off, nearly knocking Ed and myself both down as he darted away swiftly. As we waded back across I stumbled into water over my head several times but Ed caught me and helped me out each time. If it had happened going across, I would have drowned before he could have reached me. So after all, mother knew best.

But that incident didn't dampen my ardor one whit when it came to loving the river and the creeks, and it didn't even begin to affect my exultation on finding a wild animal track in the mud of a creek or on the river bank. I still feel that way. I guess it is something in my heritage that harkens back to my early ancestors.

But then I guess a lot of folks feel that way because so many people like to hunt and fish.

We used to cut our names on beech trees; others had done the same thing before because some of the names were nearly a hundred years old. There was one tall spreading beech that had limbs on it growing straight out from its body; there were quite a few of them, and there was a legend that a horse thief had stolen some animals and pulled them up into the old tree and that's how he never was discovered. The tree could very easily have been converted into a floor space to hold the horses. But then, as I said, this is legend.

But those were the days of prime enjoyment, close to nature, seeing it up close like we're supposed to, I think, and then reaping the rewards of the true nature of man to God.

Looking back on those days everything seemed bigger than it does today. The old schoolhouse I used to attend seems like a midget now to what it was back in those days. And the storms and the rain seemed more awesome and took on an austere meaning that impressed me so very much that I have never quite forgotten them to this very day. But I am proud of the memory that I have of such things. It seems to freshen up my spirit when I am down in the dumps sometime. Because they are the memories always fraught with the fond expectancy of life. Yes, LIFE in the fullest.

The first school I ever attended was called Dog Trot, and that is the only name I ever knew it to be called, although some said the real name of the school was Morning Star. It was a one-room school, and all my brothers went to it except Max, who was the oldest one of us. Our parents decided he was too old to go to school, so he worked and stayed home. Leonard and Ed were in the sixth grade when I started in the first grade. I could already read but couldn't write to do any good, so I didn't worry about that. I could name all the presidents from memory (something I can't do now), and I also could name all the capitals of the states.

I was about eight years old then, as I remember. I could also spell very well. The reason I was adept in these things was because I liked to study and I still do.

BOYHOOD DAYS

As I said, the school was one room, and when the teacher had a class you could listen to the various ones in the class and tell how much they knew. I would take part in most of the classes. Even if it wasn't my class I would still raise my hand if I knew the answer to a hard question the other members of the class didn't know.

But I always made sure none of the others knew before I would raise my hand. The teacher would then let me answer the question and make the ones in the higher classes look sheepish. There was one time that she asked the question which flower opium comes from. I happened to know that and I got to answer it because it had stopped the eighth grade cold and there I was only in the first. These little things are the things that seem to linger in my mind the same as your memories linger in yours. I especially remember one time there was a spelling match and it was on Friday. There was always a spelling match on Friday, and I guess I had taken part in them before, but this one time the champion speller was turned down on a word and the whole room tried to spell the word but none of them could get it right. I was near the end of the line and I sure was hoping nobody would get it right before it got to me. The word was "haul," and you can imagine how some of these students tried to spell it. When it got to me, I spelled it right and moved up to the head of the class and was considered the champion of the whole school. I felt sorry for the girl champion. As I passed her she looked like she was about to cry. But she already had a reputation as a good speller and I had mine to make. So I didn't grieve too much.

We never owned any land and there was a big family of us and we had to work like dogs. When I was just a little fellow about five or six years old I took my place in the field, hoeing and picking the cotton, which was the money crop. Not long ago I made a trip through the country where we lived, or rather existed, and inspected the land we once worked. The land is hilly and rocky near Elkmont and the Elk River country, and I can't see how any one can make a living on it. We just barely existed. But, looking back on those days, they were happy days and most of the time we were healthy enough and everyone doesn't get the silver spoon. So what I'm trying to do is to tell the untarnished truth about how we lived because in this day and time of plenty, I know it will sound incredible to many.

But there was one exception to the health of our family I vividly recall. My brother Ed took down with the typhoid fever. Now back in those days, typhoid fever was a very serious illness. He got bad and went from bad to worse. The doctor we had was a coun try doctor. We would shell corn and Papa would pay him that way because we had no. money. One day he came and said Ed would have to have some special medicine if he were to stand a chance against the insidious disease. My dad asked the doctor about the cost of the medicine and the doctor told him and then left. I could see that papa was extremely worried because he waited a long time after the doctor left before he said anything. He called Leonard and me out to the woodpile and asked us if we would go into town and try to get the prescription. He had no money and was afraid to leave Ed that long.

So Leonard and I started out walking in the dust of the dirt road. When we came to the place called the crossroads, Leonard went up and asked our landlord for the money to get the medicine. It was a case of life and death. My daddy had worked for this man for many years and helped him out innumerable times, but this man had forgotten all about the past. He refused pointly and minced no words. With our heads hung low we started back home without the medicine that would save Ed's life. We hadn't got very far down the road till we heard a voice calling to us. It was the landlord's youngest son. "I just heard what Dad told you," he said. "Now here is the money for that prescription and you hurry on down town and get it for that boy—" he reached in his pocket and gave my brother more than enough for the medicine; "—and listen, you might want yourself a Coke if I gave you a little over. It's really hot today." He turned and left us and we headed for Elkmont as fast as our feet would carry us. Ed had a pretty hard pull, but he finally made it thanks to the graciousness of a parsimonious landlord's son.

I had to travel up and down those lonely roads a lot, and the biggest fear I ever had was mad dogs and storms. People didn't have to give their dogs shots like they do now, and there was quite a few mad dogs every summer and sometimes in the winter. One time I had been on an errand for my mother, and it got dark before I could get back home. I was scared half to death, because there had been reports of a mad dog out and it was strongly on my mind. I turned a little bend in the road and couldn't see back of me so good, and then I heard it—the heavy panting of a dog. It was horrible. I jumped over the fence and tried to hide in the weeds, and then I saw it and heard it too. I was immensely relieved to see a neighbor on a mule that could pace—hence the sound I mistook for the panting of a dog. It was the mule's feet on the hard ground and it was a perfect imitation.

My mother was always afraid of the summer storms. There had been several people killed in tornadoes, and we were in the path of the storms that visited each and every spring and summer:

There was one family of eight people and a storm came one night and killed seven of them. The only reason it did not kill the other one—he went to stay all night with a friend and therefore escaped the tornado. It is a strange thing about tornadoes that they don't blow so hard in some places while only half a mile away they are tearing and killing. I talked to a fellow who lived close to this family (incidentally their name was Collins), and he told me it was a bad stormy night and he had to hold the door with his shoulder to keep it closed. But he didn't know it was near as bad till the next morning when he looked over to the Collins house

9

and rubbed his eyes and looked again. Sure enough the house was gone, blown away by the night's storm. They buried the whole family in one big grave through respect to them.

So you can see why we were so very afraid of the twisters. I have had a lot of experience with them, and I will also include more about the cyclones in a later page.

CHAPTER TWO

ADOLESCENT DAYS

We had been nearly starving in that part of the country. I have written how the ground was poor and we never came out on top with any money left. It had really been rough for all of us.

So my dad came in one night from Athens and told us he had made a trade with a man to move away and leave the rocks and the poor cotton. The place he had traded for was down in the southern part of the county and afforded much better land and everything else that goes with it. We were all so happy about this that we couldn't wait till the wagons arrived to pull us away.

Finally the day came when we started out for Ripley, as they called it then. It was a long hard trip and we were all worn out when we got to Athens. We had to go through Athens to get to Ripley. I remember we stopped there for a while and someone said an airplane had landed. When my brothers heard this they headed for the plane because they had never seen one before on the ground. So we had to wait for them and I felt so strange. I was totally in a new world. I didn't understand very much about anything. All the buildings seemed to frighten me inside, but I held it to myself because I didn't want the rest of them to know I felt curious.

After a while the boys all came back and we headed down the Brown's Ferry Road to get to the place we would call home.

Back in those days there was no pavement in the country, or at least there was none in our part of the country. The old wagons were rough riding and the road full of ruts and sudden jolts. We had a little old pig that rode in the wagon with me; every time the wagon would hit a rut or deep hole it would shake and jar that barrel where the pig was, and it would squeal like it had just about decided to die. I felt sorry for the little old fellow, but there was nothing I could do to help him. The trip made him sick and he only lived a few days after we got home.

We turned off the Brown's Ferry Road and headed down the Mooresville Road to the dirt road to get to the plantation where we were headed. It was even worse—through swamp country and very boggy. The water oozed from the lowlands partly out onto the road and it was very easy to get stuck or mired down in the soft earth of the dirt road. But, just as a small boy will, I kept looking forward to the end of the arduous trip for the reward I expected at the new home and its environment.

The man who owned the plantation (for that was what it was) was a college trained man. He cried to put the college into the farming and everything that he did, even fixing a fence. I didn't know much the difference myself, but I could hear the old-timers talking about it and they would actually laugh to his face about some of the things he did but that didn't faze him; he just kept right on going. He had been a military man, and he walked straight and erect every step and had the military air about him. He was really a very intelligent man but a little out of place in the capacity of a dirt farmer. I always liked him myself, because he was always kidding me about something or other.

My dad got along with the owner of the plantation very well. So did my brother Max. We were not there very long before my brother took charge of all the motorized machinery for farming the man owned. Max was a sort of mechanic and was talented to do those kinds of things. When one of the tractors broke, Max was the man who fixed it up ready to go again. I remember Max was sent somewhere off in another part of the county to return a motor cultivator back to the plantation.

ADOLESCENT DAYS

There was a lot of interest stirred up by that name, motor cultivator. The farmers came from far and near to see the contraption Max was bringing in. I never will forget it was nearly sundown when we saw him coming along the dirt with the awkward-looking machine. All eyes were glued to the strange-looking thing. Everybody had to get up close and touch and inspect it, and then they were satisfied. Their curiosity was pretty well satisfied and the man didn't get to sell a one to anybody. He had told Max somebody would buy it as soon as he brought it in. Those were good days and we were all very happy. We had more to eat and better things and land to work than ever before, but there was a big family and we still didn't commence to get rich. Not that we had any idea of getting rich, but we just couldn't seem to accumulate anything of our own.

We had four and sometimes six horses and mules to plow and could always borrow another or two from the owner if we needed them. I was just eight years old then and I had one big old mule and a young little mule to plow. I turned forty acres of corn ground with them and I couldn't even lift the plow around to turn it at the end of the row corners where you turned around. I devised a method all of my own where I would let the mules pull the plow around and do the work themselves. Those two mules were the only ones who knew the trick. The old mule, he was a good old thing but the young mule, he was just plain mean and ornery, but I got along very well with them. The old fellow would help me tame the younger one when he got real ornery. He would remain so patient and understanding that the young mule would get ashamed and quit his capricious capers. I could talk all day about mules, I've seen so many of them, but that will do for the present.

While living on this plantation I had an experience that I will never forget in all my life. The experience I'm telling about was a ghost light that roamed over the countryside, casting its eerie glow. The first time we saw the thing it had us all puzzled. And still has, for that matter.

ADOLESCENT DAYS

My father was a carpenter and also could paint. So the plantation owner hired him to fix up the house where he intended to move out with his family. The house was a nice, moderately-built country home and was above the average for that part of the country. It was a frame house and didn't need much repair as I could see, but this man was rich and had lots of money and had to persuade his wife to move out here to this godforsaken place with him. Before she would agree, he had to promise her almost a mansion, and then she decided to try it for a while, hence the ultra repair job on the house.

My dad calcimined the walls and fixed the house so nearly perfect that it really did resemble the mansion of the landlord's wife's, dream. Papa was naturally proud of the job and had charge of the house till the landlord and his family moved in. He had the keys in his pocket and nobody was to enter the house with out his permission. Now this is where the ghost light comes in. It was raining that night. There was no thunder or lightning. Just a dreary, slow rain that seemed to cast a spell over the entire countryside. We had just finished supper and it was already dark. There was a window in the kitchen facing the house Dad had repaired. This house was about a quarter of a mile from where we lived and you could see very well the entire premises.

All of us kids were in the living room playing and singing and having a good time in general, and my dad was smoking his pipe and catching up on his reading. Suddenly my mother called from the kitchen and my dad jumped and ran to her: She sounded frightened. We kids were curious, too, so we went in to see what the trouble was. My mother was standing looking through the window and when she saw my father she pointed over to the landlord's house.

"There's someone over there in that house, Charlie," she said, "and that landlord's going to hold you responsible."

My dad looked for a few seconds and then he began to laugh.

ADOLESCENT DAYS

"Why there's nothing I see over there. And if anyone was in there, you couldn't see them from here in the dark." He looked around to us kids. "No children, your poor mother is seeing things."

My mother said: "Charlie, they had a lantern. They blew it out."

So we all went back to the routine we had going before the interruption.

We had just got situated back into the midst of things when mother called out again. This time my dad got up and went back into the kitchen by himself. We heard him and listened to what he said to mother.

"Now, can you beat that? Here, I have the keys to that house in my pocket and someone has broken in. Probably crap shooters getting out of the rain to keep the game going. Well, I don't mind them having their little game of craps but darned if I aim to be their scapegoat. Everybody in this part of the country knows very well what will happen if that house gets messed up by a bunch of doggone crap shooters. They know it too. So guess I'll just have to put a stop to it."

With that he put his pistol in his pocket and started over to the house.

"Don't worry," he said, "I'm just gonna give 'em a little scare and maybe then they won't be so bold next time." He was talking to Mother, who looked apprehensive about the pistol.

Ed and Max and Leonard started to follow him, but he told them to stay there with their mother. And just about that time it happened. Papa stopped in his tracks and looked puzzled more than I had ever seen him before. We could see his face by the light of the lantern he was carrying. We knew something was wrong—bad wrong.

He was looking at a light that had apparently gone through the house like somebody running with a flashlight from room to room. And then the light had come out of the house through a window and stood still as death—changing from a red bright flame to a dull glow—then just a reflection of light without a focus.

15

ADOLESCENT DAYS

We all stared unbelievingly. I was a boy, but I could tell there was something of the unknown abqut what we were seeing. But nobody had said anything about a ghost light to us and we had been living in the community for several months. None of us could believe what we were seeing, but there it was putting on its show in the dreary, rainy night,

But the ghost light was not through yet. As we stood looking, the light gradually drifted around the house to the front gate. It paused momentarily as if someone was lighting a cigarette. Then it began a slow measured trek up the lane toward the barn. This time it took on the appearance of someone carrying a lantern. It seemed to be on the opposite side of the person carrying the lantern for we could see the motions of the arms and legs of the carrier making strides toward the barn. So we stood and watched and waited for what we did not know.

The barn was as modern an affair as the house and it was surrounded by a hogwire fence about ten feet high. A hogwire fence is one that has very small openings in it and is closely wound: as to keep the hogs from tearing out the openings and getting out of the lot. I say this because it will be very significant to what follows about the ghost light. The gate to the barn lot was about ten or fifteen feet high, and it had catches on it so it would fasten itself if pushed pretty hard.

When the light got to the gate it flew around it several times very fast— faster than anyone could possibly run and all this without even opening the gate! By this time we had settled down to watch the grim performance with an interest that penetrated beyond the imagination to a far-off dimension of the supernatural. We were seeing the act all together, and none could say that it was something of the things that make up for the hallucination or any sort of fabrication.

There was no form of a person or anything resembling a human being, but the ghost light behaved like an intelligent being and acted just exactly like it was being directed by someone unknown or unseen.

It gradually slowed down in performance and leisurely stalked around the barn, going up into the loft where we could see the hay and other objects by its pale light. It stayed up and around the barn for at least fifteen minutes and then started down the fence line to the big pond below. It moved furtively, like it was trying to escape being seen, and sometimes its light was just a glow and lit up the underbrush and weeds as it moved slowly toward the water and the pond. It finally came down to the edge of the water and waited like someone watering a horse or cow and then it really pulled something fantastic—it moved out onto the water!

We could see the waves on the pond by its light, and it continued to move across the pond toward us. We watched fascinated by the fact that we were about to catch a real live ghost or whatever it was.

The pond was about halfway between our house and the plantation owner's house, and when it had come pretty close to the ledge on our side, my dad, my brother Ed, and I started down to see if it would stand for close inspection. As we started across the lot toward the pond it stood still and waited. When we crossed the fence and moved in closer, it started retreating down the middle of the pond and to the lower edge, which dwindled down to a swampy lowland and drain for the water. There was no other outlet for the pond, and all the way down almost to the woods' edge the lowland continued. That is the way the ghost light traveled down the swampy lowland trail and into the deep woods below about a mile away that someone had named the Beckom Rough.

So my dad and Ed and I went back toward the house, more puzzled and shocked than ever. The next day my mother made some inquiries from an old Negro woman and was told that it was the spirit of some man who had lived in the house with his brother, and that on certain occasions, especially when the weather was rainy and dreary, he would come back to see about his place. The Negroes would admit that they had seen the light many times, but the white people either wouldn't talk or didn't know anything about it. It seemed the ghost light was a sort of hidden secret with the local people.

After that first night when we had seen so much of the ghost light, we began to sort of expect it on the lonely nights when the weather was dismal.

One night my brother Leonard came home from church with another boy, a neighbor, who lived quite a distance from us, and when they came to the cross-roads where Leonard had to get off (for they rode double on the neighbor boy's mule), he was still about two or three miles from home and had to walk. And it was a long, lonesome walk at night. Leonard and the other boy saw the light rise up and go down back to the ground and repeat the same over and over several times. We learned later that this was a typical characteristic of the light when it first started on its roaming over the countryside. Leonard and the neighbor watched the light for a while and then the boy went his way and my brother started his lonesome walk toward home. He had made it about halfway when he looked back and saw the ghost light about fifty yards behind, following him. He was scared stiff and he began running fast as he could, and the light went out and he started to walk again as he was pretty well out of breath. He got the light off his mind and tried to think of something else, but there was an eerie feeling inside him that he was still being fol lowed. He said he could feel the presence of something but couldn't tell exactly what, when suddenly the ghost light crossed the road in front of him only about fifty yards away. So he slowed down and the mysterious light followed here and there, front and back of him, till he got home. That was the closest any of us ever got to that light and he didn't want it to happen, especially when he was all alone.

ADOLESCENT DAYS

***

My real interest in music began when I heard my Uncle Will Williams and his family singing hymns. He could write songs and sing them too. They were in books and his name was on them and they were very beautiful. He was also a music teacher. He had taught all his children to sing and they could read music, too. I wanted to learn so very bad to read music, too, but my uncle lived too far away from us for me to take lessons from him. So I didn't know what I was going to do about that till my mother told me one day that she would teach me the shaped notes.

She told me she didn't know much about music and couldn't even sing a song until she heard someone else sing the tune, but she still knew the shaped notes and I had to begin somewhere. She taught me how to tell one note from another and that was indeed a big start. After I learned the shaped notes I began to try to figure the time, which is a very vital item in the study and performance of music. So I would try one thing and then some thing else in my efforts to make a conquest of time. If I learned a fellow could read music, I would pester the life out of him till I got his answers. They seemed to be the same with everyone who could read music. They would tell me how they did it, but I would still be lost.

I can understand now how these people who knew music felt when I tried to get them to tell me how they knew time and they couldn't explain it to me. I teach music and guitar in my spare time, and I know why so many people tried to learn music and cannot. It all boils down to the simple fact that the teacher who taught them didn't get it over in the right way. Most teachers of music know it real well themselves and can tell you a lot about music, but they just simply can't get it over to the student.

As a teacher, I don't care if my students think I am nothing but a plain dumbbell. Just so they learn the music themselves. I am not teaching just to tell them how much I know. I am primarily interested in what they will learn and what they will know when they are through with my course.

So I kept digging away at learning the time and how to put it into practice and what all the mysterious little dots and signs meant.

Then we moved again. Over closer to the school. My daddy took my sister and me over to the school the first morning. He had known the principal of the school many years ago and decided to go over with us and sort of break us in and let the man know who we were, etc. Well, when we got there he didn't remember my dad and finally, after several reminders by my dad, he remembered. But I thought I could detect a little aloofness on the principal's part. I know one thing very vividly. That principal was a hellion if there ever was, and he seemed to be arrogant and cantankerous even when there was no cause for it I would tell my dad, and he would just shake his head and say that he guessed the teacher had a lot on his mind.

By the time we moved the last time, though, there was a new principal and she was a woman. She proved to be one of my best teachers. I made a lot of progress under her and finally got to the sixth grade.

There was a man teacher at the school, but he taught the little fellows and introduced us boys to basketball. He brought in a friend of his and this man stayed about a week, coaching and teaching us the fine art of the game. He was really fine at the job and the thing I still remember about him was that he made no concessions to anyone. There were boys whose fathers were the trustees. But this man didn't care who you were just so you could learn to play the game. I learned the game pretty fast. There was a trustee's boy who learned to be good as I was too, and he got to play in all the games. That was after the man left. Had he stayed, I know I would have got to play a lot more. All of us boys on the team were real light and we lost every game we played for the first part of the season. Then one day we were going to play a real tough opponent who had beaten us two or three times before, and we were traveling in a wagon. That was the only way we had to go in those days. We had to

ADOLESCENT DAYS

go by the house of the boy who was playing in all the games and he had to stop and see his mother about something or other, and that is when I got my break to play. While he was in the house he sassed his mother and she beat him with a stick of stovewood and wouldn't allow him to go along for the game. Our coach went and talked to her, but she wouldn't budge so he came out and said he was playing me in the boy's place. Nearly all of the team were relatives of the boy and they didn't give me any pleasant words on the way up to the game. But I didn't care one whit since I felt the thrill of being at last able to start and play a whole game.

When we got there, all the school was turned out and a big crowd was there to see us get slaughtered. I knew a lot of the people and some of them were my cousins. One of my cousins played opposite me in the game and nearly broke my nose, butting me. My nose bled all during the game but I stayed in. I played center. The opposition played a really rough and tumble game, but when it was all over we had won by two or three points and that was the first game our school had won. I was not the star but I did my part and passed the ball to the other boys better than my rival teammate had done, and everybody gave me credit for winning the game. But soon as that all blowed over the other boy, the trustee's son, got to play as much as I did and what I had done to help win the game was summarily forgotten. I tell this to illustrate the chance a son of a destitute family has of receiving any recognition when there is one chance in a thousand the trustee's son, or the landlord's son, can make a showing. But I have learned that the very same principles apply all through life and apply to everything of any value that exists anywhere and in any climate. The lie is used strongly to endorse the whims of the privileged.

We moved again after two years at the place close to the school, and then we moved again, this time into a house everyone called the old Grayson place. My dad had made a trade with a man to rent and work a crop, but we didn't have any mules or horses, and Papa couldn't get anyone to back him enough to buy them

ADOLESCENT DAYS

on a credit, so we were up against it again. We lived at this place for about three months and didn't know exactly what to do because it was crop time and there we were. But the mail carrier knew my dad and liked him and told him of a place way up some ten miles from where we lived on the Florence Road. So my dad made a trade with the man up there and we moved very soon. That place was the happiest place we ever lived, and we stayed there only about a year. I joined the church while we lived there, and we all went to church regularly for the first time I could remember. It was at Valley View, the Church of Christ, and my singing uncle and all his boys and girls lived just two miles from where we had moved. They all belonged to the church and we had a lot of singings. I went with Uncle Will sometimes and helped him with his schools. That in itself was a great joy to me. I got to talk to the girls and they all liked me because Uncle Will was one of the most popular men in the whole country, and being kin to him put me in solid with everyone.

That year, we raised the best crop and had the best of every thing. It was by far the best and most happiest year any one of us had ever remembered. The people were friendlier and seemed more like neighbors than any place we had lived before.

I remember the hot days when we were picking cotton and we hired some extra help and didn't hardly take any time out for dinner. Those balmy fall days with the sweet smell of cotton in the field and corn, too. The scent of the grass and the smell of the good earth made life seem more enchanting than ever before. I also enjoyed the sounds of the insects that look like katydids and grasshoppers but conceal themselves on the cotton stalks and on the weeds so nearly perfect that one is lucky to ever see them, although they are right at his fingertips.

All this, then—the sounds and the noises of nature, the little things most people think are not worth taking up time with—are the principal ingredients that make up for what we are all seeking in the fight for happiness, peace, joy, and contentment.

ADOLESCENT DAYS

But the little dream we had possessed for that one year was to end with exactly that one year. The landlord was a very friendly person and we all liked him very much, but he decided to keep the place for himself and didn't need anyone to help tend the land for the coming year.

When I learned that we had to move, it was like hearing the clap of doom. I never felt so grieved and forlorn before in all my life. But I was not alone. We all felt that way.

Two of my brothers, Max and Ed, had gone to work in the railroad shops over in Decatur, and that is where my family decided to move, in hope that my dad and Leonard and myself could find some kind of work. But when we moved it made me feel kind of numb, and it seemed like all the ambition I had ever had was gone down the drain. It was tough moving into a new and strange atmosphere. And leaving all that I cherished so much. But I guess a lot of other people have felt like that before. in fact, I have seen my own daughters feel the same way when I had to pull up stakes and move away from a place they liked so well. I will tell more about this later.

CHAPTER THREE
HIGH SCHOOL DAYS

So, finally we made the move to Decatur, a town I dislike to this very day. If I have to go to Decatur, I go. Otherwise I stay away.

And my early memories are not all to blame, as you will find out later in the story.

When we got settled down and spent the night and had breakfast the next morning, two boys and I decided to walk around town a little while and see what was going on. We were country boys (these two boys had helped move us from over in Limestone County) and walking didn't mean much to us. So we took a long way around and finally came to the banks of the Tennessee River. This frightened us somewhat and we started to go back but we couldn't find the way. We tried several times but always were wrong, and then we all wanted to go different ways. So we split up and each one traveled his own way. I went one way. Lester went his and Robert went his way. We were three lost pilgrims.

My way carried me to a big, very big school that I was to attend, but I didn't know this yet. I came closer and closer to this awesome building till I could hear some boys in there playing basketball. So I sauntered on in and threw a few balls around with the guys there. They had never seen me before, and the same for me about them, but there were no questions asked. I finally arrived back where we live in Fairview and I was all worn out from that long trek. The other two boys got back later than I did and they were not together either. That was my first experience in a town the size of Decatur. It seemed so big for me. I was fourteen years old and had never been out of the state of Alabama, or, for that matter, had never been in a town bigger than Athens. I was completely bewildered and disillusioned. I didn't understand anything about the whole situation and didn't like it at all. That was my first lesson in adjusting myself to my environment. And I think today, after I have traveled extensively from place to place all over the United States and part of Mexico and Canada, that getting adjusted to one's environment means vastly more than some people think. I believe if one does not get adjusted pretty quickly that it may mean sickness or even death for some in extreme cases.

After we had about settled down in the new home, my next stop was to get to school. I had never been to an accredited school in my life and I was in the ninth or Junior Three grade. I knew the subjects real well and thought I would start in that particular grade, but I was to learn better in a very bitter experience.

I started to the school and the semester had already begun. So I was sent to the principal's office to get straight with the curriculum involved. The principal's name was Mr. Johnson, whom I later learned to like very much. But he was a demon to me when I first started to high school.

I marched into his office and he asked me a few questions—where I had been to school, what studies I had taken and some more routine questions, or at least I thought they were routine at the time. I didn't know what was to follow. Well, Mr. Johnson started writing out little slips and he wrote many of them, altogether about fifteen, I guess. Then he handed them to me and told me to observe them for the date on them and report when the date called for me and to the room called for in the paper, the little slip of paper.

Those innocent little slips were dates for examinations! I studied them over briefly and thought he was kidding at first. He told me to report to the classes of the ninth grade and go along with my studies just like I had passed the examinations and not to worry over the little slips. Just forget about them for the time being. So I did forget. Not for the time being but I never gave those little slips any more attention and went about my business, making very good grades and liking it better every day at the high school. Then one day the whole bottom fell out!

Mr. Johnson called me into his office and I thought he was going to murder me he was so angry.

He was infuriated because I had not taken a single one of the examinations he had so painstakingly written out for me several months previously. He pulled off his coat and rolled up his sleeves and I thought he was fixing to beat me μp for sure then. But he sat down at his desk and began to write more exams for me. I had lost or thrown away the ones he gave me before. But there was one good thing about the whole· mess. He didn't give me but about six or seven slips this time. He shoved them into my hands and told me if I didn't take the exams he would take stern measures and I believe I knew what he meant by that. So there I was, going along greatly in the Junior Three grade, and I have to take all this back stuff and maybe get set back a whole grade. I didn't understand it then and neither do I now.

But I went ahead and took all the tests and failed on only one of them and that was eighth-grade history. I have always liked the study of history and passed all the questions but one, and that was a thought question the previous year's students had had. The question was one I'll never forget: "If the Mississippi River had flowed East and West, would there have been a Civil War?"

I did quite a bit of singing back in those days. I had written my first song when we lived over on the Florence Road and it came out in a book about the time we moved to Decatur.* All the quartets knew of this, and despite the fact that I

---

*According to Alton's son Lionel, this song was "Bound for the Shore" and was written in collaboration with Alton's mother, "Aunt Molly." This song was later recorded by the Brown's Ferry Four in 1952, with composer credits to Alton and "Mrs. C. E. Delmore." —Ed.

could never sing loud they all wanted me to sing with them—that is, except the ones who had their own rehearsed group, and most of them thought they were better than they really were. There was one fellow who was so persistent about keeping a quartet that he would drive miles to pick up a singer he needed. The quartets were constantly changing in personnel. You could get a group where they could sing pretty well together and somebody would suddenly quit.

They usually gave as their excuse that the wife didn't like for them to take up so much time doing nothing but singing. They wanted them to be doing the dishes or mowing the lawn or some thing else. Back then, I just thought it was a framed-up story but now I know very, very differently. All women are vain, and they will use a man for everything from a hat rack to a whipping post. And musicians know this better than anyone I have ever talked to yet. They (women) will not actually whip a fellow with a stick, that is not every time, although I have known it to happen, but they will whip a fellow with subtle, sly, wicked undercurrent methods only Mephistopheles himself could do better. So that is the way it goes.

I already could read and write music and knew how to harmonize songs. My mother taught me the shape of the notes, and I went on from there without any teacher or anybody to help me. I figured out how to do all the rest by myself. I'm not saying this in a bragging or boastful way at all. It is meant to encourage those who are really trying hard to learn something about music. I call myself about as dumb as they come, but I learned music by myself and you can do the same if you will try hard as I did and really be dedicated in your efforts.

When I started to school I naturally felt inferior, and that's when a fellow needs a friend. I found several good country boys in school and this made me feel brighter as the days passed by and the studies of school multiplied.

HIGH SCHOOL DAYS

One of these boys, Tennis Odom, played the mandolin, and we teamed up and started an instrumental duet. We could play most of the popular songs of the day and we were very popular with the school students. I had a hard time at first trying to tie what I knew about music into the chords of the guitar and mandolin, and into the new pop tunes which were in demand and which we had requests to perform. Now I knew the harmony of the hymns and could sight read any of them in the book. And I didn't have to depend on the shape notes because I could read by the lines and spaces. But the chords made on the instruments were a little different from the chords in the hymns and that's what had me fooled. For instance, the mediant chord is used mostly as a seventh chord in instrumental music—the guitar, ukulele etc.—and when I caught on to how they made them I could apply them real well and knew exactly what I was doing. One example is this: in the key of C the mediant chord is E minor, but unless the song specifically calls for E minor, the chord you will make on your guitar will be E-7, and it mixes you all up if you don't know where to go. But it is easy when you get used to playing the country and western style.

CHAPTER FOUR

THE CAFE, THE PRINTING OFFICE

During the summer holidays away from school I worked at any thing I could find to do. I worked for a while with a Greek in his cafe. He made candy, too, and it was real good candy and he sold a lot of it. Jim the Greek, they called him, and his specialty was short-orders, hot dogs and hamburgers. He was a good fellow if you knew how to get along with him. But I didn't seem to have the knack. I worked hard for him but he was a hard man to get along with. My brothers and my daddy liked him real well but they didn't know him like I did. He had some bulldogs in the back of his cafe and he would go back and play with the dogs, rubbing them and pulling their ears and pummeling them around, and come back to the front of the cafe and handle food without thinking of washing his hands.

One time I opened a barrel of wieners and they were spoiled. I told him about them and first he would not believe me. But when he smelled them and found out for himself, he began to think what to do with them. He came up with a very good idea for him. He took what were not too bad out of the barrel and made a special sauce and served for the people at the lunch rush. People bragged on them so much that he thought he had one them a real favor. He had saved about three fourths of the contaminated wieners by feeding them to the unsuspecting customers and he was a hero for the day. He did the same thing with a roast pork shoulder he had to go bad, and it still didn't hurt anyone. He used the same sauce. It had a delicious taste and it concealed the rancid taste of the spoiled meat. Still no one got sick. But shortly after I quit and started back to school, he must have tried the same thing again and his luck ran out. He had large crowds from the different industrial plants and they patronized him regularly. So one day about half of the people he served suffered severe illness and had to be hospitalized. But no one suspected him but me. None of the people died and I was glad. I think he quit that practice after those people got sick.

I had a friend who went to the same high school with me and he worked in a printing office after school hours and on Saturdays. He used his influence and I got a job there with him. That is one of the best breaks I ever got because it gave me an insight into so many channels of life that I consider it an education far better than high school or, for that matter, some college courses. I started work as an errand boy and doing some of the repair jobs to the old building that housed the printing. When it rained the roof would leak in several places. And the next day I went to the rooftop with the tar bucket and the brush to repair the leaks. I don't know till this day how many leaks I fixed and how many I didn't fix. Because that old roof never did stop leaking. But the owner of the place was a philosophical person and he never did fuss about the leaks.

I kept at work pretty hard and finally the boss started me out throwing in type. That is done when a job is completed on the press and the type has to be put back into the cases. I never could set type by hand so good or fast but I could lock up the forms and get them ready for the press. I learned to feed the presses very fast, too. They were the hand presses and it was dangerous work if you didn't watch what you were doing. Several pressmen got hurt by letting their hands get caught in the press, but I learned to feed it without a single mishap. But I had to keep alert. I also learned to run the linotype machine. The boss's boy and me were the only ones who could run the linotype and it kept us kind of busy, because he went to school, too. The boss could run the machine a little but he never did count on himself when it came to turning out work. I also learned to fix the linotype when it got out of shape. I became so adept at this that the old man who came around on peri odical checks from the linotype company wanted me to go to the linotype school at New Orleans. But I was too timid to take him up and was afraid I would get homesick. This man worked for the company and the course would not have cost me a cent, but I still was uncertain and today I know I passed up a golden opportunity to become a first class linotype mechanic. But when I reflect back on the man's proposition, I know it was a fine compliment. The paradox of this all amounts to the fact that I can't even begin to fix my car when it breaks down now. If you've never seen a linotype, you should go and see how they look when being operated in the newspaper or job printing plant. They are really complicated-looking to the person who first sees one.

I met a lot of the fellows called "tramp printers." They have about all disappeared today, I hear, but I am glad I remember them when I was in the printing trade. They were really a colorful bunch of guys. And they all had their stories and tales of the road and the many countries they had been to. Some of them were very interesting, while some of them were just ordinary fellows. But they all had that certain something that made them what they were and that was drifting, or the "roaming fever" as some of them called it. One day I was watching one of those knights of the road as he worked setting up a form when a train whistle blew and he stopped abruptly and seemed to be in deep thought. He set aside his type slick and went out for lunch. I had an idea about him but I said nothing to the rest of the fellows in the printing office. He didn't show up when time for lunch was over and the others asked questions about where he was and what he was doing. I knew. I had learned some of their secrets. We never saw him again. He didn't even wait for his pay.

He was somewhere down the line, going somewhere, anywhere, it didn't make any difference just as long as he was on the go.

There was one of the tramp printers that impressed me more than all the rest put together. He was the best printer of them all. He had worked on the big slick magazines, *Saturday Evening Post, Ladies' Home Journal,* and many more. And he could prove it with his skill with the type. We had some very old type which was almost completely worn out, and Bill could set it up and make it look almost as good as lithographing. He was a very interesting person and congenial. He had really been somebody important, we all believed. Of course that was mere theory because we never did learn anything about his background. The boss started several times to ask him something about his past but he was very shrewd in parrying the boss's attempts at questioning him.

I never even thought of asking him anything about his life before he came to work with us, for I had too much respect for him. He took a liking to me too, and in a short time we became close friends. He told me many tales of his travels, and I've always been interested in far-off places so we hit it off real well together. One day Bill didn't come back from lunch and I was about as blue and lonely as a teenage boy could be. I had a premonition that he was leaving soon by the way he talked. I had considered leaving with him but couldn't make up my mind. He had wanted me to go. He said he could work anywhere and pay our way. And I could work also. But I heard from him about a week after he left. He had a job working at the *Louisville Courier Journal,* one of the biggest dailies in the country. He told me he was heading for Alaska. I kept getting letters from him all the way across the country, telling me if I still wanted to join him he would be proud to have me. But I decided against going, afraid I'd be homesick. The last time I heard from him he was working for one of the big dailies in Vancouver, British Columbia.

You might wonder if you were a fan of the Delmore Brothers why we sang so many songs about people with the wanderlust. Well, it was because of my knowing these wandering printers and listening to their lonely stories of the "far out there somewhere" that influenced me to write the songs and that also gave me an outlet from my burning desire to join them in their happy, carefree life of rambling.

The boss of the printing office had lots of influential customers such as lawyers, doctors, etc., and they would give him some of their business. I especially remember the law briefs we had to set up and print for the lawyers. A brief is a summation of a special case the lawyer draws up for his plea with the Supreme Court. I dreaded them very much, but I learned a lot from them because there could be not one single little error in the copy: An omission of a colon, period, semi-colon, or brackets could alter the entire interpretation of the lawyer's case. So this work was very exacting. And that leads up to what I call the turning point in my life.

One night I worked all night at the linotype to get a rush brief out for a lawyer, and as the result I took down with the flu. There was an epidemic of the flu in Decatur and I was really very sick before I realized it. I lay in the bed for about two weeks and finally got a little better. My mother had the flu also and she was just as bad as I was. We both had a rough time but came through very well. Many people died from the virus and it took me about a month of convalescing before I was strong enough to go back to work. That was the time I really learned my style of playing the guitar. I had a lot of time on my hands and nothing to do but laze around. So I started listening to the various recording artists—Jimmie Rodgers, Carson Robison, Nick Lucas, Riley Puckett, and Eddie Lang. Those are the fellows I copied mostly. I would take a little from the style of first one, then the other, till I had my own style. And besides playing some of their runs and riffs, I emphasized the melody and would play the song like anyone would play on the piano or violin or any other lead instruments, and that is where my style was different.

CHAPTER FIVE

THE BROWN'S FERRY COUNTRY

My dad and mother and my two younger brothers, Tom and Rabe, moved back to Limestone County and stayed with my brother Max for a while and kept on working at the printing office. I hated to give it up because I had it in my blood. That's the way it is with a printer. I can walk into a printing office to this very day and the smell of printer's ink brings back a feeling of comfort and security that is hard to explain.

While I was staying at my brother's house, we used to listen to the Grand Ole Opry in Nashville, Tennessee. We liked it very much.

But it was different, very different from what it is today. I had a yearning to play up there with all the fellows but never dreamed that I would ever get the chance. My brother still played some on his fiddle and I would accompany him on my guitar. But we didn't play except at his house. He never believed in going out much to play.

But I got up a little show with my school companions and we would play the local schools and sometimes we would make pretty good money doing these. We had a magician, comedian, and we all sang and played and this made up a pretty fair little show. I would print the handbills in the printing office and the boss would not charge me anything. That is the way I got my first experience in show business.

Things went from bad to worse in the printing office and my boss told me one day that I had better go home because he couldn't afford to pay me anymore. So I decided to go back to the country where my dad and mother lived. That was the only place I knew to go. I felt almost as bad about this move as I did previously when we moved to Decatur.

I had hitchhiked to Birmingham several times and always went around to the music stores, looking at the real fine guitars, the Martins and the Gibsons. I had a Martin guitar I had bought from Cincinnati, Ohio, and it was a real good one but I still wanted a better one. Then I saw what was called a tenor guitar. I had seen two fellows singing in a vaudeville show once and they had played a tenor guitar and sang a duet. They were a big hit and I liked them very much. So I decided to buy the tenor guitar on this account. I didn't have enough money to pay the man for the instrument, but I wanted it so badly that the man came up with a plan to help me buy it. The price was eleven dollars. The man said he would ship me the guitar by parcel post collect if I could raise the money when I got back to Decatur. I told him I would. So that is how the tenor guitar got into the act of the Delmore Brothers.

I packed my few clothes and my guitar and the tenor guitar and headed north to Limestone County and dad and mother and Tom and Rabe, and a future that was to take me to the "far off places," as the tramp printer says. My father operated a cotton gin for a fellow over there on the Brown's Ferry Road. He did the weighing and kept books for the owner of the gin, and I used to enjoy hanging around the gin and listening to the farmers talk and laugh. I was reared during the Depression and there was not much money to be had anywhere. Fifteen dollars a week was a good salary for the average family man. He could feed and partly clothe his family on that amount.

When I first came over to that section of the county I was not too well received by the fellows and the boys. My hands were white from working inside the printing office so long and they seemed to think I was a soft touch, especially the rough element in the neighborhood. I had to prove myself different. That's kind of like the law of fang and claw but it is the truth and it applies to every section of this country I've ever visited. I had practiced the art of boxing with my brothers and they had taught me pretty well how to take are of myself with my hands. They had been pretty rough with me and they believed in hitting solidly. I had been on the receiving end of several hard blows and could take them in style. So the preparation helped out tremendously with the lesson I had to teach the boys who were hostile with me. A boy lived across the road from us and he had a pair of boxing gloves. He was pretty good with the gloves himself and we had worked pretty regularly since I had moved into the community. Well, one rainy day two of the neighborhood toughs, both brothers, issued a challenge to fight me. We lived close to the school house. In fact we lived in the teacher's home. So these two boys had a contemptuous opinion of me, and I had to show them I was not afraid of them. We agreed on the terms and the smallest of the two first tackled me. They were all laughing about how he was going to murder me with the gloves. Since I had had some experience in boxing, I allowed the boy to put the knockout glove on his right hand and the big sixteen-ounce glove on his left. That in itself gave him the advantage over me, but I thought it best to give him the benefit of the doubt. I had the big glove on my right hand and the little glove on my left hand. So the battle began.

Although we had made an agreement not to hit hard, he began to swing from the ground, and I had a hard time keeping out of his reach. We sparred around for about five minutes and he was beginning to get out of breath. He was boiling mad. I knew I had to do something quick before he connected and I let loose the big glove to his stomach and hit him on the jaw with the little glove. He bent over forward, and I straightened him up with an uppercut and knocked him flat. He got up slowly and painfully and he was crying. He didn't want to fight anymore, though.

THE BROWN'S FERRY COUNTRY

So his bigger brother was my next opponent. He was madder than his brother. He accused me of taking advantage of his smaller brother by skillfully tricking him on the gloves. The neighbor boy from across the road tried to tell him different but he was adamant. He was strutting around like an angry rooster, puffing and blowing and bragging. So we made a change in the gloves. Now I had the knockout glove on my right hand. And I was glad of this because I knew I was going to need it against this big bully. He came at me with a lunge, and I just barely ducked his right fist as it whizzed by my head. He kept doing this lunging trick and he never did hit me.

Not a single time. He just wore himself out trying to kill me, and he proved to be an easier target than his brother. I waited for the right opportunity and I let him have it on the jaw with the knock out glove. He fell like he'd been hit by an ax. He lay on the ground dazed for a few minutes and then he was alright. I was surprised to see him smiling when he got up. He was not mad at all.

He and his brothers became some of my best friends in the community. That was number one of the tests I had to make good on before I was accepted. Some of the farmers ridiculed me because we didn't make a crop like the others in the neighborhood. They didn't know that we did not have the money to buy farm animals. After crops were laid by, they started building roads and that was work for anyone who wanted to try it. Hard work. I got a job shoveling gravel in a hot pit for one dollar a day. Those same persons who had criticized me for not working in a crop were afraid to talk work in that gravel pit. They saw some of their more sturdy acquaintances fall out in the pit and quit because they couldn't take it. I have never in all my life worked so hard in the hot sun as I did in that gravel pit. The farmer boys who had made fun of me would hang around the place waiting and watching, like vultures; for me to give up and quit. One day I ate my lunch and felt fine and went back into the pit. There was a very good friend of mine working beside me in the pit and he was sticking it out too. The loafers on the sidelines were expecting him to give out, too, but he never did. This day I have mentioned before was unusually hot and about three o'clock in the afternoon

I began to get real weak. I asked my friend if he had any food left in his lunch box and he told me he had only one peach. He said I could have half of it if I would go get it out of his lunch box. I slipped away, found the peach, and ate half of it and he got the rest. That one peach kept both he and I from giving out and quit ting. After that ordeal, I was completely accepted by the whole countryside and they had respect for me at last.

Rabon, my youngest brother, had taken up playing the tenor guitar I had brought home with me from Decatur. I taught him the first chords on it and I played it like a tenor banjo. So that's the way he learned to play it. We started rehearsing together, singing and playing. And he caught on unusually fast to anything that I showed him. All my life I had heard people play fiddles, guitars, mandolins, etc., and heard them sing but I never heard any that exactly suited me. The musicians didn't take time to get it like I wanted to hear it. I'm speaking strictly about the local music makers, not the ones I could hear on the records. The ordinary fellow who just plays for his own enjoyment and that of his friends won't take the time or exert the effort it requires to sell to the public at large.

Rabon and myself practiced a whole lot more than most acts do when they are getting started. We really enjoyed playing and never gave a thought to playing professionally. We just liked the way it sounded and we wanted to make our music sound perfect. We never tried to sing loudly. We couldn't have if we had wanted to because we both had soft voices. We would play for the neighbors and we kept improving as we went along. Everybody complimented us but we took most of all this with a grain of salt. A musician knows when he can play the way he should better than any one other person on the face of the earth. I think that will ring true in most every case where a recording artist makes a hit. No one knows exactly what is behind the fellow's career. That is the reason for the title of this book. Publicity is one thing and the truth is another. Like the old saying in show business, when an artist begins to believe his publicity he is slipping, ready for the exit.

We had mighty good times on the old Brown's Ferry Road in those days. We got to where we were invited to all the schools and churches and socials around the community and sometimes we would go over into other counties and into Tennessee. Rabon was still in high school and I didn't want him to quit school till he finished.

I had played in the old fiddlers' contests before Rabon and I started playing together. These old time musicians would gather and compete for cash prizes, and the ones who won would take home some money and the honor of being the best in the country. The school would sponsor them and advertise them all over the county and surrounding areas. Sometimes there would be between fifty and one hundred contestants to play in the contests. It indeed was a challenge for the elite in the country musical circles. Of course, some of the musicians would play just for the experience and to get in free. They (the sponsors) always had food for the contestants and a lot of fellows would enter the show just to get a square meal. * That was during the Depression and times were hard. Somebody somewhere had all the money tied up and poor folks like us musicians couldn't get our hands on the elusive stuff.

While Rabon and me were playing around the country, I got acquainted with a

*Such contests were extremely popular in Limestone County in the 1920s and 1930s and were a potent influence on the musical development of the brothers. An excellent account of these contests is in Bill Harrison's "Fiddling in Limestone County 1925-1940," in *The Devil's Box*, Feb. 15, 1972, pp. 4–9. Harrison notes that the flagship for these local contests was the annual contest held at the Athens-Agricultural High School from 1924 to the mid 1930s, and that it was this contest which was most influential on the Delmores. Other sources for old-time fiddle music in the county include square dances, ice cream suppers, and similar social activities, general store "gatherings," and, later, radio.—Ed.

girl named Thelma Neely and I liked her a whole lot the first time I saw her. We began to slip around and go together because her parents wouldn't let her have dates. We would meet at church and sometimes I would walk her home if her mother was not-at church. I never will forget those nights when the moon was shining brightly and we could walk in the beautiful silence of the countryside. She lived about two miles from the church and it was a big thrill to get to be with her and walk down the dirt road with all the night sounds, the whippoorwill singing, the katydids chirping and the frogs making their usual contribution to modify the night. Also the sweet smell of the wild flowers in the soft night breezes, especially the honeysuckles. To me, then, it was nothing much special, but as I look back on those days now it seems exotic as anything I have ever experienced in my whole life.

Rabon and I began to get popular all over the country. People would come from far and near just to hear us play and sing on the guitar and the tenor guitar. They wondered and often would ask what the little instrument was. We would tell them and they would look puzzled. But they all liked the little guitar and the way my brother played it. We practiced a lot and got better and better in our own style. But I was worried because we could not sing loud, and back in those days there was no such thing as a public address system. At least if there was we didn't know any thing about it.

CHAPTER SIX

THE OLD FIDDLERS' CONVENTIONS

The very first place we ever played in an old fiddlers' contest was down at Clements High School in the western part of the Limestone County near the Elk River.* There was a good crowd there and those people know fine music when they hear it. Many songwriters and singers come from down in that part of the county. That night, one of the judges was a singer, music teacher, and songwriter. When we went to enter the contest, the boy at the door who was taking down the names of the contestants, asked us: "What is the name of your band?"

We told him we didn't have any particular name since there were only two of us and we hadn't ever thought of calling ourselves anything. "Well then, since you two are brothers, why don't you just call yourselves the Delmore Brothers?" We agreed with him and he didn't ever know it, but he named us right there in the very first appearance we had ever made for pay or at least a try for pay. There were a lot of good musicians there that night, for they all knew that the prizes were extraordinary at Clements High School. The bands came from as far away as Huntsville, Alabama, and some were there from up in the southern part of Tennessee. There in fine tune and ready to go. Those people (some of them) were real finished musicians. They made you dig for the prize money if you were to win it.

*Bill Harrison states that Alton Delmore told him that he (Alton) was eighteen and Rabon ten when they first started playing the conventions. This would place the date of this convention at 1926.—Ed.

THE OLD FIDDLERS' CONVENTIONS

It came time for Rabon and me to play, and some of the fine bands had already been on the stage and had made a big hit with the crowd. But we were not worried. We felt the competition in our blood. The only thing was, we could not play as loud as the others had played. They allowed each band two songs and that is how they judged them. We picked out two of our best ones. I think the first one was "That's Why I'm Jealous of You." We sang it a lot in those days and it was a good duet song. When we first began to sing, the crowd was kind of noisy, but we hadn't got through the song before there was quietness everywhere. You could almost have heard a pin drop. Then we knew we had a good chance at the prize, even if there were only two of us. When we finished there was a deafening roar of applause. If the crowd had not quieted there probably would never have been an act called the Delmore Brothers. If they hadn't stopped the little crowd noise we could not have been heard. In my heart today, I am sincerely thankful we played Clements High School for the first appearance we ever made. I am grateful for all the good music lovers who live down there in that community. We took the second prize and I've forgotten what it was. Some money, though, and in those days we could use it. One of the judges came up to us at the end of the performance. He said, "Boys, you deserved the first prize and the other two judges tried to give it to you, but I held out on them because there were only two of you and I was afraid the crowd might not like it too well if we gave it to you. I'm sorry but that is the way I feel, though I know you had the others beat a country mile." We thanked him and shook hands with him, for we had not only received the most applause but we had won the first prize in a moral sense, also.

When we got home that night and told our parents what had happened they really rejoiced. They were extremely happy. And they could see now what a rewarding thing practicing can be. I began to try my hand at writing songs other than hymns. And I wish you could see the results of my first attempts at writing the kind of songs we needed if we ever were to make records. I had already begun writing some of the big companies like Victor and Columbia but didn't get much encouragement at first. So we just kept playing the old fiddlers' contests and having a good time in one of the most lovable places we had ever lived. Of course we were very popular with the home folks around our community and all over the county, too. And that is a feeling that is hard to describe for a country boy. You feel elation, gratitude, self-confidence, and just plain wonderful all the way around. When I would go to town, most people knew me by sight, and both Rabon and I were very popular. But there is one thing I have never been and for that I am extremely thankful. I never felt stuck up or egotistical in any way all through my whole career as an entertainer.

One night we played at a contest at Elkmont, Alabama, and there were two boys on the program who nearly beat us out. They didn't play their instruments as well as we did, but they sang a couple of comedy songs that got the crowd all stirred up. The judges gave us first place but we felt a little guilty about it, for the two other boys beat us some on the applause. So I decided we should do something else besides just our playing and singing. We needed some comedy songs. I kept thinking about this need and it worried me quite a lot. So, one fine, beautiful, sunny day I was strumming on my guitar and my mother was cooking dinner. I had to take my father's dinner to him down the Brown's Ferry Road.

He worked at the gin about a mile south of where we lived. That gin is still there and the house we lived in is still to be seen. It looks about like it did when we lived there. Well, anyway, I got to thinking about a song I could call "The Brown's Ferry Blues." I could work it into a comedy song. So I took a cue from an old minstrel saying, "Lord, Lord," but then I got to thinking it might sound sacrilegious if I used the words "Lord, Lord," so I changed them to "lawd, lawd" instead, and then I knew I was on the right track. I figured it out in just a short time, and the way I play the guitar was perfect for the song I was writing. Now I must remind you that I was not trying to write a song to be sung far and wide as it is now, but I was merely trying to make us up a song that would be competitive with the local groups of musicians we had to play against in the fiddlers' contests. I never dreamed it would ever be known outside of Limestone County, Alabama. Some people say that General Jackson crossed the Tennessee River at Brown's Ferry when he went to fight the British at New Orleans. I know one thing, though. Everybody in Limestone County knows of this ferry very well. So that goes for a good name for any song anytime. Rabon was off at school when I wrote the song, and when he came in and heard it he was very much impressed and he went to work on his part for the tenor guitar. We always did do things like that. We would give each and every original tune its own sound and we were very meticulous in this treatment. It was not too long before he came up with the corresponding part on the tenor guitar. We couldn't wait till Friday night when we would play this tune about Brown's Ferry at the old fiddlers' contest at the Agricultural School in Athens.

I had written two other songs before I wrote "Brown's Ferry Blues." They were of the nostalgic type and reflected the way I felt about some things in those days. I didn't have any money. No job and no way to travel except walking. I got a temporary job at the newspaper in Athens, the Courier, but I had to walk to and from work and it didn't pay too well either. Lots of times I have trotted the whole five miles from Athens to my home on the Brown's Ferry Road. I could really go in those days. It would take me about an hour to trot the whole distance and then I would not be out of breath., Just a little tired and soon would get over that after a good hot supper. Now I can't even trot around the block.

But more about that later. Coming back to the songs, the names of them were "Got the Kansas City Blues" and "Alabama Lullaby." Some of my first efforts I will spare you because of the stupidity of them. But that just goes to show a fellow has to begin some way or another. If I never had tried I would not have ever written any songs at all. Just like the old Chinese proverb: the longest journey begins with only one step. I had always wanted to write novels and short stories, but I didn't get much encouragement from the folks at home. Sometimes people just don't understand a fellow when he is trying to be something they think is away off in the stars. I would steal away to some room in the house and write for hours, and about time I really got started writing, some of my brothers or my dad would come around to warn me I was off my rocker or something equivalent to that, and then I would reluctantly decide to quit for the time being. I am still what is termed a frustrated writer. You never lose the urge to write once you have the yen for it. But my songwriting helped me to stand the push you get for being creative. The songs satisfied partially, but not wholly, my desire to do something lastingly worthwhile.

I got a job at the gin one fall, the second year we lived on the Brown's Ferry Road. The job was at the press—the place where the ginned cotton comes down into the hydraulic press and is put into a bale. This is where you take ties and bagging and put it into the press and wait for the cotton to move into the presser. This cotton must be kept in a straight even padding, and to keep it that way you must use a stick to pull the cotton over when it tends to get more on one side than the other. If this is not done correctly, the result will be a bad bale. It will be bigger on one side than the other and it looks awful. Most farmers don't mind this, but when I worked at the gin it really worried me to see one of those monstrosities turned out of my press. Once I had a lazy helper who let the bales come out like that and it made me so mad that I almost threw an iron pulley at him. From that night on he always tried harder to get the cotton smoothed out from side to side. I say "night" because we had to work way into the night to get through sometimes. And during the real peak of the cotton picking season, I hardly ever did get to sit down and eat. It was rush, rush, rush all the time. I had to chew so fast that I broke several teeth and my teeth have never been the same since. But those days were the grandest. The smell of the cotton and the gin and all the other blends of the atmosphere of the cotton ginning season will continue to linger in my make-up all the rest of my days. My dad was able to work and he was a real pal. We would walk home together up the road when we got through work and I really learned to know him during that time better than I had ever known him before. This was quite a contrast to the way he spent the last years of his life. He had a stroke that laid him low and he couldn't work anymore. For about seven years he had to kind of exist—for he never was well again. That sort of thing can get mighty boring to a man who has known hard work all his life and was always so effervescent and full of life. But that's the way fate works sometimes, and we have to get used to the verdict.

I worked at the gin just one fall and the next season the owner of the gin decided he could get someone else who would please him more than I could, so I had to get something else to do for a living. But the year I worked was a remarkable event and several things happened that changed the entire course of my life. That was the year I got married and also the year Rabon and I made our first record.*

I think the crowning point in our career came when we played the contest at Athens on that Friday night (I was aiming to tell you earlier but got off on a tangent). Now I am back again with the boys from the cotton patch, Rabon and myself, to continue on with the way we had to beat it out with worthy competitors in the music field. That's the way it was exactly, for when a fellow got up to play at one of those contests he really had to scat or he wouldn't get to first base.

*The Delmores made their first record, for Columbia, on Wednesday, October 28, 1931, in Atlanta (see Chapter 7).—Ed.

THE OLD FIDDLERS' CONVENTIONS

There was a big crowd there and everything was decorated and all fixed up like the president of the United States would be there. It was by far the biggest and most important contest of the entire country. People who had never been to a contest before gathered with the contestants at the Old Athens Agricultural School. My mother had made cases for us out of cotton sacks we used during the picking season and we had our names on them spelled out in full. I painted them on the cases with pokeberry juice. That's a plant that is typical of the South and, in the spring of the year, folks made poke sallet out of it. I have eaten it many times and it surely is good if it is cooked right. But in the fall of the year the berries get ripe and they are no good for anything except to paint with. The berries are poison but the juice makes a good lasting paint that will stick to the surface when it is used, especially on cloth material.

You know how it feels to be a combatant in any kind of contest, so we rightly felt proud of the sack cases and we were primed to go for the first in the prizes in each case. I entered the contest for the best guitarist and we also entered the contest for the best band. There were some bands there that would have given Bob Wills some strong competition if Bob had been there. We didn't think we would win that one. By then we had "Brown's Ferry Blues" down pretty pat—in fact we could play it just as good then as we ever did.

When it came our time to play, we sang just as soft as we could and just as loud as we could but we put the music in there, too and that counts as much as anything I can think of to help put an act over. You can analyze music and record hits, I mean the legitimate ones, and you will find that there is a synchronization between the voices or voice and the instrumentation.

We got tied for the first place with three pretty girls. Nothing worse could have happened because we knew the crowd usually takes sides with the singer if it happens to be a girl and those three girls could really sing. The rules were that they were to play two songs, and two for us. The girls went out first, and I could tell they had lost something of their quality on their very first song.

Their second one was not any better but they still got a tremendous hand from the audience. I knew we ha something to beat. Rabon did, too, but it just made us work harder. We could feel the challenge in the air.

For our first number we used the old song "Columbus Stockade Blues." It was written by Tom Darby and Jimmie Tarlton. It is a plaintive prison and love song combined, and when we got through singing, men threw their hats into the top of the house, and everybody screamed like they had really never before. We thought we had it won then, and we did, but we still had the "Brown's Ferry Blues" for them, and when we did it the people really went wild and we won that contest without any question or any 'doubt. And that started us on our way toward the Grand Ole Opry and the big record companies. Incidentally I also won the first place for guitar playing with an instrumental rendition of "St. Louis Blues." Our names came out in the paper and it was really swell. Of all the days of triumph in my life, there were none any greater than those.*

We had had so many compliments on our singing and playing that I began to believe we might make a start on some big radio station or some big record company. I started to writing songs more often, as I had heard that an act has to have original songs before being accepted on record. I had met the Allen Brothers who had made records for Victor** and they gave me a lot of information.

The big one, Austin, played guitar and did comedy. I won a prize over him one

*A variety of different sources put the date of this contest as February 1930.—Ed.

**For an account of the career of the Allen Brothers, see Donald Lee Nelson's biography in the *John Edwards Memorial Foundation Quarterly*, No. 24, pp. 147–151.—Ed.

time at a fiddlers' contest but that is one that I still believe I didn't deserve because old Austin had 'em hanging on the rafters when he got through with his version of the "Talking Blues." I told him so, and he just laughed and said, "Well, the only regret I have is that there wasn't more money in it for you." He was the one who told me about original songs. He said we ought to have several original songs before we auditioned for records. The Allen Brothers were a lot different from the Delmore Brothers but they surely did sell good on record. I guess you will remember "Salty Dog"—well, that was one of their smashes and I still hear it sometimes now by other artists. I don't know what ever did happen to those fellows, but they played a kazoo and guitar and were great guys. They just came along too soon, like the Delmore Brothers and a lot more of the old-timers like that. But anyway, I give them a lot of credit for giving me reliable information on the know-how of things. Lots of the old-timers wrote the songs back in those days, and somebody would just take them away from them and never even give them credit for writing them, much less any money.

I had been writing the big recording companies and also the big radio stations for an audition but they were few and far between. In fact all of them had the same reply. A polite but firm brush-off. But they underestimated the persistence of a country boy who had the love of music in his soul and craved for higher places.

Finally, a letter came from Columbia Records, the old company that recorded Riley Puckett, Gid Tanner, Clayton McMichen, Darby & Tarlton, Hugh Cross, and many, many more of the fine artists in the country and western field.* The letter was for an audition in Atlanta, Georgia. I give those fellows a lot of credit for bringing

---

*Numerous record companies in the mid-1920s were trying to create specialized "old time" or "hillbilly" lines designed to appeal to a specific regional audience, the white middle- and lower-middle-class South. Columbia was probably more successful with this than any other company. In early 1925, the company initiated its "15000 series" devoted strictly to old-time and gospel music, and met immediate success with records by artists like the Skillet Lickers, Vernon

folksongs and music a long way. They wrote their own songs in many instances and just forgot about them, not trying to copyright them or trying for any protection of any kind. Therefore they got "took" in many cases. Hugh Cross, I know, got beat out of several songs that would have made him wealthy. Please don't ask me who did it, but it happens and it has also happened to me.*

Dalhart, Riley Puckett, Smith's Sacred Singers, Darby & Tarlton, and others. Most of the records in the series were recorded on location in the South and sold remarkably well there. Many old musicians still today speak of Columbia in glowing terms, and for many musicians a Columbia 15000 release was the epitome of recording success. The 15000 series reached 782 releases before being terminated in late 1932.—Ed.

*Hugh Cross, from Oliver Springs, Tennessee, was a popular recording artist of the 1920s and later joined John Lair's *Renfro Valley Barn Dance*. Exactly what songs Alton was hinting at here is unclear, but it has been widely reported among Cross's friends and associates that he originated the popular version of "Wabash Cannonball."—Ed.

CHAPTER SEVEN

OUR FIRST
RECORD

Well, we began to make preparations for the trip to Atlanta, Georgia, where the tryouts were to be held. There were four of us in the party: Rabon and myself, our cousin Bee McLemore, and Bill Willett, the boy who owned the car we traveled in. It was an old Chevrolet and the tires were very bad on it.

But we didn't think of doing anything about the tires because we could patch them, and it was nothing back in those days to have to fix a flat. If a tire had a big hole in it, it was still a good tire because we put in boots of leather, cloth, and anything else we could get hold of to help plug up the break. The biggest and most important thing we worried about was food. So we stocked up on all the canned goods we thought it would take to make the trip. And we also took several packed lunches each from home to last till we got to Atlanta. The main fear we had was food poisoning. We were afraid to eat in the cafes because we had read so many stories in the newspapers about folks getting poisoned from food that it made us over-suspicious. Bee McLemore and myself were great buddies and we rounded up most of the food we needed on the trip.

I had the letter from Bob Miller of Columbia Records in my pocket when we left, and that was the main recognition we had as a stepping stone to the road of fame and fortune, we thought. The letter didn't promise one thing except to give us an audition, or "tryout"' as we called it, for Columbia Records. But that made us extremely happy.

OUR FIRST RECORD

It was a fine morning in the fall of the year when we left our home on the Brown's Ferry Road, starting out on the long, eventful journey. It was really eventful, and I will try to tell some of the things that happened on the way that will let you in on the way country boys do things when they are full of anxiety and know nothing much except the price of cotton and the various bootleggers in the country, where their main wares are the various types and kinds of wildcat or moonshine.

We left Athens in the morning, getting a real early start. We didn't want to take any chances on being late for that recording appointment. The first stop we made was in the town of Huntsville. But we didn't stay long. I remember I met an old gospel songwriter while there. I had led his songs many times and it was a real thrill to meet such an accomplished person. The man's name was Mr. Elgar Belue. Bill Willett introduced him to me, and when I told him how I had enjoyed singing his songs, imagine my surprise when he told me he had also enjoyed listening to my brother and me at the various contests he had been when we were present. The world was a small place.

We were not very far from home and still it seemed pretty far to all of us. I could tell by the way the others acted. They all seemed silent and there was not much conversation as we pulled out of Huntsville and headed over the mountain to the far away Atlanta. I guess we were all thinking of the trip and that we would not be back home for four or five days. And those kind of thoughts can get next to a fellow if he lets them get him into a thinking mood. But the old Chevrolet took care of that situation.

Bill had never been too far away from home and he had never driven over a mountain before. He didn't know exactly how to keep the car in hand, but he was afraid to go too fast. We could see the cliffs and rocks down below us and it gave us all the creeps. Our part of the state is level country with the exception of a few low-lying hills. And these mountains had an awesome effect on us. We could just imagine something happening to the car and it out of control, crashing down the mountainside, taking us to a swift doom. So Bill held his foot on the brake to keep the car down to about ten miles an hour. Suddenly we all began to see the smoke coming from the rear of the automobile. Bill stopped and we all got out to see the cause of our first accident. It was the brakes. They had caught on fire and we had to wait till they got cool before we could go on. We waited and continued to look around at the scenery. It is still a pretty sight going down Monte Sano Mountain, to me, and I have seen the mountains of the East and the West and Mexico and Canada.

Our course took us down through Gadsden and then into Georgia by way of Heflin and Muscadine. I thought of Senator Tom Heflin as we passed through Heflin. He was once our senator from Alabama and he was a very colorful person. I had seen him speak in Athens before he was defeated by Tallulah Bankhead's father. The whole trip began to get more interesting as we moved farther from home. The new sights and scenes were taking the place of our nostalgia. But that is what traveling will do to a fellow. You get to where all you want to see is what is on the other side of the hill. That is the way I am today. I can take a road map and begin looking at it and the first thing you know, I will have a good case of the blues. I look at the places I've been and memories kindle up inside of me and I relive the things that happened to me in the particular place I see on the map. I guess you would call that the roaming fever. I have written a lot about it in my songs.

Besides the brakes event, the time was passed pretty well with us. Even if we wanted to get bored, it was not possible, for about every fifteen or twenty miles we had a blowout. We took it all philosophically as we all knew it was what we had expected from the start. We had plenty of patching and glue to fix the ailing tube and also some extra boots to put into the tires when the hole was too big to fix without them.

I distinctly remember one thing that happened then to us that I don't believe will ever happen to any of you nor to me again.

There was the low price of gas and a major gas war. Now a gas war can and will happen every day in some part of the country. But the price is what I am talking about, as you will readily see. We had a reasonable amount of gas when it all began. The price of gas in Alabama was about twenty-five cents a gallon for the best. But when we got into the piney woods of Georgia the price began to get lower and lower. The first drop in the price was to about nineteen cents. And it kept getting lower and lower. It finally got down to fifteen cents a gallon and we decided to buy some then but debated about it and decided at last to go and see if it got any cheaper. So on we drove, carefully watching the signs along the roadside for the dropping price of gas. We were really having fun with the signs, each one we passed speaking out boldly of the diminishing prices. It seemed similar to a baseball game with the home team leading and the score going up for the home boys every inning. Bee and myself had played a lot of baseball together and we had the same idea about the comparison of the prices to innings when we were winning. So there we were, gleefully cruising along with delight. But we didn't have the slightest idea that time was running out on us.

The price of gas finally got down as low as ten cents a gallon and we still didn't stop. We thought it might finally get down to a nickel a gallon and we would have something to tell when we got back home. So we kept going. Bill looked at his tank and it was almost empty! We drove and drove till we came to another station and the price was posted in big black letters along the highway—twenty cents a gallon! We had gone too far to turn back and had to pay the fellow twenty cents a gallon for each and every drop he put into the tank. We really were a crestfallen gang. We had been caught in our own little game of bluff. We knew we could not make it to Atlanta the first day, so we took it leisurely and didn't think much about where we would spend the night. The Georgia pine woods and the other trees were a pleasant sight to see in the fall of the year and we had plenty of time to look. Bee and myself rode in the rumble seat of Bill's old Chevrolet and Rabon rode in front with Bill. We never gave it a thought about what we would do if it began to rain. And our luck held out good. All the way there and back it never rained. When we got ready to eat, we would pull over to the side of the road and have lunch in the shade. It seems ridiculous now, that anyone would take a trip like that, as ignorant as we were of urban life then. But as I look back on that trip now, I can't recall any I have ever taken that afforded any more pleasure. There we were, living out in the open with the sky as our only shelter, plenty of fresh, clean air to breathe and plenty to eat. What more does anyone need?

After we had passed through the gas war and acted so foolish about passing up the bargain prices, we didn't look for any more breaks. We just traveled along lazily, drinking in the marvelous sunshine and wondering what the recording man, Bob Miller, would think of our act.

Night came on and we kept going till Bill got sleepy and we began to look for a place to sleep. We had enough sense not to stop along the highway. We didn't know exactly why but we were guided by our instinct I guess, so we kept a sharp eye for a suit able place off the road where we would not be trespassing. We finally came to a dirt lane that turned off the highway. Bill turned into this trail and we came to a nook that just pleased us about half a mile from the main road. So there we spent the night, thinking we were not trespassing on anybody's property. All of us were weary and tired, so we went to sleep without any trouble.

The next morning we were up with the sun and we had almost slept in a man's sweet potato patch. The house and barn were only a short distance away and we could see the man out feeding his livestock. But he didn't say anything to us and we thought we would let doing well enough alone and pulled out quickly and headed

OUR FIRST RECORD

for the highway. We stopped along the way and had breakfast in the shade of the trees by the roadside.

We got into Atlanta about ten o'clock in the morning and went right to the building where we were supposed to meet Mr. Miller. I forgot the name of that building but it was somewhere near the Wurlitzer Store. It was in the afternoon before we were supposed to report but we decided to go early and find out about the time and check it for sure. A man told us we were scheduled to be there all right and he had the time down on a book.

While we were waiting to get in to see the man, we were gawking at the recording stars. They were an interesting sight.

Something we had not expected to see. They wore the best of clothes and had diamond rings on their fingers and presented an atmosphere that simply bewildered all four of us boys. There we were with old dress pants on and cotton sack guitar cases and we began to wonder why we had come over here at all. We began to lose confidence. These people had something and were not the kind of folks they sounded like on the records we had at home. There was Clayton McMichen and he really was a dandy. All tailored up in the finest clothes, and they fit him perfectly. We had listened to his records and he sounded like a true mountaineer. And Riley Puckett, who was blind. But he dressed immaculately and clean as a pin. He couldn't see, but his knack for good-looking clothes must have been instinctive. So we saw them all and we had heard them all on record. I can't remember all the names that were there but there were enough of them to cause us no end of anxiety. Gid Tanner, Lowe Stokes, Hugh Cross, Tom Darby, Jimmie Tarlton, Fiddlin' John Carson, and Rev. Andrew Jenkins (who wrote "The Death of Floyd Collins," "Ben Dewberry's Final Run," and many, many, more song hits back in the late twenties and early thirties. Many of his songs are still used widely, especially his wonderful hymns like "God Put a Rainbow

OUR FIRST RECORD

in the Cloud," etc.)

All those famous recording stars ignored us, or we thought they did, till we learned better. They were just acting normal. They didn't have time to take up with such guys as us but nevertheless we felt plenty hurt for a while. But something happened I'll never forget to cause us to feel much better and entirely change our minds about the whole gang of recording musicians. But I'll follow the sequence of events so that I'll not leave anything out, for the time ensuing, in-between, is one hilarious memory to me now in retrospect. We were really country boys.

When we left the recording building we didn't know exactly what to do. Atlanta was the biggest city we had ever been to and we were like a bunch of wild animals in captivity. We had the idea of self-preservation, though, for we began to look for a place to spend the night. Hotels were out of the picture, for none of us trusted the big town and its ways. We drove for a long while and finally came to the place where the city began to play out and the traffic was not too thick. We kept on driving till we came to a quiet road and there was an old sawmill on the left side and there was plenty of room to drive around and park. The sawmill must have been still in operation, for there was sawdust and the machinery was all there and it looked like it had been used that day or not many days away. Anyway, there was not any rust on the wheels and it afforded an ideal place, we thought, to spend the night. It must have been about eight o'clock at night when we discovered the sawmill, and that was not long till bedtime according to the way we lived in those days.

Each of us had money but we preferred this quiet place to the hotels. In fact, the one main reason we liked to go off like that to a secluded spot, none of us knew how to get into a hotel. We didn't know you have to register in. And frankly, we just didn't know how to go about it. So that night we all found us a place on the sawdust, and after eating some of the cold food—pork and beans and Vienna sausage and cheese—we found our blankets and quietly went to sleep under the stars, out in the open country, where the wind rustled and the nocturnal birds and insects set up their wild chorus to put us in a dreamy mood. I lay awake for awhile and listened to the night sounds and thought of what lay in store for us the next day. I had gained some of my confidence back since I was out in the open where I could breathe easy and get my thoughts together. The other boys felt the same as I could tell by the way they talked.

The next morning we woke up bright and early so we could get away before the sawmill men showed up. We didn't know whether it was illegal or not to sleep on a sawdust pile but we didn't mean to get caught. We could not afford to let anything interfere with our date with the record man. The dew was still on the weeds and grass when we took off from our Saw Mill Hotel. We stopped along the way and ate some more of the food we had brought along and it was really good after a good night's sleep on the sawdust. We felt like a new gang of guys after the rest and we determined to make the best of the tryout for the record man.

Our date with the record man was in the morning somewhere around ten o'clock, and we had a lot of time to kill before we were due. So we cruised around in the old Chevrolet and saw some amazing sights. The location was near Decatur, Georgia, and we saw the Stone Mountain Memorial. It was really a fascinating sight and it still is. But we didn't know what it was then. If you're ever near that part of the country you should see it, for it is one of the few scenic wonders that I really was thrilled to see. I cannot describe it without a lot of words, so I will just say it is a granite hill and it looms up like a gigantic joker when you first see it. Honest, it's that unbelievable.

We fooled around till about nine o'clock and then went up to the recording place. We didn't want to be late for this appointment. We didn't dare! When we got up there, there was already several people waiting with guitars and various instruments.

OUR FIRST RECORD

They were waiting to be heard. Altogether there were over three hundred musicians wanting to get a chance to make records. We didn't know how many there were then but the record man told us later. We knew we had an appointment to be heard, but after seeing this large array of people waiting, our hearts sank a little. We were still afraid and untrusting. But we were confident and determined to play the string out.

The record man kept coming out and beckoning different ones and groups to come in for an audition. Some of them came out looking really glad and some not so glad. But they all had confidence that maybe someday they could make it and be on record. Most of them didn't make it but they all had alibis—a sore throat, indigestion, failure of the record man to recognize or appreciate extraordinary talent, etc., etc.

Some of the recording stars came in and they still were aloof to all of us there to get an audition. We didn't know any of them except when some of the other hopefuls would tell us who they were. But we soon learned they didn't cater to the ordinary fan and that is precisely what we were. I didn't understand them at all then, but now I understand perfectly how they felt. They were not "stuck up" like all of us thought but were acting perfectly normal. They were all wonderful, finished performers and artists in their own right and they didn't have much patience with the riff raff. That is just a normal attitude for a professional performer, I was later to learn.

It was near ten o'clock and the record man finally looked over our way and beckoned us to come in. We instantly obeyed him and he led us into a funny-looking room which had drapes and curtains all around on the walls. It sure was a fantastic-looking place to a bunch of country boys like us. But the record man was real friendly and introduced himself.

"I'm Dan Hornsby* an assistant to Mr. Bob Miller," he said. "I'm listening to you boys and will tell you what happens after I have heard you play a few songs. You boys sing?"

"Yes sir, we try," I said.

"Do you have any songs you wrote yourself?"

"Yes sir."

"Well let's get on with the audition. I just wanted to save some time. And by asking you these questions I find you are at least eligible for what we need on Columbia. We are interested in original songs and singers. I have turned down many good musicians because they didn't have anything original. Now I want you boys to just relax and sing like you were back home in the cotton field or in church and among friends. I hope you are what we are looking for."

The first song we played and sang was one we called "Got the Kansas City Blues."

He seemed impressed but we still didn't know what he had on his mind. We stopped.

"Just keep on singing song after song till I tell you that's enough," he smiled.

So we sang another song, an original we later used for our theme song, "Alabama Lullaby." After that, we sang "The Girls Don't Worry My Mind" and several more songs I had written myself. I began to doubt the quality of my songs and he told us that would be enough.

"Now would you boys like to hear what you sound like?" he asked. We had been playing in front of a little stand that had something that looked like a can on top of it. We didn't know it was a microphone.

"We sure would."

*Dan Hornsby was a Columbia studio musician who worked in the field with Bob Miller. The team had replaced Frank Walker and Bill Brown, the team that had pioneered the idea of field recording sessions for Columbia. Hornsby was a trained musician with a good baritone voice who himself made quite a few novelty and "event" songs for Columbia. He also acted as sort of a music librarian for Columbia, seeing over the Atlanta studio's substantial collection of sheet music. He would work with artists, help them find words to old songs, and on more than one occasion would sing the vocal with stringbands if the band had no suitable singer. Hornsby can be heard singing on various records by the Skillet Lickers and by Jess Young's Tennessee Band.—Ed.

OUR FIRST RECORD

So he turned on the machine and we began to hear ourselves sing the songs we had just put on the wax. We recorded on wax for years before they started making them on tape. But when he started the music and we heard what we had played and sang it didn't sound real. It sounded like something far superior to what we thought we were doing. We could not believe it was us! But we were tickled pink and so were Old Bill and Bee. And for that matter, so was Dan Hornsby. He showed it in every way that a man can. He really bragged on us and went immediately in to see Bob Miller. Before he went to see Mr. Miller, he told us he thought we were "in," but he had to make sure because he didn't have the last word.

While he was gone in to see Mr. Miller, we sat there dreaming and hoping. Everything seemed like a nightmare. It just couldn't be. Country boys like us getting a break on records—but then, we sounded much better than ourselves on the wax—that is, much better than our real selves, we thought. There was something divine in that little can, as it looked like to us, that helped us immensely and changed us from two country farm boy singers to something "up town" and acceptable to listeners who bought records and listened to radio programs. That was the whole secret of our good luck. Our voices took well to the microphone.

Dan Hornsby came out beaming. "Mr. Miller says for you boys to come in this afternoon at five to make records."

We were walking on air when we left the studio. And we never gave money a thought. We were just sublimely thrilled to get a chance to make one record. There were so many of the stars of records and I had met some of them—Uncle Dave Macon, the Allen Brothers—and had seen but not met personally Gid Tanner, Fate Norris, and Claude Davis when they played a personal appearance in Decatur, Alabama, one time. And now we would be on record!

It was hard to believe it was real as we went into the place where all the musicians

61

were gathered. It was kind of a lobby. Not many seats, but plenty of room for everybody to move about and everybody seemed impatient. Especially the recording artists. Some of them were shooting craps to pass away the time. They had appointments, too, like us. It was hard waiting.

We had already decided to leave immediately after we had got the word that we would record. We wanted to get off somewhere to think it all over and get our bearings. We were really all shook up.

The professionals were still paying no attention to any of us guys that were auditioning. They didn't know the good from the unfortunates until they heard them, and they were taking the right attitude, I know now. You can't fuss with every opportunist who comes your way and wind up with any rest, or any nerves, or much of anything else if you do.

We had our old picksack cases around our instruments and were going out when two old gentlemen standing by the window stopped us and began asking us questions. We hadn't heard who they were and we were in a hurry, but we stopped and tried to be friendly to them, deciding that we could at least be more friendly than the great stars had been to us. One of them looked at our guitar cases and read that we were from Athens, Alabama. He misread it and thought we were from Athens, Georgia.

"Hey, boys," he looked at the recording artists gathered in a group. "We have two boys from way over in Athens, Georgia, come here to try out and I'll bet you they can beat us all put together." He laughed. He was really a friendly person, and the recording stars paid attention to him when he spoke. They knew him but we didn't. He looked over directly to where the record stars were congregated and shook his finger at them.

"Now if you want to hear some real singing just shut up and lis ten to these two boys and then I'll bet you'll be glad you did." He had never heard us but he was there going to town for us in front of the nation's best-selling hillbilly record artists. I guess we looked a little impatient to him.

OUR FIRST RECORD

"Now boys, I'm old Fiddlin' John Carson and this is my friend, Rev. Andrew Jenkins, who's wrote so many pretty songs. You may not have heard of him but he sure does write pretty songs. Now, as a favor to me and Rev. Jenkins, will you boys take your guitars out and play a song or two? We are old men compared to the rest of that bunch over there," he pointed to the record stars, "but we appreciate good singing and playing." Before he was through with his talk we had our guitars out and were ready to play. I had heard of those fellows all of my life.

"What would you like us to play?"

"Oh, just anything you boys want to sing and we'll help you." I was dubious about the last part of his statement, but we fired into "Left My Gal in the Mountains," and before we were halfway through all those record stars were over there with us, singing along just like a choir. It was, and still remains, one of the biggest thrills of all time in the show business. And it all started with one old considerate fellow, or rather two, who wanted to make a bunch of country boys feel welcome.

I never saw either one of them after that, but I'll always have a warm place in my heart for those two old-timers, Fiddlin' John Carson and Rev. Andrew Jenkins. To you fellows who are reading this, I want to say right here and now that whatever cloud seems to be insurmountable will always have its silver lining if you pursue in your ambition long enough and try hard enough. It will never be dished out to you on a silver platter unless you work to get it. We had worked like field hands for this chance and these two old-timers put icing on the cake for us. That is the way of show business. The whole gang of record stars began to accept us as one of them and that was another big thrill. They didn't ask a lot of questions or anything like that, but we could sure tell a difference from the freeze we had been used to before.

We sang several songs together before we had to leave and everybody joined in.

OUR FIRST RECORD

Even the ones who were waiting for an audition. Suddenly we realized there had been no animosity all along. We just simply had misunderstood the guys and we didn't know exactly how the world went. But then, on the other hand, we were all very young to be out looking for a recording contract. It's a funny thing, though: we didn't care about a contract. We just wanted to sing. And I think the whole gang in the building that day finally realized our zest and our honest ignorance which bordered on the sublime. We were not looking for money. Singing and playing was all that was interesting to us, and the "pros" there wanted money. They all wanted money. And there was trouble about money and some of them left without even making a record. We didn't know it then, but we learned later what it was all about. The old Columbia company was going broke. You see there was no money around in the pockets of the common man who buys records: It was the Great Depression that was causing all of this. And that is when we got started. A dime then looked as big as a dollar does now. Most everybody was hungry but rich folks and the people who had government jobs in Washington and other high places. They didn't suffer, but if I mash my finger does it hurt you? No. So it was in the hard times when we made records. Hunger stalked the land like an evil phantom. But strangely enough, we enjoyed ourselves more then than I can recall later. We had to forage for food, the absolute necessities of life, and we had to get it any way we could. Anybody who went through those days of hardship can tell you the same as I'm telling, and there's lots of people still around who can vouch for this. If you have any doubts just ask a few of the old-timers and learn first hand. Pardon my little dissertation on the Depression, but there was a depression all the time Rabon and me were at the crest of our career. So it kind of reminds me of the cartoon: "Born Thirty Years Too Soon."

We sang several songs with the gang before we took off to relax and wait for the five o'clock date to record. We got away and drove around the town some more, but we were extremely excited about the good fortune that was coming our way. There were many pretty sights around Atlanta. We went in a lot of stores and bought a few little things, but we all guarded our money very carefully. We soon hit out for the open road, for the sights of the city didn't calm us down and we wanted to be at our best when we faced Mr. Miller. As yet, we had not even met him and we wondered if he would be as good and friendly a fellow as Dan Hornsby. We didn't think it was possible but we had hopes.

We traveled to a remote section of the highway and stopped the car to rest. After we relaxed a little and talked a whole lot, Rabon and me got our instruments out and rehearsed the songs we had sung for Dan Hornsby. They were very easy songs to sing but we didn't want to miss the words or music to them. The time finally came when we had to start back to the recording building. We were still wondering what we would find in Mr. Bob Miller.

When we arrived at the studio, Dan Hornsby was there to meet us and he took us in to meet Mr. Miller. We saw a kind of heavy set, ruddy, round-faced, friendly man who put us at ease immediately. He was even friendlier than Dan Hornsby, if that could be possible. The first thing he did was compliment us on the style we had and he called it "wonderful." He told us of many things we could accomplish if we kept going like we had started out. He told us, although he lived in New York then, he was originally from Memphis, Tennessee. He was trying to make us comfortable as Southerners, that he also was a Southerner, and maybe we would feel more at home. But we didn't know the significance of such a thing then, so his try there met with a blank.

We went over the songs again for him for timing, and every one of them timed out just right. He tested for balance and then we were ready to make our first record. We had begun to realize what the little can meant by now and I began to be slightly afraid of it. I never asked Rabon, but I don't believe he was a bit nervous because he seemed to be in a relaxed mood.

OUR FIRST RECORD

Mr. Miller showed us the little red light that would come on and then we were to start singing and playing, making the recording. That was the part that made me a little more nervous. A little light, a mechanical gadget that seemed to be telling me what to do. That was the way I felt. But I soon got used to it. The first recording was "Got the Kansas City Blues," and then he played it back to see how we liked it. We liked it all right, for we had made no mistakes in it. And in those days, if we made one little sputter on a string or didn't get the tone of voice just right we would never have let it go at all. Mr. Miller said that was fine and he said: "Let's go into the next song." He brought out a gallon jug of white liquor or moonshine and asked us did we like a drink. Rabon and Bill didn't drink so they refused. Bee and myself drank some but we didn't take him up on the free offer. l was afraid there might be some catch in it somewhere, and although I could have used a little nip for my nerves, I let it pass by and we went ahead with the records. Mr. Miller kept telling us what a wonderful future we had in the record business. And I know that he was sincere in what he said, for he didn't know then that the company was going broke a bit more than we did. He told us we would be able to get the best of guitars and drive big cars and live really high.

"You boys make me think of Carson Robison and Vernon Dalhart," he said, "and they have all that." That made us feel mighty good because we had some of the records made by those artists and they really sounded good. We knew we couldn't sound good as they did, but it helped a lot to hear somebody like Mr. Miller say that anyway.

We went on ahead and made another song. This time it was "Alabama Lullaby," "Oh, Carry Me Back to the Land of My Dreams," which we used so long for a theme. In fact, we always used it as our theme, unless the sponsor wanted us to make up one about his product. And you can't tell a sponsor what to do unless you want to start looking for a new job.

OUR FIRST RECORD

We made two more sides "The Girls Don't Worry My Mind" and "Smoky Mountain Bill and His Song," a song I wrote in the place of Carson Robison's song "Smoky Mountain Bill."* The reason I wrote it was because I heard it on the radio and couldn't find the song anywhere, so we liked his song and that is the rea son. I offered him the royalty on the one I had written later, but he wouldn't accept it. But when we got hold of his song, we used it instead of the one I had written and I guess he got performance royalty on it. We liked it and used it a lot.

There's one thing that stands in my mind about our first record session that I'll never forget and that is about Bob Miller. You see Bob Miller was a famous songwriter, but I didn't know it then, or I'd never made the faux pas I did. During the talks we had, he asked had we heard the song "Twenty One Years." We had the record of Mac and Bob singing and playing it. The boys did a good job on the record but somehow I just never did like the song too much. When Mr. Miller asked about it, I was supremely ignorant of any songs I didn't like, so I blurted out, "Yes, Mr. Miller, I've heard that song and never have liked it, though my folks are crazy about it," and they were. He didn't say any more and he didn't change a bit in his expression. "Twenty One Years" was an all-time great prison song hit. Bob Miller wrote it.**

*The titles "The Girls Don't Worry My Mind"and "Smoky Mountain Bill and His Song" were never released by Columbia, nor do they appear in the Columbia files of unissued masters. The only two Delmore masters Columbia shows from this 1931 session were the two released sides, "Got the Kansas City Blues" and "Alabama Lullaby." It is quite possible that the brothers made several test recordings for Columbia that were never assigned a master number, then later sanded and possibly reused. "Smoky Mountain Bill and His Song" and "The Girls Don't Worry My Mind" were among the songs later recorded at the Delmores' first Bluebird session. —Ed.

**Miller's interest in "Twenty-One Years" may have been related to the fact that Riley Puckett was recording his version of the song at this same session. Puckett, in fact, recorded his version the day after (October 29) the Delmores recorded.—Ed.

OUR FIRST RECORD

It didn't take long to get the four songs made and that was a session. I think we made all of them in less than an hour. When we got though Mr. Miller said he would mail us our contracts and he gave us twenty-five dollars, to help pay expenses he told us. "Now you boys just sit tight, and wait for me to write, and we are going to be on top before very long, I'll guarantee that," he said. "And tell everybody back home you are real recording artists now. We'll get this first record out in about a month and you can hear yourself while you are walking down the street." He smiled and shook hands with us and told us good luck and we were on our way after the first record. But we still had a long, hard, row to hoe although we were oblivious to the fact.*

*True to his word, Miller released the record in December 1931, but the issue sold only 511 copies. This was not especially a failure, as most of the issues during that year sold around this amount—an indication of how the Depression was affecting the record industry.—Ed.

CHAPTER EIGHT

WE AUDITION FOR
THE
GRAND OLE OPRY

We took our time and traveled leisurely on the way back home. There were a lot of pleasant memories and we wanted to think everything over, so that is the reason for the leisurely return. We still didn't take to hotels and the cafes but slept out and ate in the open. You know that's a lot of fun if the weather is good; it is real healthy because you get fresh air. That was before the atom bomb. Now, I don't know what you'd get if you stayed out in the open too long, that is, in case of fallout. Anyway, there was no contamination at all in that Georgia region of the piney woods country—nothing but just pungent purity with a pine twang.

The twenty-five dollars Bob Miller gave us was not even considered as any kind of payment compared with the lift it had given us music-wise. We were still too flabbergasted to get down to earth. What we needed then, and always did, was a manager. But they did not have them then like they do now. At least, managers were not available for poor country boys like us, who didn't even have a change of clothes except overalls and work clothes. That is why it was so strange to us. We couldn't get it through our heads that we were now traveling in a different world than we were when we were in the cotton patch. And that was bad. It was always bad for we never did fully accept the responsibility of business. We were emphatic on the side of artistry and not on money.

WE AUDITION FOR THE GRAND OLE OPRY

In other words, we did not ever accept the bread and butter side of things till it was too late. We knew we had to eat, but we thought and took it for granted, like the verse in the Bible that says something about the birds of the field that never worry over the things of tomorrow for they will be taken care of anyway.

I had an old typewriter and I kept it busy writing to various radio stations and asking for a job of some kind but the answer always came in the negative.

We came through Anniston, Alabama, on the way back and we found out there was a radio station located in town so we decided to go by and put on a program for them. In those days you could do that—just go in at any time of the day and tell them you wanted to put on a program, and they would listen to see if you were capable (and you didn't have to be too capable) and in about fifteen minutes you would be on the air. That is the way we did there in Anniston. Rabon had never played on the radio before, but I had played several times as I have mentioned before. So we got together a thirty-minute program and went on the air. Bee could play the harmonica and he helped out on the program and we had a big time. The announcer gave us lots of plugs about our records and it was a great big boost all the way around. They were glad to have us, and we certainly were glad of the opportunity to advertise our records and get the big publicity. The announcer was a real friendly chap, and we could have worked indefinitely with a fellow like him, but we had to get on our way. We didn't know it then, but we were to see this young announcer again in the near future. He was still the same friendly young man we saw in Anniston and he still is today—Ott Devine, general manager of the WSM Grand Ole Opry in Nashville, Tennessee. Of course Ott was several years in coming to the Opry, but he made good when he did.

When we got back home all the people were mighty glad to see us and to know we had made good. The two county papers put a big story on the front page and we were really recognized in the home county. I couldn't walk down the street without someone coming up and shaking hands and telling me how they appreciated our putting the hometown on the map. But we still didn't have any money and times were hard as I've said before. We had everything except money, and we had to get that some way, so we still competed in the old fiddlers' contests, although we didn't consider it quite fair to the other contestants, since they had no publicity like we had. But we had to make money some way and that was better than nothing. We could have started a show, and we eventually did, but at the present time we still had the contest lure.

And, too, it was a good way to advertise our records, when and if they were released. But we still couldn't make enough money to make ends meet. Of course, Rabon was still going to school and that had to be considered, too. And he was nothing but a kid. I was not much more. We had the fire to be entertainers but we didn't know quite how to go about it. If we had lived in a city, it might have been different. But not in the lonely country, where the only outside connection with the other world is the daily rural postman. I kept writing letters.

We finally decided to get up a show and start playing personal appearances. There was a good blackfaced comedian, George Smith, who worked with us and he had a car for us to travel in. He used his brother as a straight man and we had a good little show with music, singing, and good comedy. Before I go any further, I want to say I have never seen any blackfaced comedian any better than George. He would have made the big time if he had tried.

Sometimes his brother would not show up and I would have to play the straight man with him. It was hard for me to do because he was so funny; I would get tickled and spoil the joke. He didn't like that at all. So I learned to control myself, although it was a job sometimes. He was really great. But all he wanted was the laughter of the crowd, not his straight man. We made good money on a lot of school dates. Being known, like we were, it was easy to book most of the big schools without any trouble. George did the booking and advertising and we split three ways, after paying for his gas, and he payed his brother with his part. I look back on those days, and review the other days, and they remain some of the happiest. So you see you may have gold at the end of the rainbow without knowing it.

We listened to the Grand Ole Opry a lot in those days and we longed to be there on the program with the other entertainers. It was an obsession with me, and Rabon felt about the same way. He always loved music so much that he would do almost anything just to get to play a little with someone or be on a program with other artists. That's the reason we liked the old fiddlers' contests so well. We always felt the challenge to play a little better, and any way we could improve, we did it. We would watch other performers and pick up something from them. You can always pick up something if you are wanting to go places. It may be just a little something that seems terribly insignificant. But it may make the difference in a hit song or record later in your career. For example, the guitar style of Johnny Cash. That's his trademark. Merle Travis, Chet Atkins, Sugarfoot Garland, and all of them have little characteristics that are their own style. And it completely sets them away from the average run-of-the-mill guitar players. Any true artist is that way in my opinion. Songwriters are, too, and a real good musician or songwriter can pick out another's style. I can tell you the style of lots of the composers just by hearing their songs, because it sounds like them. Some of them have told me they can tell my song style. I learned and still learn from other songwriters. When I first met the late Fred Rose, he helped me a lot in writing songs and I copied some of his little twists in my songs later, but I didn't mean to be stealing his style. If I had wanted to, I couldn't have, because it is impossible to really steal a songwriter's style. But you can learn something from him just like I said above. Writing songs is the most rewarding thing I know of, except writing a novel. That's why I took up music. I didn't want to sing, I wanted to write songs. That was the main reason and that satisfied my creative urge. I have talked to a lot of songwriters and singers, one especially, Ernest Tubb. Ernest told me one time he would never die happy unless he could write a story and have it published, or a novel. That remains a mystery to me about artists and artistic people. They always want to do everything, and they might come close to succeeding if they would pursue along those lines they want to so badly.

So you see we had a dedicated attitude toward the Grand Ole Opry. It was like something like Cinderella felt when she made her big splash. It was ambition with an amazing intensity—just longing for something that is seemingly impossible to attain. I still remember very clearly how I felt and I'm sure Rabon felt the same way. Two country boys longing for the chance to perform in what was, to us, like heaven. Now this all brings me up to the day of our audition at radio station WSM and the famed Grand Ole Opry.

I had written Harry Stone, the manager of WSM then, and asked repeatedly for a chance to audition for the Grand Ole Opry, but every time came the same answer. Nothing open and the program was full, and he was right. The program was full; and with the good musicians they had they didn't seem to ever need anybody like us, but I kept writing him letters. And there were rumors, some of them wild and discouraging. For instance, we were told that only people from Tennessee were allowed to play on the Grand Ole Opry, and those rumors, fantastic as they sounded, were depressing to us. I never mentioned this to Mr. Stone in my letters because I did not want to believe it, and I was afraid if I mentioned it, he would confirm it and then there would be nothing left but chaos for Rabon and myself and our heartfelt ambition. Times were hard and we were lucky to have food on the table, and the winds of winter and summer can be dampening if you give up in your ambition.

So I stuck by my guns (or rather my typewriter) and kept on writing letters,

WE AUDITION FOR THE GRAND OLE OPRY

begging for an audition, to Mr. Stone.

We were still playing schoolhouses and any other place we could book, and still the old fiddlers' contests, and we brought home some money nearly every time—precious money that kept some food on the table, along with daddy's help. We were treated almost as celebrities then in our home, Limestone County, Alabama, but we didn't have the money to make the thing real.

That's always been my trouble; I have never had the money people thought I was supposed to have. But you know people get stunning ideas about somebody that is known, although the party known may not have enough for the next meal. That's the tragic part of being known. If you have no money they will say: "Well? He used to be a millionaire, but he drank it all up and now look at him." Or, if an entertainer goes with women they'll say: "Now look at him. He used to be worth a cool million dollars but some little strumpet got it and then let him down and there he goes, full of sin and meanness." Gossipers ... you try to figure them out and let me know how you do.

As you can see, I digress from my subject too often maybe for some people, but I hope you will forgive me, for I am trying to be very frank in this account of my life story. You will be amazed and really thrilled later on in the following pages if you will bear with me.

As I said a page or two ago, I kept writing Harry Stone in Nashville, trying to get on the Grand Ole Opry. So one day the letter came. We were to come up for an audition on Monday of the following week. That was a big thrill and my heart felt the impact. At last, we were to be given a chance to show them what we could do.

We began making preparations to make the trip. We had no car or any means of transportation, so we had to look around and find somebody to carry us to Nashville. My cousin, Jake Williams, agreed to take us if we would pay for the gas up there and back. So we made our plans to go swiftly.

74

WE AUDITION FOR THE GRAND OLE OPRY

Mr. Stone said plainly in his letter that we were to come on Monday for the audition, but Jake could not make it for some reason and we had to wait till Tuesday. We didn't know how he would take it but we didn't think one day would make much difference, so we headed for Nashville without giving it much thought. And there's where we were plenty wrong. We had to learn the hard way.

It was in the springtime of the year because the Southern League baseball season started on the day we arrived in Nashville. And Nashville was always one of the strongest clubs in the league, fanwise. Anyway, we asked several people where the radio station was located and finally parked the car and headed for the National Life Building on Seventh Avenue. It was a five-story building then and WSM was located on the fifth floor. We were really thrilled as we caught the elevator for our audition.

When we reached the fifth floor we went immediately to Mr. Stone's office. We were awed and afraid of the big things we saw all around us, and we had a fear that maybe we were not ready for so big a place after all. It was all business, too, and that helped to excite us. For we had expected an air of relaxation like it sounded on the Grand Ole Opry. But here we were, in a huge atmosphere of big time and with nothing to fight with but two worn guitars in cotton pick-sack cases. No kidding. That is exactly how I felt, and Rabon told me later he felt the same way. But then, I was older than he was and I don't believe the impact on him was as terrifying as it was to me. But the old determination was there and it was fed by the ego every country boy has of whipping someone in the big city. Our work was cut out for us and we knew it.

When we went into Mr. Stone's office he was not there but the girl told us to look around, if we wanted to, and he'd be back in a short while. So we proceeded to look around from one studio to the other. There were only two studios in those days but they were the highest we had ever seen. We didn't go inside the studio but stood on the outside, just looking and marveling. I wondered if we would ever make the grade for a plush place like this. We were standing outside the biggest studio when someone spoke to us: "Are you the guys who were supposed to come in yesterday for an audition?" He was a tall man with a dark, serious complexion. The suit he wore was of the very best, and he had on a tie and his shoes were shined and he looked like a lawyer to me. As he spoke I could tell he was irritated and that didn't help anything. "I'm Harry Stone," he said, "the station manager, and I specifically told you guys in my letter to come up yesterday. Now tell me what happened?"

"Well, we don't have an automobile, and Jake here couldn't make it yesterday so we thought one day wouldn't make any difference." I spoke the truth but it didn't have any effect on him. He was mad at us. He asked us could we come back the next day.

"I want to go to the ball game and I won't have time for an audition before the game. Besides," he said, "you guys are going to have to be prompt or learn to be prompt if you ever intend to be regular entertainers on a radio station. These programs don't wait on people. You are either here or you're not here. I can't afford to fool around with people like you, who put things off and think nothing about it." He was *so* right then, but I was not to understand this till way later.

"Well, Mr. Stone, we just don't have the money to come back up here any other day this week. But we could give you the songs real quickly as we have them all rehearsed very well, and maybe you could hear us and still have time to go to the ball game." I was desperate when I told him that.

He wheeled around to leave, took a few steps and turned around again. He was still angry.

"Well, you guys get into that big studio and do it fast. I'll be back in a minute or two, and you better be ready to play, for I don't want to miss that game." He stalked away and we slunk into the big studio to do as he said. This was a bad break in itself,

WE AUDITION FOR THE GRAND OLE OPRY

I thought, if we had the bossman mad at us before we had ever started. I'll be frank with you. I didn't think we had a ghost of a chance after we had fouled up the way we had. But I still could not realize the full impact of his anger about a trivial thing like not being there on the day he stated.

We went into the big studio with some misgivings, but we got our guitars out of the pick-sacks and had them in perfect tune in about one minute flat. It was about five minutes before he came back and he was not alone. He had five more men with him and they were as elegantly dressed as he was. They were all dressed like movie stars. I never dreamed they were so ritzy around a radio station which sounded so homespun to the listener. I didn't like the idea of so many listening to us for just an audition but I didn't say anything. If I had known who they were at the time I guess I would have passed out. But luckily, I didn't discover who they were for several weeks. Or at least some of them for one week.

They all sat down around the walls of the studio, except Mr. Stone. He sat down at the announcer's desk, where the microphone was. "Now you guys just play like you do back home and relax. Play me some of your original songs first. When you finish one song go right on into the next one, 'cause I'll be damned if I'm gonna miss that ball game on account of you fellows."

Some of the men around the walls smiled a little when he said that, but he didn't. He meant it, but I was grateful that we were getting a chance. We fired into "I Ain't Got Nowhere to Travel," "I'm Mississippi Bound," and several more of our original songs. And then he stopped us.

"How many original songs do you boys have?"

"I guess about twenty-five or so," I said. He told us that was enough original songs, and for us to play some request songs.

We looked at the men grouped around us for any clue as to how they were liking us, but we couldn't tell anything about them.

WE AUDITION FOR THE GRAND OLE OPRY

Their faces, as a whole, were inscrutable as statues, and Mr. Stone was even worse. None of them frowned, but he was frowning and my heart sank for I thought we had made a faux pas. A failure.

He told us the request songs were something like "That Silver Haired Daddy of Mine," etc. We started singing "Silver Haired Daddy" and I forgot he words. Rabon didn't but I did. I had to think quick so I pulled one of my first professional tricks on the audition. I didn't know it then, but I do now. I stopped playing and Rabon stopped. And I began to tune a string that was already in tune to cover up for the mistake I had made. It worked like a charm. We went on through the song after that, and never missed a word. Mr. Stone got up to go. He yawned and stretched. But I begged him to let us sing "Lamp Lightin' Time in the Valley," a song written and sung by the Vagabonds, the hit act on the station. He reluctantly agreed and three of the fellows got up to leave. "If they're gonna sing that damn thing I don't want to hear it," one of them said. And they stalked out like somebody had hurt their feelings. That made me feel bad again. I couldn't understand anybody who didn't like a beautiful song like that. Mr. Stone said for us to sing just one verse of it and that would be all. He had heard enough. So we sailed into it and sang the one verse, although it is a ballad song. When we got through that one verse, Mr. Stone and the other two men left without even looking at us one time. So when that happened I got mad. Jake had been in the studio with us all the time and I think he felt just about like we did. That we had gotten a raw deal. We just couldn't understand how people could act like that without being provoked. They were all cold as ice. Of course Mr. Stone, we thought, had a right to be a little tough, but he had already been and he had agreed to give us the audition. So we were quite bewildered.

"Rabon, put up your guitar and let's get out of here the quickest way we can. I would still like to get a job on the Opry but they don't have to treat us like we were suck egg dogs."

"I don't like them either," Rabon said.

Jake said: "They acted like they were mad all the time, didn't they?"

"Yes, Jake, they sure did, and we don't have to be treated like that. I'd rather plow, hadn't you?"

I was pretty bitter.

So we all headed for the elevator with our faded old clothes and our guitars with the pick-sack cases. We still had spunk.

When we got to the elevator it was not there. There were some steps leading down and we began going down the steps. The quickest way out for us was too slow, we thought, as we started down. We hadn't walked down the first flight when someone called us.

It was Mr. Stone.

"Where do you guys think you are going," he asked.

"We're just going home, I guess. Can't we walk down the stairs, is there any rule against this?" I asked him.

"You boys come back. I want to talk to you." He ignored my question.

We went back up. His expression still remained the same. There was no elation, no welcome look as we could see. Still the same old poker face. He didn't mince words.

"Can you guys be up here Saturday night at nine o'clock?" he asked.

"What for?" I asked him.

"You will take the Pickard Family's spot on the Opry. They are leaving for Chicago and we need you to fill their place on the show. You will have a thirty-minute program to do. Now, you have a lot of original songs in your repertoire, but don't play too many of them at first. Kind of mix them up with the old songs and request songs, and we'll see how this does for the first program. So be in town by about six

WE AUDITION FOR THE GRAND OLE OPRY

o'clock Saturday afternoon, and let us know you are here."

He still didn't brag on us but he had given us one of the greatest thrills we ever had.

We were on the Grand Ole Opry!

CHAPTER NINE

TRIALS AND TRIBULATIONS

We felt kind of numb at first. And nobody said much to each other. We all knew that the Grand Ole Opry was the greatest show on the air at that time. Or, at least people in the South thought so, and we were Southerners.

Jake got the car started and we headed for home with the proverbial bacon, we thought. But we were later to learn very much more about the business of entertaining, or show business, they now call it, than we suspected. There were pitfalls along the way and snares that catch you and treat you worse than a rabbit because a rabbit just dies, but you live on after the snare treatment, wondering sometimes out loud, talking to yourself, "What did I ever do to him that caused him to hurt me with a lie like that?" or "You just don't know who will damage you and hurt you to the quick," or "Well, I helped him when he needed a friend, and now look what he does to me."

The above statements remind me of the late, eminent Hank Williams, who was the victim of many false statements that cut him deeply and hurt him permanently, and was one of the direct causes of his premature departure from this earth. There are many more besides Hank, and I will mention them later on in this book, but I will never tell who did the satanic dirt. I don't have to. Other musicians know who they are without me sticking my neck out. Because they always are, and they always will be, as long as there's show business in this old world. Some of them make big names for themselves by climbing, like a monkey, over the shoulders of someone already known, damaging reputations till they are in the driver's seat. Then, they are content to drift along, like a beneficent angel, in the comfortable breeze of big money. More about this later.

To come back to the scene of our first visit to Nashville, when we first felt our supreme elation of the great Grand Ole Opry: We were divinely innocent. When we came by the WSM radio tower going up for the audition, there was a feeling of awe, and it reached to the seemingly impossible act of ever going on a station with that big a capacity.* It was one of the world's tallest radio towers and it still is, to my knowledge, and it gave off a seeming challenge to anyone who wanted to go far and do things. There it was, blinking and flashing its facility out to some little person or persons, who thought they deserved the plaudits of the great Grand Ole Opry audience. You look at it when you pass by sometime. It is on Highway 31 between Nashville and Franklin. Think of what I have written and put yourself in my place and I'll bet a horse you'll feel the same as I did when we came by on our way to the audition!

It is a strange thing for me to say, but the manager of the station and the others there who heard our audition didn't add up to anything like the challenge that tall tower did. It was a tall tower, and it takes a lot to stay tall like it does. But we tried it. Our listeners thought we were tall, like the tower, but we never felt we quite made it to our own way of thinking and judging. And I, personally, don't think anyone

---

*WSM started operating in 1925 as a 1,000-watt station, making it one of two most powerful stations in the South and more powerful than 85 percent of the other stations in the country. In early 1927, as more and more radio stations began to spring up around the country, the WSM power was upped to 5,000 watts. The next year, with the formation of the Federal Radio Commission, WSM was assigned a national "clear channel" status, and given a new low wavelength of 650. The famous tower that Alton sees as such as important symbol in his own life was used a great deal by WSM publicity in the early 1930s, and photos of it were often printed on postcards with pictures of Opry performers.—Ed.

has ever made it, and I don't believe they ever will. That old tower is a gigantic and magnificent object to live up to. To me, a former Grand Ole Opry entertainer, it represents the Bible of radio achievement. I will quit on that, but I do hope you will get the idea of my inspiration and the inspiration that absorbed the Delmore Brothers as we tried to do our best to get over to the public and our friends just exactly how we felt when we started out, hoping and praying to be liked and to make good and also to make some money.

Back home, everybody went wild about our chance on the Opry. The *Alabama Courier* and the *Limestone Democrat* had big stories about us. We were celebrities there in Athens, Alabama, and we were happy, delighted and proud, but we never felt we were any better than any one of the country people who were our neighbors. I am very sincere about this. And I am thankful to God that we always felt like that to other struggling entertainers we met. Some of them now are the great stars you hear every day on record and the other mediums of show business.

But there's something I want to say here and now that I know will be hard to believe. Prominent people and those of the upper class and some of the middle class were ashamed to let people know that they would stoop to listen to music like it was played on the Grand Ole Opry. Some of them thought it would lower their standing socially. I know this is true because I have been a victim of it. One time a lawyer wrote a condescending letter to Rabon and me about a song we sung that was similar to his name. The song was "Brown's Ferry Blues." His name was such that when the song was sung it sounded just like his name. I remember he didn't say he ever listened to the song, but somebody else had heard it and told him about it. The letter he wrote had a threatening tone, so I replied immediately telling him the name of the song and its origin, and I never heard anymore from that particular person.

I also remember meeting the great Nick Lucas, guitar wizard, whom I copied to some extent and admired very much. He was playing a theater in Nashville and when we went up that day, we left a little earlier than usual so I could catch his show. I had seen him in the movies and listened to his records many times. I felt inferior when I approached the stage door to wait for him to come out. Finally he came out and I shook his hand, telling him how much I had enjoyed his show, which, I thought, was truly wonderful, and he was a very gracious person. But he was in a hurry, so I didn't get to talk to him very much. I managed to tell him, however, that I played on the Grand Ole Opry and made records, but he got in a bigger hurry and I sadly thought: What a jackass I've made of myself now.

If that incident could be repeated this day and time, and Marty Robbins, Eddy Arnold or Roy Acuff or, for that matter, most any of the Opry stars could take my place, what would happen?

Would he be unknown, politely brushed aside? I truly wonder what really would happen. I will leave that for you to decide.

When we started on the Opry, we just took our places with the rest of the gang who played each Saturday night. We liked them and they liked us. They were truly our kind of people and still are for that matter. I can go to the Opry any Saturday night and stay backstage till I am too tired to move and still will not have seen or talked to half of the fine people I would like to. It was home for me for close to seven years and it still feels the same. The atmosphere is still there. It seems to be contagious. You ask the entertainers and they will tell you the same thing.

There was one thing, though, that we didn't tell to many of them. I had taught music before I ever sung on the Opry. I made our arrangements arid they were correct from a harmony stand point. I had written songs and knew something about harmony. That makes a lot of difference when it comes to singing correctly. Rabon didn't read music then and he never did learn to read it too well. But he had such a good ear he could do without it very well, although he depended on me when it came to the new songs. And I helped him finish a lot of the songs he composed. Now, that is one point I want to make to all of you would-be composers: learn to read music if at all possible because it will help you to keep up with the various trends that time creates in the music and show business world. It might seem a little hard for you to grasp, but it will really pay off in the long run and you will enjoy music so much more.

As I have said before, we didn't own a car when we got on the Opry, so we had to get some of the neighbors who had a car to take us up there to make our program. But that was an easy thing to do because they (the ones who took us) would get to see the Opry and be there with us and they enjoyed this tremendously. I can say one thing and really mean it: if it hadn't of been for our friendly neighbors, there never would have been any Delmore Brothers act.

The people in Limestone County, Alabama, still have a pride in the way we got our start from scratch. They knew we were poor folks, like they were, and they saw it happen. It's kind of hard to describe the way I feel about them, too. They contributed enough to make it possible for us to do what we did. They would turn out to our shows when we were nothing more than two unknown boys, struggling to keep going. I remember some of the wealthier farmers who liked to hear us sing would send for us in a truck or car to come and play for them till bedtime, which was never later than ten o'clock. They would all listen—and I mean *listen*—and not say a word till we were through with our song, then they would ask for another one. Now I can tell you this. If you are reading this book, and I don't care how much money you have, or have made, your supreme happiness is in moments when you have your audience captivated like I have stated above. Without the show of appreciation, the old show can't, just simply can't go on very long. That is the bliss you have hungered for, if you are a true entertainer.

When we knew we were on the Opry for sure we began to practice harder and harder so we could make a favorable impression. But you know, a funny thing about the way we thought: we were practicing for the people who listened to WSM, not the bosses. That's the way we always were and sometimes I wonder if that was the right approach, because we never did make any money on the Opry. We just barely existed and were always deeply in debt. I know that I have answered a multitude of questions from the general public by that last sentence. The Grand Ole Opry does not pay a good salary. It gives you a chance to go out on your own and make the hay from your personal appearances. If you didn't know how to do that, in those days when we went there, you were sunk. Now, they have managers in Nashville who can take you out on a shoestring and make money with you—that is, if you have made records and have had a pretty good seller. But back in those days of the debut of the Delmore Brothers, you didn't have a manager except the station manager and he didn't give a damn if you sank or swam.

I was just reminded by Thelma, my wife, a night or two ago that when we got started on the Opry it was WPA days. She said that those men only got three dollars a week to help keep their families from starving. It was a government project and the work these men did seemed unnecessary then, but every now and then, today, one can see some of the very good and lasting work they did. But three dollars a week! But you know something? I am coming to something you won't believe when you read it. Rabon and me started on the Opry for five dollars a week each, and we had to pay the man or person who took us to Nashville five dollars of that, which left us two and a half bucks each. And I mean we worked for over a year without asking for, or getting, a raise. We were living on the manna of inspiration. But now, you think it's over. We could not buy any clothes or a car on that kind of money, and personal appearances didn't pay like they do now. And the uptown folks, who always have the big money, didn't turn out in those days at all. So there we were—living on glory alone, the glory of just being on the Grand Ole Opry.

TRIALS AND TRIBULATIONS

And there is the key of the whole thing. We were just two country boys, very young and green and timid and never had coped with the cruel world of reality. And the cruel world took advantage of it.

In Nashville, Tennessee, in those days, nobody in the country and western field had a manager. But there were people in New York, Chicago, and Hollywood, and I think St. Louis, that had managers. The people in the North accepted country and western music much sooner than the people in the South. There are too many "Southern aristocrats" in the South. They would listen to the Grand Ole Opry on the sly and pretend to their friends of the upper bracket that they didn't listen at all. Or they would pretend that the kids had turned the radio on and they didn't have a chance to turn it off. Now I hope you get the idea, because with their attitude, there was no prestige. Rabon and I played just as correctly as any of the large bands on the networks. We read music and made our own arrangements, but we were still classified as "hill-billies" by the long-nosed guys who looked down from a pedestal of superficial knowledge and preference. But nowadays, let Roy Acuff, the Louvin Brothers, Ferlin Husky, or any one of the other stars of the Opry come to town and you can't get near them for the big shots who used to take Uncle Dave Macon, Sam and Kirk McGee, the Fruit Jar Drinkers, Arthur Smith, and others with contempt and scorn. And I might add, also, the Delmore Brothers. The Kingston Trio are classified as popular singers. The Everly Brothers are, too, but if they had been on the scene when we were, you know what the label would have been? HILL-BILLY.

I hope I don't sound bitter by these comparisons. It is just a means of clarifying the difference and appreciation in the changes and trends of the times in respect to quality of the performer. Stephen Foster was not appreciated in his time. Neither was Edgar Allan Poe. So I guess we might as well write it off to the strange acts of man and his seeming stupidity of presence of mind. Don't get mad, now, for I am in that class myself. What little I know was hard to come by. I had to struggle like hell to learn to read music. And anything that requires deep and thoughtful concentration has always been difficult for me. And, oh yes, I will add this as a last reminder: What was the man's name who made the long speech at Gettysburg?

What I have been writing sounds like a chapter in a book that could be called "Futility." And that's exactly how I meant it to sound. You will find the best singers, musicians, and composers either working in a trade that is outside their realm or blind drunk in the local saloon. These people are the true artists but they are not dependable. So they go marching through life with a heart that is eating at them constantly and driving them almost insane, until they get killed in an accident or die by their own hand. I figure alcohol goes high on the list to contribute to the dereliction of the true artist or composer. I talk from a personal viewpoint, because I have seen this with my own eyes. Here are two examples of what I mean:

We were playing a theater in some little town in North Carolina, I forget the name, when a young Negro man came and met me at the stage entrance. He had heard our show and wanted some information on how to get started in the entertainment business. At first, I was doubtful about him, like Nick Lucas was with me.

But I talked to him and had some time to give him. He and I talked for a while and then some of the other boys in the show came back and stopped to listen. They were interested in him and so was I. We took him backstage with us to listen to him. At that time we were under contract to RCA Victor and the A & R man, Mr. Eli Oberstein had told me to round up any talent I could find for country and western or sepia, as they called it in those days. Sepia was listed as Negro talent. So I had some authority to help this young man if he could produce. He played a harmonica and guitar at the same time. He had his harmonica with him and I let him use my guitar. The boys in the band accompanied him and he began to play and also sing. His voice was good and sounded commercial, and I almost was positive after he had gone through his first song that he was a natural. The first song he rendered was

TRIALS AND TRIBULATIONS

some old song that he had picked up somewhere in his travels around the country and we had all heard it before. Then I asked him if he had any original songs, and he said he did, so he went into one of those. It was a great thrill to watch and hear this song he had written. It caused us all to get goose bumps. It would make your hair stand up. He was that good. And he didn't stop at that. He sang and played about six or eight more of his original songs. And they were all very good. He had the true heart of a superb entertainer. I thought to myself: How Mr. Oberstein* will like this guy! He's got everything it takes and then some. I was not getting one red cent out of the deal but it made me happy to help this old boy.

Naturally, he was tickled pink that we all liked him so much, but he rated. I must say that he was one of the best prospects for a hit I have ever run into before or since in my more than twenty years of show business. I cannot put it on paper or describe his style, because I don't have that word power. But I can say this one thing: He was simply great. And now I don't even remember his name. He gave me two or three addresses to locate him when I had anything definite from Mr. Oberstein. So when we got back to the hotel, I called Oberstein and he was greatly interested. I wrote a letter to the place where he said he would be and the letter came back, so I wrote another to the other addresses and they all came back. I sent telegrams and tried to call him but he could not be found. I went through this for several months and never did find him. Someone said he might be on a drunk, but he surely was not drinking when he performed for us. So, you can see where your very best talent is hard to catch up with. As long as I live, I will never forget that boy and the haunting

*Eli Oberstein had by the early 1930s replaced Ralph Peer as Victor's chief talent scout for both blues and old-time music. Oberstein, following Peer's methodology, spent much of his time touring the South, locating suitable artists, and setting up field recording sessions in local warehouses, hotels, and radio stations. Oberstein was to supervise many of the Delmores' sessions on Bluebird and also helped them work out their publishing and copyright arrangements.—Ed.

way he played and sang. I have never heard anything to compare with it.

Another memorable occasion was in Memphis when we were playing on WMC. We had an early morning radio program, like we always did. It was at six o'clock and lasted for thirty minutes. We had lots of visitors from time to time. One time Johnny & Jack happened by with Kitty Wells, who is Johnny's wife. They had their band with them and were booked in that locality for several show dates, so we just turned our program over to them and they put the whole show on with the exception of one or two numbers. That was before they ever made a record but we liked them and always did. But the particular incident I especially refer to in the above sentence is much more startling because we knew Johnny & Jack were good musicians, and the guy I will tell about was completely unknown to any of us boys on the radio program. He was a tall, skinny fellow and his clothes looked a little shabby. On this particular morning, we didn't have any other visitors but him. He was sitting in the studio when we got there about ten minutes till six.

He was real friendly and he asked us if it would be all right for him to stay for the program. We told him we would be glad to have him, and he smiled and sat back down. He didn't say another word till after the program. And he seemed to like our program very much.

You know that's pretty early in the morning for a radio program, so we usually left the studio immediately after the show and went back to bed for a little sleep, for we were playing somewhere every night except Sunday. So we started picking up our instruments making ready to leave when the stranger asked me if I would let him play a tune or two on my guitar. I didn't feel too good about it but I stretched my feelings and told him yes. The radio announcer looked at me and shook his head. The seedy looking stranger had his back to the announcer and didn't see him when he made the gesture. But I understood well enough what he meant. Of course he was just the announcer and didn't have any thing to do with what we wanted to do. But it was plain to see he didn't like this bum hanging around and didn't think he could play. But I always figured you don't know and can't judge what a man can do by his looks alone. So I handed the old boy my guitar and he sat down to play.

"Do you boys have anything particular you would like to hear?" I told him no and he said, "Well, I'll play you one of our favorites down in old New Orleans, 'Honeysuckle Rose.'"

With that remark he started to play and he was simply a one man band. I have never seen his equal on a guitar. His hands moved rapidly all up and down the neck with a smoothness that was hard to believe. We couldn't believe our own eyes! And he played very softly. He played five or six tunes for us, mostly Dixieland, and if he ever missed one single note, Rabon and me and Wayne couldn't tell it. That old radio announcer's face was plenty red; He couldn't hardly look me in the eyes for two or three days. When he had finished several tunes, the stranger politely handed me back my guitar and said he had caused enough trouble. He really was polished in his manners, even if he was dressed poorly. He told us his name. But I don't believe he gave it to us right because I thought we ought to know and recognize a man's name who could play that way.

Anyway, he went out into the lobby with us and we talked a while. We all figured he needed some money or some help some way, but he didn't ask us for a penny. Rabon and Wayne [Raney] told him to wait for us while we went back into the studio a moment. So we retired to the back of the studio, where he could not see us, and we agreed to give him five dollars each. When we got back to the lobby he was still waiting for us with an old friendly grin, like a dog wagging his tail. One of us, I forget which, gave him the money and he said:

"I wasn't gonna ask you boys for any money but I appreciate it very much. You see my guitar is in the pawn shop over on the next street. I have a dance job tonight.

TRIALS AND TRIBULATIONS

And when I get through I'll pay you fellows back. This is certainly wonderful of you."

And with that, he disappeared out the door, into the foggy Memphis morning, and we never saw him again.

So that's the way it is with your best talent. I have many more incidents like the two I have just related, but I think they will give you a pretty good idea of what I mean by the hidden jewels.

Now this chapter has been a rambling chapter. I feel like that is the only way I can tell this story, for there are so many things I would leave out otherwise which I think should be told in the line of public and folk interest. There are things I have told here that happened long after Rabon and I left the Grand Ole Opry and I am ahead of myself, way ahead, but in the next chapter I will get back on the relative events that coursed destiny when we first went to the Opry. And I wish to say here and now the Grand Ole Opry was not, by any means, the most interesting of our experiences. It proved to be the most costly, healthwise, and it is a hard driver of talent. I would say from my experience the Opry is a killer of people who play so hard making personal appearances.

Nobody but the ones who play them can tell you just how hard it is on your health and physical condition. That especially was true when we played there. The management of the station would not allow us to stay out and miss a single Saturday night. We had so many commercials, important commercials, that meant so much money to the station that we just had to come back each weekend. I begged them to let us stay out maybe for two weeks at a time, but they would not do even this. I was told we would be fired if we didn't show up for each performance. Now the acts can stay out for indefinite periods without showing up and that helps out some. But the old road of personals is still a very rough and rocky one to travel.

Still, regardless of the threat to your health, the Grand Ole Opry grows on you

TRIALS AND TRIBULATIONS

once you have played on it for a while. And that is what Rabon and I both wanted to do at that time. But if I could recall my decision, knowing what I do today, I would never have gone up there to play. Of course you fans of ours and the ones who stood by us with their fan mail, I am deeply grateful and always will be. And if Rabon could say so, I am sure he would be the same. The people were always our best friends. And this, Mr. Entertainer—I don't care how big you are, and how much money you are making, and how much you are worth, even if you are a trilionaire—is true also of you.

Now I will get into the next chapter. But stay with me. There are several more rambling chapters to come.

CHAPTER TEN

THE WAY THE OPRY WAS IN THE EARLY THIRTIES

We were two mighty happy boys when we headed for our first program on the Grand Ole Opry.* We made a deal with one of our neighbors to take us up there each Saturday night. He said he would do it for expenses, but we didn't know how much they were going to pay us. So he took us on his own expense. His name was Richard Harper and he was a grand fellow and he liked to get out and travel anyway. So, all and all, he was the perfect man for the job. He never failed us. But he told us we could get anybody else to take us if they wanted to. He knew everybody in the county, it seemed, and some people would ask him about it, for they thought he had a contract to take us each week. Now that's the kind of a fellow he was, sharing the joy of the trip with his neighbors. He was always like that. He has now passed into

*Though it has been widely reported that the Delmores joined the Opry in 1932, I can find little documentary evidence that they were on the station before the spring of 1933. Alton has noted that when they went for their audition the baseball season had just opened, and that they replaced the Pickard Family. Both of these events point to a date of spring 1933. The Delmores appear in the WSM Opry radio log in the Nashville *Tennessean* for the first time on April 29, 1933. (They appeared in the 9:15–9:30 slot, following DeFord Bailey and the Four Boys and preceding Mrs. Cline, the dulcimer player.) They continued to appear regularly through spring and summer 1933, usually between the time slots of DeFord Bailey and the W. E. Poplin stringband.—Ed.

the Great Beyond but I'm sure he will get along all right up there.

Mr. Harper had an old Dodge and he would coast down the hills on the way to Nashville. And there are a lot of hills. Of course, now the highways have been widened and changed and there are not near so many now as there were back then.* But he told us he would save a lot of gas with the coasting and I suppose he did.

Some of the neighbors would not show up when they were supposed to, and it would worry me nearly to death. I remember one Saturday afternoon we waited in Athens for someone, I forget who, to show up and it was after three o'clock. We were frantic and just waiting. I decided I would try to find Richard, for he always stayed in town pretty late on Saturdays. So I started out around the square, looking for him. I finally found him and he looked surprised. "What are you doing here, boy? I thought you would be in Nashville by now."

I told him and he said, "Just stay where you are and I'll be ready in fifteen minutes. We got to get rolling." So if it hadn't been for him that day we might have got fired. But that was not the only time he came to the rescue. Regardless of what he was doing, or how busy he was, he always took care of us. In fact, we owe Richard Harper a lot that I personally feel we never repaid. Jewel Black was another one who took us up a lot, and he was a very fine man and still is today.

We passed that old tower I have spoken about earlier [WSM's radio tower], and we felt a particular elation, knowing that in a few hours we would be singing and playing on that giant of radio broadcasting.

On the audition, the only person we knew was Harry Stone, and we didn't know the others who listened in. But we learned who they were when we went up the first Saturday night. One was George D. Hay, "the Solemn Old Judge." Another was

---

*Athens in 1933 was well over 100 miles from Nashville, and the trip included a difficult drive over the Cumberland Plateau.—Ed.

THE WAY THE OPRY WAS IN THE EARLY THIRTIES

Tiny Stowe, famous announcer for WSM. And the three lads who walked out on us when we sang "When It's Lamp Lightin' Time in the Valley" were the Vagabonds, the leading act on the station at that time.

They had all been in the show business for many years, and I can understand how they acted then, now that I, too, know the ropes a little better since that time.

But the real friendly people up there who were more like us were the fiddlers and banjo pickers and guitar players who played in the stringbands, like the Fruit Jar Drinkers, Uncle Dave Macon and Dorris, and the Possum Hunters, etc. On our first broadcast we sat down in chairs and didn't have a single word in front of us. We had seen Uncle Dave earlier and he sat down and so did we. But the second time we played we stood up like we were used to, and never again did we sit down for a broadcast on the Opry.

The regular entertainers on the Opry, the ones who started it in the first place, were just plain old country boys like Rabon and myself. But the Vagabonds were a little uptown for us. They had all been to college and they knew the score and they were making the money on WSM. They didn't have to play personals to get by. But those boys could really sing. And they wrote a lot of songs. I forgot to tell this before now, but they wrote "When It's Lamp Lightin' Time in the Valley." One of them later told me the reason they walked out on our audition was they had sung the song so much that they couldn't stand it anymore. I later learned that that can be true of a song. For instance, I wrote "Brown's Ferry Blues" and we had to play it so much that I got the same way. Of course I don't feel like that now. But neither do I have to sing it once or twice or three times a day on personals and the radio. Yes, you live and learn in the show business. You don't have to try, you just do it.

We always traveled back and forth and never stayed in Nashville overnight till we moved up there and stayed with our Uncle Prater Williams. He lived on Fourth Avenue and we finally moved up with him and stayed till we could afford a place of our own, but that was nearly a year after we had gone on the Opry.

We had a thirty-minute program at first, just the two of us, when we first went on, and we sang and played and waited for any response from the people. They read and acknowledged all telegrams in those days and we got several the first night, which was a good sign. We felt mighty proud of them too. The old-timers would come around and say, "You boys are gonna make a big hit, just keep up the good work."

I know on our first program we sang one of Bob Miller's songs, "Twenty-One Years," and that was the last time we ever sang it. The manager of the station forbade us to sing it and I told him Bob Miller gave us our start on record. "I don't give a damn if he did give you your start—he's an S.O.B. to me and I'm telling you not to sing it again." So we didn't sing it anymore on the station but we got a lot of requests for it and always had to substitute something else. I learned later that the Vagabonds wrote a song almost like it called "Ninety-Nine Years" and Miller sued them and collected. That was how the Vagabonds stood in at the Opry and WSM.

Every radio station had their so-called pets in those days and I guess some of them still do. We never played on but one station without pets. That was WLW, the Nation's Station, Crosley Corporation, in Cincinnati, Ohio.

Anyway, that admonition about "Twenty-One Years" was enough to tell us that Radio Station WSM was not a bed of roses to us and it never was. We got on but we never did "get in."

It is a lot different now. I know it is, because I go up there occasionally and see and talk to the artists. The pay is still not as good as the public thinks it is. But the management has realized this: the Grand Ole Opry is the best place in the world to build up a good name and a good record artist may have on the market. They allow the artist to stay out when he or she has a good-selling record, so they may make the hay while the sun shines. The management at the time we were there didn't care what happened to us just as long as we made the weekly appearance. So, through the evolution of time, they have become sane enough to know that a man cannot stay on the road all the time behind the wheel of a car and hold up very long. It didn't matter how far we were from Nashville—we had to drive all the way back. Even if it were over a thousand miles and on a Friday night we still had to come in. I have done it—how many times? I cannot tell because there were many such occasions.

We didn't play any personal appearances for over a year after we went to the Opry because we did not know how to book anything up there. I tried to book some theaters when we needed money very badly but the managers always would shrug me off with: "The people who patronize my theater won't appreciate your kind of music. You wouldn't make any money and neither would I, so what's the use of fooling with it?" I would tell him we used to draw down in Limestone County in North Alabama and also in southern Tennessee. He would shrug again. "Well those people down there are your friends and they know you. That's the reason they turn out." So that would be that and the deal was ended. I would go my way and he would go his. But I would hate him because I knew with the proper advertising and publicity we would make money and he would make money. But he was afraid that people, that is some of them, would laugh at him for booking "hill-billies" that would contaminate his plush theater.

When we were staying at Uncle Prater's we were getting fifteen dollars a week between us. Thelma, my wife, was staying with my mother and father. And we were getting so much fan mail we didn't hardly have time to read it. The station was making plenty of money off of us, and we were living on the crumbs.

Here is an example of how we were treated by the bosses up there:

One Saturday night, Harry Stone called us off and whispered to us confidentially: "Boys, I understand that some WLS big shots are coming down next week to make you a lot of promises and tell you a lot of lies. They will be trying to get you to come to work on WLS. Now, here's my advice to you. You have a good future here on the Opry and WSM and I don't want you to leave. I have sold you boys on a good commercial and you will start next week. I am raising your pay. You, Alton, will get twenty dollars a week and Rabon will get fifteen. Now don't have anything to do with those sons o' bitches when they come down here next week. They just want to pull you away from us because you are so popular. They will keep you two or three months and then they will let you go and where will you be then? I can tell you—without a job because if you leave I will never take you on the Opry again. Your career will be ruined."*

Needless to say, we were very pleased with what he had said. That was more than he had ever talked to us before and everything looked really wonderful. We both felt like we were floating on air. That was a lot of money in those days. And now I could move to Nashville. Thelma had been waiting too for a long time. You see, we were going to have our first baby.

Well, Saturday night came and, sure enough, the WLS bosses came to the Opry. We had met some of them before. Mr. Fred Foster of the Foster Music Co. came along with them, and he introduced us to all the ones we did not know. They were all the big bosses: the WLS station manager, the program director, etc. Altogether there were five or six of them, and they just went about having a good time and enjoying themselves. We were shy of them, just like Mr. Stone told us to be, and we didn't even let them get very close to us. I could see Mr. Stone watching them and us too. And he was not very friendly to them either. But guess what? They didn't try to corner us or even act like they wanted to hire us. To me, that showed how big time

---

*There was no slight rivalry between WLS's *National Barn Dance* and WSM's Grand Ole Opry. The *Barn Dance* had started in 1924, a year before the Opry, and Judge Hay had received some of his early experience in country music by working with the show. Furthermore, the *Barn Dance* was picked up by the national network in 1933, six years before the Opry went network. The music of the *Barn Dance*, being designed for the Midwestern as well as Southern audience, was less "pure" and more sophisticated than that of the Opry. Some Opry staff apparently felt they had been "raided" by WLS when that station lured the very popular Pickard Family away from WSM. But given the quality and type of music that flourished on the *National Barn Dance*, the Delmores probably would have fit in very well with their vocal style.—Ed.

they were. They were just too big to stoop low. But I did learn later that they had a very good paying job to offer us.

We got the raise in pay and the commercial as promised. And then we thought we had it made. I moved Thelma up there and what little furniture we had, which was not much, just things our people had given us when we set up housekeeping. We bought a few more things—a bed for Rabon and a stove—and we went in debt to do this. But we could have made it fine if everything had gone right, but it didn't.

About four or five weeks after we had moved to Nashville, the station had some trouble with the sponsor. It seemed like they didn't pay their bill, or at least that was what we were told. Anyway, the commercial ended and we were called into Mr. Stone's office.

"Boys, I have bad news for you. We're gonna have to cut you back to the regular rate for the Opry entertainers." I was stunned and so was Rabon. I almost got down on my knees and begged him to do something to help us. The regular Opry rate then was five dollars a week each. We couldn't live on that and we didn't know anybody to play personals with. So there we were, right back where we had started from, except we now lived in Nashville and couldn't go out and catch a rabbit or squirrel to eat. I was desperately grasping at straws. And I came up with an idea.

"Mr. Stone, why can't we play three mornings a week like Paul and Bert* do and maybe we could exist better if you would not cut back so much? I will have to move back to the country if something can't be done." I was begging in earnest. He shook his head and didn't say anything for a moment.

"I will have to talk this over with my bosses, but that is a thought and maybe I can

---

*"Paul and Bert"—Paul Warmack and Bert Hutcherson, who called themselves "the Early Birds" and had a popular early morning show on WSM. Paul played mandolin, Bert the guitar, and both sang. They also both played regularly on the Saturday night Opry as members of Paul Warmack's band, the Gully Jumpers.—Ed.

do it." He said he would let us know in a few days.

So we left his office, wondering what had become of that sweet promise he had made us not long ago about the future, and also thinking if all our practicing and work on our act had really been futile.

We were beginning to learn that money is the keynote to the whole musical world. Like I have said before, we were green, ignorant country boys, and we didn't have a real friend to turn to. If we had had a manager, he could have put Mr. Stone in his proper place and we would not have felt so low. But that is the way the ball bounced in those days.

Mr. Stone knew how crazy we were about staying on the Opry and he always took due advantage of it till the very day we left. But he still had some good qualities and he helped us some later on, just to keep us from leaving before we actually did. I could have gone out and got a job as a printer, but we couldn't have practiced like we should and I wanted to devote my entire time to playing and singing. Mr. Stone called us and told us he had arranged for us to play the early morning show three days a week. I would get ten a week and Rabon five. That was fifteen a week to live on and pay rent, and my wife expecting a baby. It looked pretty dark but it was five dollars a week more than regular Opry pay and that helped us to get by till we started to playing personals with Uncle Dave.

Before I start to tell about Uncle Dave Macon and our years together, there's something I feel I should tell you about the WLS men coming down to hire us. As I have said before, we took the Pickard Family's place on the Opry when they left to go to Chicago. They were on the network and also WLS and they were making real money, not playing any personals, just making a good salary for broadcasting. Everybody at the Opry, the old timers included, said Obed Pickard was just a lucky man. And they were partly right, but he made his own luck. We had never met him but had heard the Pickards many times on the radio. So the next summer after the

THE WAY THE OPRY WAS IN THE EARLY THIRTIES

WLS men had come down to see us, the Pickards came home for an annual vacation with pay. Now when they came home, "Dad" as they called Obed, would make a few personals with the WSM gang on the big jamborees. We were lucky to be playing on one of them one day and met "Dad" and talked to him some. After he got to knowing us pretty well that day and thought he could trust us, he called Rabon and me off to one side to talk to us. We didn't know what he wanted to say at first, but we liked him so much we didn't mind. When we got off to ourselves, out of earshot of the rest of the entertainers, he looked at us both for a moment and then he said: "Have you boys got good sense?" He didn't smile either.

I said, "I reckon so, why?"

"Well, why didn't you take that job I recommended you for at WLS last winter?"

I told him what had happened and he snorted.

"Those fellows are the finest, and they wanted you and Rabon very badly. They were going to offer you a hundred a week each and would have gone as high as one hundred and fifty each to have got you up there. I heard you boys when you first came on the Opry, and I recommended you to them but they said you would not talk to them."

He said they wanted us permanently, and we could have stayed there as long as we wanted to.

Soooooooooooo, you live and learn, but sometimes it is too late when you learn. That has happened to me too many times.

CHAPTER ELEVEN

PERSONAL APPEARANCES— UNCLE DAVE MACON, SAM & KIRK McGEE

When we found out we could not make enough money to live on at WSM and the Grand Ole Opry, we started to look around and talk to people about making personals in earnest. My wife was going to have a baby pretty soon after we moved, and we knew there was going to have to be more money to help through that. Alloway Street in south Nashville was the first place we moved to and it was a duplex apartment. A fine Catholic family, Mr. and Mrs. Mathews, lived in the other side with their daughter and we got along with them fine. After we got settled down we got used to living in town and were quite happy except for money problems.

Rabon and I started playing the early morning shows and we enjoyed them very much. But Mr. Stone would not allow us to announce our own programs. I can't tell why to this day, because he would allow others who were from the country and used incorrect language and did most everything else to do their own announcing; I guess he knew we wanted to so bad that he just held us off. But we had good announcing boys up there. David Cobb was one of the early morning announcers. And he would let us talk as much as we wanted to. He often told us he wondered why they didn't let us announce our own program. Sometimes he would be a little late and I would put the station on the air and hold down the fort till he arrived. David was real young in those days and a fine fellow to get along with. He still remains one of my very best friends in the business and he is still working on the Grand Ole Opry. Percy White was the engineer or control man in those days.

On those morning shows I would try to bring in guests when I could find one whom I thought would be interesting to our audience. We had Baby Ray, a football great from Vanderbilt University, several times and he really was a swell guy. Sometimes we would have as our guest one of the wrestlers and we got to know a lot of them in person. We had the late Dorv Roche on, when he was in town and was available. I tried to get Bill Terry, the famous baseball player, on the program but that was a mistake. I didn't even know him personally, but I was making a shot in the dark. The New York Giants had played the Nashville Vols in an exhibition game the day before, which was Sunday, and I personally knew two of the pitchers, Dick Coffman and [one other] whom I had met in Black Mountain, North Carolina. Dick was from my part of the north Alabama hills, Elkmont and Veto. My father knew his father and my brothers went to school with Dick up in Elkmont. I would have liked very much to have had the two boys on our programs but they couldn't go on without the permission of Manager Terry. So I tried to call several times at his hotel and he was not in. I called just before I went to bed and he still was not in. So l went on to bed and decided to call him the next morning. I had talked to Dick and he told me they had to leave early and would have to get up anyway, so I knew Mr. Terry would be out of the bed and I would not cause him to lose any sleep. So when I got up to go to the program I called his room. He was in alright, but he sounded irritated. I asked him would he let the boys come on the program and here is his answer: "Not for the Statue of Liberty." I then asked him would he come and make a little talk and he told me that was ridiculous. He said he had to ride herd on the whole baseball team and he didn't have time for radio talks. With that he hung up. Of course I had a bad impression of him and the newspapers were after his scalp, giving him bad publicity which I believed, till I met and knew him, in West Memphis, Arkansas, several years later. I will tell more about him later. But I will say here and now: Bill Terry is one of the finest gentlemen I have ever met and I like him very much because he does not want a lot of praise for being a baseball great. He just wants to be a natural human being and to be a regular guy like you and I. Newspapers can cut the very hell out of you when they want to be sadistic and distort little things into big ones. And that's what they did to Mr. Terry, and I have also had it happen to me.

Anyway, we had a lot of fun on the morning show. And it helped our popularity. We were getting a lot of fan mail and we got some requests for personal appearances. We got a request to play Red Boiling Springs, Tennessee, and that was the first one we ever played after we got on the Grand Ole Opry. We got Kirk McGee to play that date with us and Kirk is one of the finest guys you will ever run into. But I got twisted up somewhere along the line and didn't advertise the date like I should have, and we didn't have much of a crowd. I guess I'm about the dumbest guy who ever was in show business. I had supervised the dates we had played before we came to the Grand Ole Opry down in north Alabama and southern Tennessee and I advertised real well with handbills and posters and anything else it took, but on this one date I depended on WSM to take care of all that with the announcements we gave on the morning show and also the Grand Ole Opry, but that didn't work. The know-hows at the station said it was just useless expense to spend money on posters and handbills when we had announcements on such a big station. So I took the same view because it seemed logical at that time. But it took several years later and some convincing examples of promoters to prove our theory was entirely wrong. Here are two examples:

PERSONAL APPEARANCES

We all played Memphis, Tennessee, at the big auditorium there and we didn't draw enough to pay expenses. I mean the whole Grand Ole Opry played there in person. There may have been a few acts that were not with us but we had the ones who drew the most telegrams and fan mail. And still we failed to draw. But we didn't use any posters, handbills or anything else except a little two-inch ad in the Memphis papers telling about our appearance. The Solemn Old Judge was the MC and we had the real Grand Ole Opry just like it sounded on Saturday nights, but we didn't know how to advertise. We were all disgusted and bewildered but we didn't know what was wrong. We all began to think that it was not the kind of music Memphis liked. Just like I have said in the first chapters of this book. But we were all wrong. All we needed was some good promotion, as it was later proved by some experienced showmen. The Grand Ole Opry is the greatest medium of advertising in the world, if it is handled right. But can you imagine the chagrin we all felt when we went into a town and didn't draw enough to pay expenses? Everybody was singing the blues.

Another example of how we failed to advertise the Grand Ole Opry was when we played the big auditorium in Louisville, Kentucky. That was another time we had the genuine Grand Ole Opry with us, most of the ones that drew the biggest fan mail and sold the best on commercials. I would venture to say that there never was as complete an Opry taken on the road than we had then, and again we thought we would draw big. We had that place booked for three big days and every one of us kept hoping that the next day would be the big on·.

The Solemn Old Judge again was the MC and we put the show on just like we did every Saturday night. Still no crowd. And it was pretty weather. We knew we had listeners there in Louisville, because our mail was great from that part of Kentucky. But we sure didn't draw flies on people either. Everybody on the show had the blues individually. We just simply felt worse than hell that we had a show that was so well liked nationally, and still couldn't draw in our own back yard. But, again, I chalk this whole thing up to our ignorance of the way of big time promotion. We all had the same idea. Since we had the real Opry performers and so many of them, we thought that was all that was necessary.

I think we had another little two-inch ad in the Louisville papers and I don't really believe we advertised in all of them. At that time, there were several dailies in Louisville, but we didn't believe we needed newspaper advertising of any kind and that's where our tail flew up. So we abandoned the idea of the Opry drawing, big as it was! The ones who booked the show were afraid that they would never get out of the hole if they did a lot of plastering when it wasn't really needed, and then didn't get them out after all. But therein lay our downfall. If they had plastered the town with posters and newspaper ads it would have brought our prestige up to where it belonged and we would have had packed houses the whole three nights. It was not long after that when Judge Hay got sick.*

Now Uncle Dave Macon had people all over the country, school teachers and people in the chambers of commerce in lots of little towns all over the South that knew him personally, before there ever was a radio station in Tennessee or, for that matter, anywhere. Uncle Dave had been playing for tobacco auctioneers, and political rallies, and various other events for years and years. And that is how he got to know them. If he wanted to play a week in a certain part of the country, all he had to do was write someone a letter and they would book him up and he always made good money.

One Saturday night Uncle Dave came up to Rabon and me and showed us his fan mail. It was a lot of mail. He always did get his part of the letters, and I would say he was just about leading the rest of the country music makers.

---

*Throughout his career at WSM, Judge Hay experienced several prolonged periods of illness serious enough to cause him to have to take a leave of absence. Grant Turner recalls that during one such illness Harry Stone was named acting manager of the station in Hay's absence, and when Judge Hay returned he found that Stone had been named permanent manager.—Ed.

PERSONAL APPEARANCES

"Boys, I am told that you are getting more fan mail than anyone else on the station. Is that the truth?"

"Well, I don't know whether we are or not. We haven't asked anybody about it," I told him. In fact, I really didn't know who to ask about such things. All I know was, we were getting a lot of mail, and we were both proud of that. Uncle Dave continued: "Well, I know you are getting more telegrams than anybody else and that is a good sign. You boys would make a good team to work with me on some show dates. Do you need the money?"

Did we need the money? That was a staggering question. We were simply desperate. Rabon and I both told him we could surely use the money. That would be a life saver. He told us to think it all over and he would talk some more about it later. So he went on to another studio to rehearse his program with his son, Dorris. Of course, we didn't know him too well then. I had met him down at a theater in Decatur, Alabama, and he had seemed very friendly then. He was just dropping through and knew the manager of the theater, Mr. Baniza. I told him I had a fellow that played with me and we wanted to play the theater and the manager would not allow us to. We were just high school boys then, but Uncle Dave persuaded the manager to give us a chance to play in the near future. Neither of those men had ever heard us play but Uncle Dave told him, "They have got to start somehow, just like you and me did. Somebody had to give us a chance, didn't they?" Mr. Baniza then told me he would give us an audition and if we could play good enough he would put us on the stage. We later played for him. He thought we were real good.

Now that's about all I knew about Uncle Dave, and Rabon hadn't ever met him before we came to the Opry.

Uncle Dave Macon was a real "pro" before the day of the so-called hillbilly. I remember I kept up with the theaters in their advertising and always was on the lookout for any country musicians who played the big theaters. One act was the

PERSONAL APPEARANCES

Weaver Brothers & Elviry. Another, and one of the greatest was Britt Wood. These people played the big time before there were any radio stations. One time I noticed an ad about Uncle Dave and Fiddlin' Sid Harkreader. They were to play a week in a big theater in Birmingham. They were held over and wound up playing about six weeks or maybe longer. The people were not ashamed to go and pay to see them in person, but when radio came along they denied ever listening to such music. I guess they thought the theater lent prestige to the act which was nothing of the sort. But there was a change or trend on its way to happen, and Rabon and I were caught right in the middle of the whole thing. We got the fan mail and the telegrams but the prestige just simply was not there. Sometimes, I liken our plight to the well-known newspaper cartoon, "Born Thirty Years Too Soon." That just about captions us when it came to the deserved prestige we needed so very badly. But, as I have said before, the trend was there and even Uncle Dave Macon could not play the big time places he once played so often and so successfully.

So we started playing show dates with Uncle Dave and, I must say, that they were some of the happiest, if not the very happiest days we knew as long as we were in the show business. There were only three of us and we all traveled in the same car. We made all the necessary business agreements. I was to drive the car and Rabon and me would own it and Rabon and Uncle Dave were to split the upkeep of the car. That was in exchange for my driving. Most of these arrangements were advanced by Uncle Dave, as Rabon and I had never really known how to figure out things like that. But it all worked out fine. Everybody was happy and we began to make some pretty good money right at the very beginning. Now there is one thing I want to say about Uncle Dave. He knew how to operate and he was honest as the day is long. He didn't want a penny that wasn't his, and he didn't want you to have a penny that belonged to him. For instance, when we checked up, that is, counted the money, sometimes there would be an odd penny. We split three ways and of course you can't divide a penny into three parts. But Uncle Dave would put it down in his little book and remember every time who the odd penny belonged to. We thought at first that it seemed a little too much trouble to go to, but we later learned that big business is conducted along those lines down to the very fraction of a cent. And when you do that, your dollars will take care of themselves. Yes sir, we simply learned a lot about business, honesty and many, many more things from that fine old fellow.

Many of you will remember him for his jokes. He always had plenty of them and he could tell them better than anybody I've ever seen. But he never kidded anyone and he didn't like being kidded himself. I can't remember how many jokes I have heard him tell but he never tried to pull one on another person. He just didn't like it, period, and he didn't mind telling anyone about it. Several times I have seen men who tried to pull a joke on him and he never would have any use for them afterward. He would just avoid them. He would never get mad at them. He just considered them a bore after they tried to do that to him. I remember one particular occasion when we stopped at a cafe, one of his choice, and, he thought, the best. Uncle Dave had known the operator of this cafe for many years and had always stopped there to eat when he passed, if he wanted to eat at all. This particular restaurant specialized in country ham, steaks, and plate lunches, and it was a good place to eat.

I remember, we were going down to Athens, Alabama, our home, for a few dates and to see our parents. Uncle Dave was particularly fond of our dad and mother. He called them Uncle Charlie and Aunt Mollie. And he felt just as welcome at our house as he did at his own home.

So we headed down the line from Nashville to Athens and were about half way when we came to this cafe. Uncle Dave always got up real early in the morning and he had become hungry when we started to travel. It was only about one o'clock in the afternoon but he still wanted to stop and eat. We told him we had rather wait till we got home but he said he was afraid he would take the headache if he had to wait too long. So we pulled up at the cafe and went in. Uncle Dave introduced us to the owner, and the owner of the place seemed to like him very much.

"Yes, boys, Uncle Dave has been eating with me now for many years and I am always glad to have him back again."

Naturally Uncle Dave was very pleased with what he said. "Well, Cap (he always called people he liked Cap) I just brought the boys in to show them some real food. And it's all on me, for they wanted to keep on till they ·got home and eat some good home cooking for a change. And I told them to let their mother rest a bit and enjoy them coming down and we could eat here and she wouldn't have to go to work cooking soon as we got in." With that over, we ordered our food. Rabon and I both ordered a plate lunch, but Uncle Dave ordered a big steak of some kind. But it was the biggest and best on the menu and he tried to get us to eat the same but we didn't feel that hungry. That was another thing about Uncle Dave Macon. He always believed in eating the best. It would be some little time before his steak was ready, so we settled back to wait and do some talking and planning about the dates, etc.

There was a good crowd in the place and most of them seemed to be just taking life easy and asking us questions. They all seemed to know us. I guess they had heard Uncle Dave when he introduced us to the owner. They were all real friendly and we all enjoyed talking to them. Uncle Dave was always a gregarious person and was at home wherever he hung his hat. Then too, he always wore a gates ajar collar and Stetson hat and he had gold teeth and a contagious smile, and a goatee. His clothes were tailor made and he wore the best he could buy. He didn't have a suit that cost less than one hundred dollars.

But the gang at the cafe had something up their sleeve and were doing something on the sly. I could easily tell this by the way they were acting. But Uncle Dave never thought of what they were doing. He never suspected anything. But I was suspicious. The owner of the place was in on what was fixing to happen because I could see he was talking to them and nodding his head and laughing at the same time.

A well-dressed man got up from a table, not too far away from us and came up to our table. "Uncle Dave, I'm a salesman from Nashville. I've listened to you and the Delmore Brothers many times on WSM. In fact, I listen every time I don't have to work too late and you are my favorites. Now I'm having a little trouble with the proprietor of this cafe about some preserves I'm trying to sell him. He says if you will only taste of them and let him know how you like it, it will determine his decision. If you like it just say so and if you don't say no. I will abide by your decision and he will too. So if you don't mind helping me, I will appreciate this from the very bottom of my heart. I may make a sale. Will you help me, please Uncle Dave?"

Uncle Dave straightened up in his chair. He felt honored. Uncle Dave always felt himself somewhat of a good connoisseur of good food and I can vouch for the fact that he was. He did know good food when he tasted it. On this particular occasion, he really felt grand because he was going to be a judge of fine foods and also help a struggling young salesman at the same time.

The salesman handed him the jar. It had a big red peach pictured on it and the label really looked delicious. I began to wish it was me instead of him that was tasting the preserves. Uncle Dave took the jar and handled it very carefully like he was caressing it. He began to twist the top off. He had not turned it around but about twice when the top jumped off and a big, worm-like thing as long as your arm jumped out and began to weave back and forth in front of Uncle Dave's face. He was so terrified he couldn't hardly let go. It seemed he was frozen and his hand would not drop it. But he finally dropped the thing and hit at it as he pushed his chair back from the table.

The whole gang in the cafe was roaring with laughter and some of them were shouting and laughing and slapping their thighs. They couldn't have hoped for anything funnier if they had planned it over for fifty years. The way Uncle Dave looked, scared and pale. It was really going over big.

Everybody in the cafe was laughing and really howling except Uncle Dave and Rabon and me. We knew he did not appreciate a thing like that. His goatee was sticking straight out from his lower lip. He always wore a goatee. A goatee is a little short whiskered mustache on the lower lip and it used to be real stylish in the old days when Uncle Dave was growing up. When he was excited or hurt, his goatee always would stick out in a straight line from his lip. That was always one way you could tell when he was ill or hurt in some way. I could say he was mad but I never did see him get mad at anyone, anywhere. He had very good control of himself and, as I have said before, he always avoided the things that were not pleasant to him. So, when Rabon and I saw how he looked, we knew the owner had made a very grave mistake.

They had already brought our plate lunches and the food looked very good. We had been waiting for his steak to come in before we started to eat. He looked at us both for a moment and then he whispered: "Boys, let's go."

Without a word, we both got up with him. We both felt he had been the victim of a very undignified trick and we resented it almost as much as he did. It certainly was not very complimentary. He laid a five dollar bill on the table. The cafe owner came up. He had quit laughing. So had some of the others.

The cafe man was real worried now. He had known Uncle Dave for many years and had heard him tell many hundreds of jokes but he didn't know that his old customer didn't stand for kidding. I don't imagine that man would have had any part of a thing like had happened here today for his right arm if he had been a little more observing. He tried to apologize every way possible but the old troubadour was adamant. Uncle Dave didn't say anything much at all. He did ask the fellow if the five dollars would take care of the bill and the man tried to make him take the money back but he could not move Uncle Dave Macon. He got his overcoat and hat and started out and we followed him. The cafe man tried to get us to talk to the old banjo picker but I told him there was no use. So we left the restaurant and headed down the line toward home. I asked Uncle Dave if he wanted to stop anywhere else to eat.

"No, Alton, I feel too nervous, and that back there made me a little sick at my stomach. If I were to eat now it would make me really sick. We'll just wait till we get down to your house and maybe Aunt Mollie can cook us up some real country eating."

That was all he ever said about the cafe. He just stayed away from it after that time and he never went there again. By the time we got home he was his old jolly self again. But he always had a soft spot in his heart for the state of Alabama. He gave Alabama people a lot of credit for his start in the show business.*

Our first car was an old 1928 Chevrolet. Rabon and me both bought it together. I forget how much it cost, but it was not good enough to make long trips in. So we decided to buy one a little better that would make the trips and not keep us stranded on the road. We knew we had to have a better car if we were to make the trips with Uncle Dave into Virginia, Kentucky, and far away states like that.

We knew a salesman who used to work with us, Sam Jones Anderson. We had taught music schools and put on shows together and we knew we could trust him. He worked at Bitting Chevrolet Company there in Athens so we went down to see him. He looked our car over and found one we could afford. It was a Plymouth and it looked real well to us, so we traded with him.

We hadn't paid much attention to what fuel it used, but we did notice it burned quite a bit of oil. But its appearance offset that with Rabon and me. We thought we

---

*Uncle Dave's first fully professional engagement was probably a booking at the Loew's Theater in Birmingham in 1923, and he continued to play north Alabama regularly during his early career.—Ed.

had a real good buy till Uncle Dave made a trip with us.

I remember we played Hillsboro, a little town over in Lawrence County, Alabama. It was one of the first we had played with him. When we left to play the show he took out his little book and put down the gas and we had the oil checked and everything was full up and we went to play Hillsboro. But on the way back somehow the oil gave out and we had to add some to make it back home.

"Boys, we're just gonna have to do something about this oil situation," we heard him say. My heart sank because we could not buy another car right now. But I didn't know what he had in his mind.

"Who did you fellows buy this car from?" We told him and he said we would have to go up there and see them first thing in the morning.

"Now don't you boys be worried. I know something about buying cars and I can help you a whole lot in picking out something we can travel in. Why this thing would break up a millionaire." And that is all that he said. It was remarkable how he could dismiss something unpleasant and completely quit thinking about it till he got ready to settle it.

The next morning we got up real early and headed for town. My parents lived out in the country about five miles from Athens, still on the Brown's Ferry Road. We went straight to the Bitting Chevrolet Company to get the deal all settled, for that was the business we had to get right. I was real worried because I didn't know whether we could afford another car. But that was during the big Depression and things were a lot different than they are now. Cars were not high at all but they seemed high in price for that particular time.

When we went in the place, Uncle Dave received his usual commanding attention. He was a walking commercial, advertising himself and making money by the effort. He was not a show off but he knew his unique personal appearance was responsible for every dime he had in his pocket. Sam was there and we told him our troubles.

"I didn't know that car burned oil like that, so let's look around and find another one that you like that won't eat you up on fuel. We just took it in a few days before I sold it to you boys but we'll make it all right."

But we didn't have any money to pay any difference of prices and we told him so.

"Now don't let that bother you at all. We'll just go along like we never did trade in the first place and we can make it fine like that."

So we began looking around the car lot, trying to find something that was capable of making the long trips we knew waited in the near future. In the meantime Uncle Dave had made the acquaintance of Mr. Bitting, the owner of the place. Now Mr. Bitting himself was some character. He had a keen sense of humor and he reminded me of the great Will Rogers. He had a real wealth of stories to tell and they were just as good as the ones Uncle Dave told. So they had a grand time just talking to each other. One would tell something and they would both laugh a lot and then the other would tell one and vice-versa. They were not smut, but just plain old down-to-earth that would tickle anyone who listened. I don't believe I have ever seen any two persons enjoy themselves so much. They weren't paying any attention to us, apparently, so we finally picked out a car we thought would take the rough travel we had to do. We came up to get Uncle Dave to look at it and he didn't seem to hear us when we told him we had one picked out. He spoke to Mr. Bitting.

"Cap, let's see what you have in a new car you can sell the boys." And they both headed for the new cars. I had never owned a new car in my life and this simply mystified me. How could we buy it? He talked to Mr. Bitting a moment, then he said: "Now it's up to you boys if you want a new car or not, but if you want one, just go on out there and pick it out. I will help you to pay for it, then you can pay me back later when we get to making some money."

Imagine that! It seemed that heretofore everybody had been trying to take away

PERSONAL APPEARANCES

everything we had and along comes this ole country banjo picker offering to stake us to a new car. It was incredible.

I picked out the car that would haul us the best, I thought, and then asked Rabon and Uncle Dave what they thought of it. They liked it, and then I didn't know what to do. How would we pay for it or how much down and so forth. There was no discussion at all. Uncle Dave asked Mr. Bitting how much he needed for the rest of the down payment and he wrote a check for the whole thing. That was the way he did business. He was strictly big time.

CHAPTER TWELVE
PERSONALITIES AT WSM

There were two classes of entertainers at WSM. The staff members, the ones that got paid every week and knew they had a good job and security, and the other class was the Grand Ole Opry talent, who played only once a week and were paid a very token fee for each Saturday night.

Rabon and me found ourselves in the middle of the group. We didn't get a good salary but we played three times a week on the morning shows and sometimes on other programs they had when they needed someone like us. But most of the time we were simply left out of anything important that the station promoted. For instance, we never did play for the National Life's agents' convention. The station bosses just left us out and that always did hurt my feelings, and Rabon's, too. We felt it would add a little prestige to play on that, but we never did quite make it. You see, there is devilish politics at work on a fellow who makes good at anything, and it was the same thing there. We didn't want to believe it, at first, but it happened so much to us that we finally got the wind of it and knew we were being discriminated against. That always made me simply furious. But if I said any thing to Harry Stone he would shrug his shoulders and tell me if I didn't like it I could go somewhere else. That always put a scare into me for I didn't know anywhere else to go. His excuse that he always left us out was that the company and radio station made a decision that the agents didn't appreciate our particular kind of "hill-billy" music. Well, that decision may have been correct from their view point. But here is the bare fact: The National Life agent always showed up to see us when we played his town and not only that, he would help advertise our appearance. If we had been allowed to play at the conventions it would have helped our personal appearances tremendously. We could have met the agents and contacted them about their town and it would have worked out fine for everybody all around. And that being our biggest source of income, I will leave it up to you to decide how much it hurt us.

But most of the girls and fellows on the staff of WSM liked us very much. Fannie Rose Shore was a cute, little dark-eyed singer who was going to Vanderbilt University when we first landed on WSM. We saw her nearly every day. She was helping to pay her way through school, singing on the station. She was always a pleasant, smiling person and she could really sing. At least Rabon and I always thought so. Sometimes we would make personal appearances for various benefits in some big building there in Nashville. The whole staff of WSM would appear on these, free gratis. Fannie Rose was always one of the very best to sing at these occasions and she always went over big. Most of the time she would steal the show and nobody was ever jealous of her, for she was so friendly to everybody. I understand she went on and finished college and then went to New York to become the celebrated Dinah Shore you know today on every medium of entertainment. They changed her name to Dinah when she went up there. I believe Eddie Cantor is responsible for the change, but I still remember her as little Fannie Rose Shore.

Fannie Rose Shore (or Dinah) was always very friendly to Rabon and me, and she was classed as a popular singer or "pop" as they now call it. Back in those days we were classed as "hill-billies" but the real musicians recognized our style as authentic and legitimate, musically. Now some of the other pop female singers would not even speak to us when they saw us at the station. They would make out like they didn't even see us. We were "old hill-billies." But not Fannie Rose Shore. And you know what? I don't even remember their names and I'm sure you don't—but if you've ever listened to the entertainment mediums of today you have heard of Dinah Shore. She was big when she was little. That's the way it goes.

There was another very popular fellow on the staff of WSM when we went there whom we learned to like real well. He was Francis Craig, the staff orchestra leader for the station. He is now very famous for his tremendous hit called "Near You," but he didn't have any laurels when we knew him, except for the fact that he was an accomplished musician and leader who had an uncanny way of picking out big time stars.* You might say that he was unsung in those days except for the friendly news writers who remembered the greats he gave a start to. Some of the names you will recognize: Snooky Lanson, James Melton, and Fannie Rose Shore sang some in Francis Craig's band. On the surface, he appeared to be a poker face type of performer, but he was not that at all. He was a very warm, friendly person as Rabon and I learned when we made his acquaintance. The way it came about, he had a song called "Red Rose" and he had written it himself and he gave us a copy. He had learned that we read music and could do the song. I didn't know how he wanted it done and he said: "Do it just like you do the rest of your songs and that will be good enough for me." I was greatly relieved, for I thought he would want some fancy arrangement, being an orchestra leader, but he just wanted to hear our interpretation in our own way. He knew we would get it correct musically, in our

*Craig, who was related to the Craigs who controlled National Life and thus WSM, had been a popular fixture at the station since the mid-1920s. His orchestra made numerous records for Columbia in the mid-1920s, some of which have considerable merit as examples of early big band jazz. Among the members of this early band was Kenny Sargent, who later became famous as lead vocalist for Glen Gray's Casa Loma Orchestra. Craig's reputation on both the local and national level was well established by the time the Delmores knew him.—Ed

way. And that made us think a lot of Francis Craig. We went right to work on the song and all we had was the sheet music he had given us. We liked the song very much but it was a little out of our line, I must admit. So we practiced a whole lot on it, and we hoped it would please Francis. I don't know just exactly how long it took us to get the song where we were satisfied with it, but one night we called Francis up and told him we were doing it on our next program and to be listening for it. He was overjoyed and he said he would be down to the station immediately and hear it in person. So he came down and was there in person to hear the song the first time we sang it. He was elated to hear the way we did it and gave us some real fine compliments on the way we did it. Now, we did the song correctly but we didn't sing it in a so-called "pop" way. We were real thrilled that Francis Craig liked the way we did it in our own style. It gave us a big lift because we were suffering from a lack of prestige and this gave us a great boost. Francis will never know just how much he added to our get up and go spirit, but he was a frank man and a noteworthy musician and people like that don't discriminate when it comes to performance, if the performance meets the correct level. That is more pervading now than it was when we came along. We always sang "Red Rose" when we made programs on various radio stations. We never did record it but it was not considered our type and you don't argue with a recording director. (Now they call him an A&R man.) But Francis Craig stands tall in my book of real fine fellows and entertainers, and I am sure Rabon would echo my regards too.

We met those guys every day because we went up every day to get our fan mail. If we didn't, we'd get so far behind we would never catch up. We took the requests down and listed them and tried to play as many of them as was pos-sible. To us, the fan mail was our real boss. And I have answered many letters from would-be entertainers asking for information. I was the one who answered the fan mail because I could use a typewriter. They gave a course in high school and I took advantage of it, although I have never been a real good typist. One of the famous singers of the day in the country and western and gospel song field is Martha Carson. She gives me credit for helping them (her sisters and her) get started in the professional radio work. I didn't ever remember the letter I wrote them but I always told them all the same, I know, because I told them all the same, how we got started and it was rather easy. I just didn't deviate from the original program and it worked for some and it didn't for others, but basically I think it would work for anyone wanting to become a successful entertainer. I know you are going to take issue with me for using "entertainer" instead of "singer" or some other word that would best describe the person I am talking about. But that word is the word I use because you don't have to be a good singer to go way up high in the field of entertainment. Some guys can't even sing and still the public thinks they are the very best and will fight you if you say otherwise. But the ones I refer to are the stylists. They take a song and can't do it at all like it's supposed to be done, so they change it around and get a good rendition out of it and maybe a hit record, just because they do it different. That's the truth. The public buys what they want to buy, not what some official wants them to buy. So, in the final analysis of the music business, I would say that the guys who can't sing a lick are the ones who make the big money. They are simply just stylists. Now, don't get me wrong, I like them, too.

Beasley Smith was one of the staff musicians around WSM when we went there. He could do most anything they wanted done. Make a special "Dixie Land" arrangement, lead an orchestra, or get a small combo that could have a lot of punch. He was a great and grand guy. He helped me a lot in musical arrangements. He was the first fellow who showed me how to write "swing" music like the way Rabon and me sang it. I remember one day I went up to the station and told him I had written a new song. He was working in the music library at the time. He asked me to sing it for him. So I did. When I got through, he said: "You're not singing that song like you have it written down."

I didn't understand what he meant at first but it didn't take him long to show me. I had it written straight out and he said if I wanted to write it like I sang it, I would have to change it. He told me I should put a quarter-note on the left side of the measure bar and then I would have it right like I was singing it. I thought it over a long time and carried the idea home with me and finally realized what he meant. I really was swinging a note on the left side of the bar but I was not writing it. I told him the next day that I understood his idea and he was pleased. After I had explained it to him he knew that I knew what I was doing and since that time, I have been pretty well able to put my music down like I want it to be performed by other artists.

Beasley didn't write any songs in those days. I asked him why and he said he just never did have the desire to write songs since there were so many already written and so many songwriters that could beat him. But he always thought my songs were good and he really meant it. There was no flattery about Beasley Smith. But he must have changed his mind later because since then he has written some very outstanding songs. You will remember, "Lucky Old Sun," "The Old Master Painter," "I'd Rather Die Young," and "Night Train to Memphis." Well, Beasley had a big hand in all those and some of them he wrote entirely by himself. Sometimes I wonder if I didn't help awaken something inside him by my feeble efforts in songwriting. I haven't seen him in years and I think when I do see him, I'll ask him.

Rabon and I were already on WSM when a young man from Anniston, Alabama, joined the station. He was a real friendly fellow and said he remembered us when we came through Anniston and put on a program. He was working on the station at the time and somehow or other he just happened to remember the day we came through on our way home from Atlanta, after making our first phonograph record. He was 100 percent correct. Anniston, Alabama, was the first radio station we ever played on. I forget the call letters of the station. But back in those days, you could blunder into most any radio station and put on a program. They had trouble getting entertainment for the listeners. We did a lot of that and it was great fun. We would just go in and ask for a program and they would look at the schedule and sometimes we would get right on with a thirty minute or an hour broadcast. There were a few times we had to wait but usually we made out a program and just started in singing and sung for requests.

Those really were the days. They didn't look at your clothes or question you about your ability but just put you on and let you go. If they had paid any attention to clothes, we would never have got a program. But usually the manager would come around and thank us and ask us to stop in again when we could make it.

The young man I am writing about was Ott Devine, who is now manager of the Grand Ole Opry. And I understand from what I have heard of him from other entertainers up there that he is the very best they have ever had. I am not hard to convince about that because Ott Devine is one of the best and he is honest—a hard worker and sincere and considerate of the people who work on the show. I know Rabon and me were always crazy about Ott when he used to announce for us and all the time we were at WSM he came nearest to being the same all the time than anyone else we ever worked with. That considerate attitude goes a long way when you are nervous and driving like made to please everybody. And when criticism is always your undesired companion. It is simply refreshing to think of how we got along with Ott Devine when we were at WSM and the Opry.

Another person whom we liked a great deal was Jack Harris, now manager of KPRC in Houston, Texas. Jack was always a genial fellow and he was a good announcer. He became a top sportscaster on the station. I will have more to say about Jack in a later chapter.

Then there was Snooky Lanson, whom I saw not long ago when he played

Huntsville. Snooky was the main vocalist with Francis Craig and his orchestra. He was one of our best friends up there and he used to take up a lot of time with us. At first, we were surprised to think that he, being a pop singer, would take up time with two "hill-billies" like us. But he learned to like our singing and he listened and heard that we sung the harmony correctly and that makes a whale of a difference when it comes to a man who has studied voice and music like he did. Some people are just naturally born with a true ear and can learn to play and sing much quicker than others who are less fortunate, and they are content to roll along and accept anything they hear and will not study music. They don't know that it would greatly increase their ability if they would try to learn but there's no use trying to convince them. They are too ignorant to know the difference. I have never yet been able to teach anyone who could play real well but Merle Travis.

Bobby Tucker was another musician on the staff who would take up some time with us and treat us like fellow musicians. He was a real pianist and he had several programs each day and he played a lot of variety in his arrangements. I remember we picked up some of our best spirituals from him. We would listen to him and when he played one we liked we would go and ask him where we could locate it, if we couldn't find it ourselves in the music stores.

All of the ones I have mentioned above were a big help to two lonesome boys green and fresh from the country who needed a little recognition from fellow workers, who would treat us like someone or somebody. That is where jealousy brings a lot of grief. And we had plenty of the "big shots" up there who were jealous of us. They wanted us on the station but they wanted us to feel just like a couple of bums and they succeeded very, very well. I know it sounds like a diabolical trick but it sure will happen to you when you are a victim of vultures.

Our records were selling real well at this time but we were having trouble collecting all we were due and we never did get a proper accounting from the people who were representing us. These people had a publishing company, or made up a name for one and tried to get us to sign a contract with them but we didn't trust them. They tried every means of duress they could think of to make us sign but we never did and I am thankful today that we did have enough sense to keep from signing that contract. They took us to Chicago, and we made records and they made records, too. But we never did sign a contract with the RCA Company up there. We recorded seventeen sides the time we went to Chicago, and Rabon and me had written every single song we recorded. But the record man didn't say anything about us signing anything. But we heard him talking to these people over the speaker. I don't think they would have said anything about it, if they had known the speaker was on. But when the recording director, Mr. Oberstein, asked them who wrote the songs one of them told him they did, and that just simply burned me up. I didn't want anybody claiming my songs when I wrote most of them myself. Rabon didn't seem to mind too much but I just wouldn't stand hitched. The main reason I had started in the show business was to get started out as a real songwriter. And I didn't want somebody else's name on my songs.

When the people went out to get coffee, I simply raised hell with the recording man. I told him before I would let someone else claim my songs I would not sing another song on record. He didn't know what to do, so he waited till they all came back and he had a long talk with them. They got real irritated but they waited a good while before one of them came out to talk with us. He was full of soft soap and other things in general, and he said they didn't mean to tell the man they wrote the songs. He said they were trying to protect us from having our songs taken away from us. He said our name would appear on the records as the composers. That was good enough for me so we proceeded with the recording session. But we still didn't sign anything with Mr. Oberstein. It really took a long time to get that situation straightened out.

Every time we went up to broadcast on Saturday night they would jump us and try to get us to sign their contract. In the meantime I talked to a good lawyer down in Athens, Alabama. He read the contracts over and told us if signed, we would lose all our copyrights and it would not be just partial. It would be for as long as the songs made any money. So I knew we weren't going to sign, if it meant our losing out on WSM. They used that to put a scare into us. They knew how much we loved the Grand Ole Opry and one of them told me:

"Now you can do what you damn please about signing our contracts. I don't care either way. It's up to you. But I'm gonna tell you one thing." He got up real close to me and almost whispered, like a snake hissing. "If you don't sign those contracts, Harry will run you off the Grand Ole Opry." With that he walked away and let it soak in. I was afraid to say anything to Mr. Stone because I knew they stood in very good at the Opry and I thought maybe if I said anything that soon, it might be a mistake. So I just went on and Rabon and me made our programs and left.

Now when we went to Chicago, they didn't say anything about our songs or their songs or anything else. They just told us the company (Victor) would like for us all to come up together in the same car so that they could save expenses. I would not have minded giving them 10 percent for their efforts as an agent's fee. But they scoffed at that. They wanted the whole title to all the songs.

I thought it over for a week and didn't go up to the station, except to get the mail and make the morning shows, and I didn't stay long then. There was trouble and I didn't know how to meet it. But I finally decided that we would quit WSM and the Opry if it came to giving up our songs. So, with my mind made up, I went in to see Mr. Stone. I took the contracts with me. I told him what had been said and how they had threatened us. He flamed up and was real angry.

"Don't you guys sign anything unless you want to. And my advice is not to sign anything. You don't work for those people, you work for WSM and they have no right to try something like this. Just wait till I see them. Somebody's gonna get a hell of a bawling out. No, don't you sign a g—d—thing."

That settled the matter for the time being. But that bunch did everything in their power after that to hurt us, and they hurt us plenty on the station and the Grand Ole Opry.

The name of the act was the famous singing group, the Vagabonds. They were one of the best and most accurate singing groups I have ever heard since, or before. They were leaving soon for their annual vacation away from WSM, as they always did. And we got the crumbs when they left. We were never recognized by the bosses like the Vagabonds were, but they were never recognized by the people like we were. So I figure it was a tie in our favor.

Mr. Harry Stone had come through for us and in great style. That was the first time we realized that he did not hate us. In all that he did he was only trying to be fair-minded. Of course the old "pros" like the Vagabonds knew how to twist things around to their own liking. They knew a lot of tricks of the trade that we did not know and they took full advantage of it. Now, looking back over the years, I can't say that I blame them too much, but they sure did make life miserable for me and Rabon, especially me when they tried to force us out of our songs. It was just like someone trying to take your own child away from you. I never gave the money part a thought. I was afraid they would get credit for what I had written. In that bunch of songs was "Brown's Ferry Blues" and it took me about two or three years to get it all straightened out.*

There was one thing, though, I'll never forget about the Chicago trip. We had a wonderful time and except for the argument over the songs there were no hitches. The Vagabonds had worked in Chicago and they knew a lot of the entertainers up there on radio and clubs and on record. I never will forget the night we got the news that Utah had voted wet and Prohibition was a dead duck. That was when we were in Chicago and I believe everybody in Chicago got "tight" when the news came in. There were people on the street I had never seen before that stopped and shook hands with me and the same went for Rabon and the Vagabonds. We made a lot of the clubs and the Vagabonds sang several songs in each one. Then we would hurry on to the next one till we got so tired we had to go back to the hotel. You know, I think it's a sin and a shame for the government to suppress their people so much when they do not want it. Just a few big-mouthed people who want their way and force it on their neighbors. In other words, they slip up on their blind side till they have something pulled that can't be stopped till it is too late. The people didn't want Prohibition in the first place, but they got it just the same. But that's one thing you cannot ever

*The exact details of the Delmores' dispute with the Vagabonds over the Delmore songs are still not entirely clear. Apparently the Vagabonds formed a song publishing company shortly after they came to the Opry in 1931. This company was called Old Cabin Co., Inc., and was located in the Hitchcock Building in downtown Nashville. In January 1932, they published a folio, *Old Cabin Songs for the Fiddle & the Bow as Sung by the Vagabonds*, which within a year went through ten printings and which contained eighteen songs, none of them Delmore compositions. The company also issued records on the Old Cabin label; only two different recordings are known to have been issued by Old Cabin Records. Victor session sheets from the Delmores' first Chicago session (December 6–7, 1933) indicate that virtually all the original Delmore songs, including "Gonna Lay Down My Old Guitar" and "Brown's Ferry Blues," were copyrighted in 1933 by the Old Cabin Co., Inc.—the Vagabonds' company. Sometime later the rights were transferred back to the Delmore Brothers themselves, though just when is uncertain. As late as 1936 appeared a Curt Poulton and the Delmore Brothers songbook, *Sentimental Songs from the Heart of the Hills*, in which over a dozen Delmore songs appeared with composer credits given to the brothers; however, Poulton was a member of the Vagabonds and the fact that he included his songs with those of the Delmores might well indicate that Old Cabin had some control over some of the early Delmore material three years later.—Ed.

do successfully: try to make the people do something they are opposed to. They submit for a while but when the seams start to bust there's going to be trouble, plenty trouble.

CHAPTER THIRTEEN

THE PLACES WE LIVED IN NASHVILLE

The places we lived in Nashville afford me a guide to what we did when we were there. Without the places I could not remember the events because I associate them with what happened. For instance, we lived on Alloway Street when our first commercial ended with disastrous results. That was the first place we lived when we left our home in Alabama. It was a duplex apartment and was pretty nice for people who had lived in the country all their lives. But it took us a long time to get used to the plumbing facilities. It just didn't seem like home. We had hot and cold running water in the house, and we thought that was nice but the toilet was on the outside and in a house just like the one we had in the country but you had to flush it and it just didn't seem right somehow. Seemed like we were getting a bit lazy by having to use a thing like that. But then we finally got adjusted to it and it worked out just fine and we learned to appreciate that little gadget more than we thought we would.

My wife was going to have a baby. And that didn't worry her or me any at all. We didn't realize just how serious it was till it caught up with us. We knew we had to have a doctor so we got an old doctor who used to be our family doctor when we lived in Veto, Alabama. His name was Doctor Tom Whitfield and he really was a fine man and a good doctor. He had told us the baby would not be due for two months the last time he came to see Thelma. But it was not long after he left that she got to feeling bad. We didn't think much about it. But she was not well all night long and the next day she was still not doing any good at all. We kept waiting, hoping she would get to feeling better, but she didn't. She was gradually getting worse all the time. I waited till after dark and I went and called the doctor and told him how she was. He got real excited and rushed over as soon as he could. I don't guess it took him over ten or fifteen minutes to get to our apartment. Thelma had gone back to the toilet like she had been doing all day and the night before. When she came back in, he examined her and said the baby was on its way and nearly here. He didn't wait to call the ambulance but took her in his car. He was afraid the baby would be born on the way to the hospital. He didn't tell us then but he did later. I followed behind in my car. So when we reached the hospital he rushed her right on into the delivery room. The baby, a little girl, was born shortly after. I was simply bewildered. Being a father was a curious experience for me and I didn't know how to take it. I felt at first that the baby was some kind of an intruder. I guess it was because it had come early and surprised, and excited, and scared us. She was a seven months child and everybody always said you have trouble with a premature baby. And we did have. We nearly lost her.

We named the baby Billie Anne and she was a cute, normal little thing, but she had a hard time getting started. She would cry at night and when she took her bottle she would vomit or spit it up and she was simply starving, but we didn't know it and the doctor thought she would catch up and start growing soon. But when she was three months old she still hadn't caught on. She was just about skin and bones. She weighed less then than when she was born. We were alarmed but we didn't know what to do.

The Mathews family lived in the other side of the apartment. I have mentioned this earlier but didn't tell all that happened. They were Catholics. They were sweet people, Mr. and Mrs. Mathews and their daughter. They were really a blessing to us.

One day out in the back yard, I was holding Billie Anne and walking around in the sunshine, thinking maybe some sunshine would help her to get on the road to being a hardy little girl like she was supposed to be. Mrs. Mathews came up along the side of the fence that separated our lots and started talking to me. She showed her anxiety over Billie Anne. She asked me to let her hold her and I did. When she took the baby she caressed her a little and then she turned her head away from me. She didn't say anything for a few minutes but when she turned around I could see tears in her eyes. She had a heart. "Mr. Delmore, will you let me try something with Billie Anne, you and Mrs. Delmore?" Thelma was in the house cooking or something else but I told Mrs. Mathews to come into our house and talk to us both, for we needed any help we could get to help our little girl.

She kept the baby in her arms and came in the front door. She seemed as upset about Billie Anne as we did. I guess she knew we didn't know anything about children and she was glad to help us out. She spoke to Thelma.

"Mrs. Delmore, I believe Billie Anne is starving to death and she won't last the way things are going. I love Billie Anne and I want to help. I believe I can." She was a lot older than we were and we realized something had to be done. We had faith in her. She said: "Will you let me try?"

Thelma assured her we would be glad to have any help we could get and then Mrs. Mathews turned to me.

"Mr. Delmore, I want you to go to the grocery and get me two quarts of Jersey Farms milk and a half gallon of white Karo syrup. That's all I want but I want you to hurry and bring it back so I can feed this starving little thing." I jumped in the car and was back in no time with the milk and the syrup. Mrs. Mathews went right to work. She knew what she was doing. First, she mixed the syrup and milk together and put it on to boil. She stirred it while it boiled and then she let it get lukewarm before she gave any of it to the baby. Then she put it in a bottle and gave our little Billie Anne the first real meal she had ever gotten since she had come to the earth. In a very few minutes she was asleep and she slept soundly for a long time. Maybe three or four hours. And when she woke up she was not ill and crying like she was before. She began to gain weight from day to day and in a week she weighed twice as much as she did before taking the milk and syrup formula. She slept well at night and didn't keep us up, and we were very thankful and still are to a wonderful Catholic lady who passed along a remedy that saved the life of our first child. Without the kind help of this Catholic lady, Mrs. Mathews, two young parents would probably have had sad hearts and empty arms. There is always someone to turn to in the time of storm. I have always found it that way myself and that belief is a major part of the way I believe about religion.

We had lots of visitors in the entertainment field when we lived on Alloway Street, even if we did live in a little, crowded apartment. There was nearly always someone from the Grand·Ole Opry coming to see us. Of course, they were the little ones, or they at least were considered the little ones by the big shots at the station and the acts that thought they would lower their elevation by coming out to see two country boys who didn't know the score like they did.

Yes, although we weren't making a lot of money, we still had friends, and they showed it. If we had just been able to get a manager like they have today, we would have been making some real money. We had the best commercials on the station, with two of them on Saturday night before the Opry began and then we had from two to four programs on the Opry after it started, and we still had to go out of town each week to make a living. Our fan mail was really tremendous but we were young then and could take it, we thought. But that kind of a schedule will finally kill any person who attempts it. I know by experience. I had rather face anything now than a crowd. It is not that I don't like people. It is the fact that I have seen so many of them, at so many given times, and kept a big smile on my face, knowing that I had to drive nearly a thousand miles to get back to Nashville for the Saturday night programs.

Some of our guests and friends who came to call on us while we lived on Alloway Street were Zeke Clements and Texas Ruby.* They played together then and were a big hit with the fans all over the country. They would come out and we would play and pick and sing till it was quite late in the evening or rather early in the morning. Just to show you how hard times were in those days, Zeke and Ruby came out one night and had dinner with us (we always called it supper). Anyway, it was night and they brought their band along. There were three or four of them. And we cooked up a meal. It wasn't fancy or anything like that, but we all ate and had enough and then we enjoyed some real good music by Zeke and Ruby and the band. They were playing the Opry, like we were, but they were not getting rich either, but they had a string of theaters, the Crescent Chain (or as we always called it, the Sudekum Circuit) booked and they knew they would make some real money on that. But they hadn't started playing it yet and times were hard. They told us later that on this night they had eaten with us they were flat broke and couldn't eat otherwise. But you would never have known it by their actions. They knew how to keep the old chin up. And a lot of times, it takes that in the show business. And that is just about true for any business you get in. If you tell the truth to somebody and you are real desperate for help, nine times out of ten you will get laughed at. Nobody loves you but your family.

---

*Zeke Clements was at this time leading a band called Zeke Clements & His Bronco Busters, one of the first "western" bands to establish itself on the Opry. Texas Ruby, of course, was later to achieve more lasting fame during her marriage and partnership to fiddler Curley Fox.—Ed.

THE PLACES WE LIVED IN NASHVILLE

And, sometimes, it doesn't pay to let them know if you are really in a tough spot.

Rabon and I later played some dates with Zeke and Ruby. But they were the stars, having top billing, and we were advertised just as guest entertainers. They had a good show but I never did like being a tag along. So we just filled in on some dates when they needed us. And they understood perfectly.

Uncle Dave Macon and Sam and Kirk McGee and Herman and Lewis Crook were some of our visitors. Also Dr. Humphrey Bate and some of his band came to see us.

Some of the kinsfolk usually stayed with us for days at a time. They just liked to come up there and watch us and go to the Opry with us on Saturday nights.

The next place we moved was called Grove Avenue. It was a house to ourselves and it was kind of isolated from the other houses on the street. It suited us better than Alloway Street because we had trees and more room and it was cozier. It was on this street where we got to traveling too much. By that time we had learned how the land laid about personals and we made some pretty good money with Uncle Dave and various others. But mostly with Uncle Dave till the station stopped us. There were only three of us, Uncle Dave, Rabon, and me, and we were making out better than any of the others on the station. We would make long, hard trips into the mountains and coal camps of Virginia, West Virginia, and Kentucky. We would always come back to town with some money in our pockets. We were very happy. We took good care of Uncle Dave and saw that he got his necessary rest. He had a habit of getting to a place early and going to bed for a couple of hours before show time. This meant we had to leave real early in the morning for some of our dates were several hundred miles apart. And even though Rabon and I wanted to sleep later, we had to get up and get the Dixie Dew Drop (Uncle Dave's publicity name) to his place of rest. Sometimes it was hard to do, but we both knew he couldn't hold up if he didn't get his rest. And we never bickered about this habit of his, and that is one reason he liked to play with us. Now, as I look back on those times, we would have been a lot better off, healthwise, if we had done the same thing. He used to tell us that himself, but we had to learn the hard way. He believed firmly that rest was one of the most important elements in the line of keeping healthy. And I can now see that he was just about 100 percent correct.

It was on Grove Avenue, or while we lived there, that I first began to have trouble with my nerves. All those hard trips and hard driving was beginning to catch up with me. I can also say that it was when we lived on Grove that I first seriously began to think of leaving the Grand Ole Opry. On our trips to various parts of the country we could see other radio entertainers who were not on the Opry and were making more money than we had ever thought of making while we were in Nashville. And most of those we talked to were on stations of but maybe 1,000 watts and just played locally and didn't have to make the long trips like we did. Some of them were on 5,000-watt stations and some maybe a little higher. But the more power a station had, the more they thought they owned you and could make you do like they said do, or get fired. So I began to figure that we could have more happiness and be at home more if we left the Opry and traveled on to some other station.

We had a lot of important company while we lived there in the trees. They didn't seem to be so important then, but if it were today, they would certainly be important. Nearly all the time there was somebody dropping in to see us or to talk business.

I remember a frequent visitor to our house there was the late Fred Rose. He had once been one of the most popular songwriters of the day when he was writing songs in Chicago and New York. He knew a lot about songwriting and could tell you more in a minute or two about songs than most so-called writers can in many months. I learned a whole lot from Fred myself. And Fred Rose was not jealous of someone else who could write songs. If there was any way he could help a beginner, he would do his very best.

THE PLACES WE LIVED IN NASHVILLE

I first met him at the Grand Ole Opry. He had come down just to see what it was like, and he played a program on the organ. When he got through with his program, Rabon and me waited around to meet him. We thought he was the same one who wrote "That's Why I'm Jealous of You," but we wanted to be sure. Fred was near-sighted and he didn't look like a great songwriter to us. So we just waited and bided our time. When we caught him free of someone else, we approached him doubtfully. We told him who we were, and he was glad to meet us. He said he had heard our songs from Chicago or St. Louis, one. I forget which.

"Are you the same Fred Rose who wrote 'That's Why I'm Jealous of You'?" I asked him. He gave me an odd look.

"Sure. Why, do you know it?"

We then told him how much we liked it, and that we sang it on a lot of our programs. And we told him we never expected to meet so famous a songwriter as he was. He just kind of laughed. But he seemed pleased. He never bragged on the song. He just told us he was pleased that we liked the song and appreciated our singing it on the air.

We had sung this man's songs since we first began singing together. It was a real thrill to meet him, because he was the first big time songwriter we had ever met in the pop field. This meeting was long before we moved to Nashville. I remember not long after we met him I asked him to look at some of our songs. They were on record but I couldn't get anybody to publish them. He told me to bring four or five up the next Saturday night and he would pick one out and have it published for us. Boy! That was what would add to our prestige, I thought. So I got a bunch of them together, the ones I thought he would like, and showed them to him. He picked out one song and told me we would start from this one and then there would be others if this one was satisfactory. The name of the song was "I Ain't Got Nowhere to Travel." He said he liked it very much. He sent it up to Chicago, to his publisher, and assured me that it would not be long before it would be on the market in sheet music form. We waited and waited and finally Fred got a letter rejecting the song on some sort of whim or another. I was bitterly disappointed and Fred could tell it. And there was something else he saw. He saw or, at least he thought he saw, something in my attitude that made him think I thought he was giving me the runaround. He was plenty mad at the publisher. Here is what he said: "I'm sorry you boys are so disappointed about this thing. And just to prove to you that I am no jerk, I'm never sending another song to that publisher again."

That was the sincerity of Fred Rose. He never did send that publisher another song just because he had broken up the promise he had made to two green country boys. And this publisher was a powerful influence in the publishing world at that time and his songs are still sung and played. That publisher has some mighty popular songs in his catalog. But Fred Rose had principle and he wouldn't compromise with anything less than true blue. That is why he is in the Country Music Hall of Fame today. I feel it an honor to be one of the voters. There are one hundred of us. And I voted for Fred Rose on the first ballot. He belongs there with the greatest.

Yes, there on Grove, it was a beautiful little place. The trees were high and spreading and the birds sang almost as much as they did in the country. And, that is what made it seem so much like home. I believe our visitors caught the spirit of the place because they liked to come out so much. We really had a fine place. The rent was not so high, just fifteen dollars a month. But that is the way things were priced in those days. Most of the fellows who had a staff salary lived in much better places and paid much higher rent. But they didn't look down on us for living in a low-rate house. It was a clean house and I find it to be the same everywhere you go. If you live in a mansion and don't keep it clean, it takes on the status of a hog pen. I know the government has taken away the slum sections of a lot of cities and built beautiful and ultra-modern housing projects. They have moved those unfortunate people into these uptown places, and left them to live in comfort far beyond their means. But they can't change the slum attitude of about 90 percent of those poor "unfortunates." A visit, or a short stay, in most of those projects will show how callous some of those so-called "unfortunates" are behaving and how they are tearing up their homes just like they did before they left the slums.

Like I have written before, we were raised poor people but we were taught to be clean and decent. The creatures of the wild that inhabit the forest are a good illustration of what I mean. A squirrel, for instance, lives in an old hollow tree, but you won't find a cleaner animal than him. Of course he has opposites. The opossum, for instance.

While we lived on Grove, Uncle Dave was our most frequent visitor. When we were not hooked up and had a week off, he would always go home and said he wanted some real rest from those long trips we had been making. He would stay up in Readyville (that's where he made his home) for about three or four days, or till the middle of the week, and then he would get one of his boys to bring him down to Nashville to our house. He would then stay and enjoy himself for the rest of the week. He always liked to go to the Market Place and buy from the farmers gathered there. He knew most of them by their first names and he just about knew who had what he wanted, and also the best. He always liked to pick out sausage and country ham and fat, middling meat. He would bring it back with him and share it with us. He would buy chittlings, pig's feet, and other parts of the hog and bring it in. Sometimes we would not eat it, but Thelma would always cook some up for him. Lots of times he would have to tell her how to cook it and he always would eat it.

Looking back now, I can see lots of things that should have been changed when we lived on Grove Avenue in the little green house. I guess one reason it seemed so much like home to us was because of the color. It was in keeping with our experience in the entertainment business. I have said earlier that it was on Grove that I

THE PLACES WE LIVED IN NASHVILLE

first began feeling nervous and tense and I can see the reason now. I never did get enough rest. I wanted to do so many things and I wanted to do them all personally. That was a big mistake. I answered all the fan mail that required an answer myself. I could type and Rabon couldn't, so there was the difference. He should have been given some of the assignments and it would have kept him from getting on the wrong road and with some of the wrong people he associated with, to the detriment of our popularity in Nashville. Of course our many fans didn't know a thing about lots of the things that happened, but the Nashville bunch did, and there in that little old town of Nashville, you can have a hell of a lot of trouble, when you're supposed to be a star on the Grand Ole Opry. It cuts like a sharp knife when it hits you. And then there's always somebody to add to, when it comes to gossip. Like Hank Williams once told me. He said: "Alton, if they'd only tell the truth it would be bad enough. But why do they go out and deliberately tell a malicious lie?" I answered this time from experience.

"Hank, it's because they're jealous of you." He looked at me kind of curiously, then he shook his head. "I guess you're right but why? I've gone out of my way to help some of the people who tell the worse things on me and I just don't get it." I said "Hank, how many of these people up here can write and record hit after hit like you're doing now?" Then he understood what I meant.

There's a little more I would like to add to what happened while we lived on Grove. Our second baby was born and I'll never forget it. Rabon and I had been off on a long trip with Uncle Dave. We let him out of the car at the Merchant's Hotel, where he always stayed while he was in Nashville, when he didn't stay with us. But on this particular Saturday, we were all just about worn out. We had come about a thousand miles from our last show date and we didn't have time to stop to rest any at all. I had driven all the time and I felt just like a dried-out sponge. You get to feeling like a vegetable or something like that when you drive that far. But it is not much better on the guys in the car with you, because you can't put a bed in a car. I never could get any real rest in a car, so I guess I was just as well off driving. Anyway, when we got home, Thelma was feeling pretty ill at ease.

My dad and mother were up there, luckily, and that helped out some, in the things that had to be done. I felt more like lying down and sleeping a week than I did going to the hospital with my wife. We called the doctor and then we took her to the hospital. They said it would be some time yet, so I went back home after they assured me I could do nothing else to help. I lay down on the bed but I couldn't sleep. I was so nervous I just rolled and tossed. I knew I had to make the Opry, but I sure didn't feel like it. Rabon didn't have any trouble going to sleep and he jumped back to normal pretty quickly. But I had to tough it through. I went out and got me some strong spirits, and took a drink or two of that, and it got me through all right. I knew I just had to make the Opry. Now that is what makes people think musicians are all sots. They are not sots but they have to have something to brace them up occasionally to help them make up for the beating they have taken on the road. You can't get on the radio or stage and start apologizing for the way you feel. You've got to get up there and smile and look fine, and put them on a show, or they won't like you and they'll think you are a heel, and you *will* be.

Rabon (*left*) and Alton during their Grand Ole Opry days at WSM,
Nashville, 1930s.

Rabon (*left*) and Alton, as they appeared on the cover of their *Songs We Sing* songbook, published during their tenure with the Grand Ole Opry, late 1930s.

Rabon (*standing, left*) and Alton with Curt Poulton of the Vagabonds, ca. 1936. This photo appeared on the cover of a songbook that Poulton published with the Delmores, *Sentimental Songs from the Heart of the Hills.*

Rabon (*left*) and Alton at WIBC, Indianapolis, ca. 1944.

Alton (*left*) and Rabon at WMC, Memphis, ca. 1945.

Alton, Wayne Raney (*seated left*) and Rabon, late 1940s.

Rabon and Alton. Photo by Riggs Studio, Fort Smith, Arkansas, ca. 1949.

A Delmore Brothers songbook, published in 1951 by Lois Music,
which was owned by King Records magnate Syd Nathan.

CHAPTER FOURTEEN
BEHIND THE SCENES—NO. 1

Like I have said before, Zeke and Ruby played the Sudekum Circuit of theaters and other acts drifted in, having never played on the Opry before, and would play the whole Crescent Amusement Circuit, as long as they drew well enough, and most of them would draw well enough to play what they wanted of it. That is, the theaters where they could make the most money. I remember Salt & Peanuts played the houses and stayed busy for a long and profitable time. They had a good show. So did the others. Asher & Little Jimmie Sizemore also played some of the choice houses.

But nobody would tell me how to book the circuit. When I would ask them they would only say it was very hard to book. I don't think I ever asked Lasses White how to book them. Lasses & Honey had played them, but they had a good and well-known minstrel show that was aired on WSM every week and it was an hour show. Lasses was an old-time showman. He had been in the business for a long time, nearly all his life, and he really rated. He was a prince of a fellow, too.

Rabon and I, with Uncle Dave, wanted to play the circuit too, so I was very persistent with my questions about how to get to play those theaters. I knew we had a show that was going over everywhere we played and I was sure we could go over with those houses too. We had played many theaters in the coal towns and cities in the mountain sections, but they were so far away that we wanted to get a little closer to home.

Finally, when Frank Salt came in to town with Peanuts, his wife, I asked him what to do. He was a fine guy, too. All the old timers are good guys. When I asked Salt, as we all called him, he didn't answer me at first, but thought it over for a moment.

"I'll tell you what I would do if I were you. I'd see Russell Parham down at the Princess Theatre and see what he says about it. He stands in with Mr. Sudekum as well as anybody I know of, and he can help you out, I believe."

I told him I was afraid to see a big-time theater manager like that. He said he would go down with me, but he had to go out of town.

"And if you book the circuit through him, just you, by yourself, you will feel like you've got a feather in your cap, and you will have, so just go on down and talk to him like you are talking to me. He's just a man like you and me."

I was really scared stiff, but I decided to go through with it. I couldn't face Uncle Dave and Rabon if I didn't. So I went down to the Princess and asked to see Mr. Parham. I got to see him right away and I got right to the point.

"I tell you what I'll do. Next week I have some room on the stage for a little act like yours. I'll put you and your brother on with this big vaudeville show and if you go over, I'll recommend you to play the whole circuit."

That was something I didn't expect! Rabon and me playing the Princess Theatre, where the big time stars played! I had to hold on a moment to get my mind straight before I could say anything to him. He didn't wait for me to answer.

"I'll pay you boys thirty-five dollars each to play Thursday, Friday, and Saturday. I would pay you more but I have my budget for that week and just put that much in an extra and charge it to something else. And then I'll have blow-ups made from your pictures and put them in the lobby, and I'll also put you in the newspaper ad and that will help you around here, locally."

I couldn't believe my ears. He was doing all this just to give us a try at a big theater circuit, which would mean everything to us and nothing to him! But Russell Parham was a good man and he was a real showman. He wasn't the manager of that big theater through politics. He had earned every bit of the position he had advanced to, and he was completely unspoiled. I said something about playing Uncle Dave on the bill with us but he shook his head.

"No, we don't need Uncle Dave to play with you boys. He has played on this stage so much that we are used to him and we know what he can do. All I want is you boys and, hey, drop by and leave me a picture so I can have the blow-up ready when you play."

I left that theater walking on air. Here was something unbelievable. It was really a great break he was giving us. I went straight up to the station and got the pictures and gave them to him. Then I went home to break the good news to Rabon, Thelma, and Uncle Dave. He happened to be with us at the time. We all agreed to keep it secret till we found out if we were going to get the full circuit or not. Uncle Dave was simply delighted.

"Now, boys, this is the big chance we've got to make some real money. Did Russell say anything about what kind of a show he wanted in the theaters?"

"No, he didn't say anything about that but evidently he has plenty of confidence in you, because he said he knew what you could do."

So, at last, we were to make some real money on the strength of our radio and record publicity. We were all very happy with the turn of events. We had been going out of town every week to help make a living and it had become a sort of dread to us like drudgery or something of the sort. Uncle Dave said: "Now you boys do your very best to go over with the crowd because that's what Russell will judge you on. And I'll be out there in the crowd, helping to cheer you on. Yes, I'll be there at every show, and I'll lead the whole crowd in applause because this is something big."

We had a few small schools to play down in Cheatham County till we were to play

145

the Princess. That kept us busy till the time of the big break. But it didn't keep our minds off of the great opportunity. We didn't know exactly how we were going to play it, but we knew we were going to try as we had never done before. Our anticipations were as wild as a March hare.

Mr. Parham did as he had told us he would do and he advertised us real well. Thursday was our first show and we were to play through Saturday. So we were there bright and early Thursday afternoon, and we found out when we were to appear and how long we were to be on the stage and everything was squared away real fine. The big show was in full progress. They had been in town since Monday and had got used to all the angles around the Princess. They (the show people) didn't pay us any attention, just seemed to take us in stride.

Pete Brescia of the staff of WSM had the pit band and he said he would introduce us. Pete was a fine fellow and an arranger for the station. He could lead a band and do most anything that it took to run a big radio station, and he liked us. I remember many a time when we went to make our morning shows on WSM, we would meet Pete going home for some rest. He would stay up all night to catch up with his arranging. He said he could work better at night with no noise or people to interrupt him.

We went over fairly well on the matinee show, though we didn't set the woods on fire and we were better on the supper or second show. We had to take a couple of bows. Mr. Parham had told us not to take too many encores even if we got them. He said he didn't have the time to spare and he didn't want the show to run overtime. So we didn't try too hard to make a big impression. We only took up about five or six minutes. And we knew this was only a try-out anyway.

But on the night show we really went over big. We had three encores, and the people on the big vaudeville show began to pay some attention to us. That made us happy, and we were really looking forward to the next day, Friday, for we wanted

BEHIND THE SCENES—NO. 1

Mr. Parham to think well of us. I apologized for the encores we took when I saw him and he just laughed. He said it was quite all right, and if we continued to get encores the next day he would take some time off some of the other acts that were not going over so well. That made me happy, and when we left to go home we really had something good to tell Thelma. Uncle Dave was in the crowd and he was delighted to see us go over so good with so little time on the stage. We took Uncle Dave by the Merchants Hotel and then we went home to get some rest. Everybody was happy.

The next morning we woke up and I felt real good, looking forward to our second day at the Princess. I wondered how we would make it today. I didn't have long to wait to find that out.

When Rabon woke up he had something wrong with his throat. He could not speak. He didn't feel like he was sick but he just couldn't talk. After he had breakfast, I carried him to the doctor. The doctor examined him closely and said even if he could sing, he must not for he might injure his throat permanently. He gave us a prescription and it helped Rabon some, but he just could not make it. At first, I felt real low about it, but then I realized it was something that could not be helped. Then I called Mr. Parham.

I didn't know quite how to tell him about it. I thought he would be mad or badly disappointed. But he was not. He was more concerned about how Rabon was getting along. He told me to take good care of him and do what the doctor said, and he hoped he would be all right soon. I never will forget one thing he said to me: "It's pretty bad when someone in the show business has his living taken away from him." That's how concerned Russell Parham was. So we didn't get to play out the try-out date, and I thought everything had fallen through and forgot about it. By Saturday, Rabon was lots better and could sing pretty well but that didn't save the day. I was thankful we could make the Opry that night. I decided to go uptown and get the blow-up picture Mr. Parham said we could have, after we had played the date.

BEHIND THE SCENES—NO. 1

He seemed glad to see me, and the first thing he asked me was about Rabon. The blow-up picture was still in the lobby. He pointed over to it.

"I just let it stay up, because there wasn't anything else I knew to do. Some people asked why you were not on stage, and I told them you were on just for a try-out and that got me off the hook. But there's the big picture and you may take it with you when you leave. I want to see you in the office a minute." I followed him and he sat down at his desk. "Yes, that's real bad when someone gets sick and can't go on, but you boys have your radio job, and that's a good thing. I've seen entertainers get ill and have to quit work indefinitely. That's the worst. Most of them live from day to day and don't try to save any money and then they are really up against it."

He then wrote me out a check for the entire amount he had promised to pay us. I was amazed. But somehow I got out my thanks to him and told him I sure was sorry we didn't get the theater circuit.

He looked straight at me. "I told you if you went over well enough you'd get the circuit, didn't I?" I didn't know how to answer that one. But he didn't wait for me. "You went over plenty good that night, and you get the whole chain of theater. You couldn't help it because you couldn't go on. That happens to everybody. I've already called Mr. Sudekum and arranged for you to start playing the houses. But I want to give you a little advice. You two boys and Uncle Dave will be plenty of show for any of our houses, but it will look too small for just three people to show up to play some of the bigger houses. So you get together with Uncle Dave, and hire you about two guitar or banjo pickers or fiddlers and take them along with you, just for the looks of things. That is all I'd take if I were you, and you don't have to pay them too much either. So I'll be seeing you about further arrangements."

I left that Princess Theatre walking on air again.

I just couldn't hardly wait to tell Rabon and Thelma and Uncle Dave about the good news. Here, at last, was an angel in disguise, and his name was Russell Parham.

BEHIND THE SCENES—NO. 1

But I was to meet many more good people in the theater business later just like him. The show business is not all cut-throat. There are far many more good ones than there are bad ones. And the bad ones don't last long at all if they don't change their ways. You can't fool everybody all of the time.

When I got home and told everybody about our good luck, they could not believe it at first. It was such a good break and came in such a good time. But our joy was not to last very long.

Nobody knew of the prize at stake, when we played the Princess, that is, nobody but Rabon and me and Uncle Dave and Thelma, my wife, and we all agreed to keep it a secret. We knew better than to let it out, because somebody might get some ideas that we might not like. But the news leaked out some way. We had not hardly got used to the idea of playing the Sudekum Circuit when we got the bad news. We had not even thought of selecting the two extra musicians Mr. Parham said we needed, when we got a call to come up to the station for a conference on a new road show. George D. Hay, the "Solemn Old Judge," was the artist manager of the station, a newly organized office at WSM. He was the one who called us.

That was the early part of the week, Tuesday or Wednesday, I think. We did not know what it was all about, but we had premonitions of something that boded no good for us. We went up to the station and Judge Hay had a whole bunch of the Grand Ole Opry gathered in the big studio. There was eight of them, and Uncle Dave and Rabon and I made eleven people. Mr. Hay and the manager of the string-band had gone over to see Mr. Sudekum and offered him the big show to play the theaters instead of just three with the two "extras." I don't know to this day how they found out about our playing the circuit of towns, but they had heard about it somehow. Hay had the thing all figured out, how to divide the money and who was to manage the show and everything. This man stood in with Judge Hay, and Mr. Hay told us we could do the way he had it planned or he would recommend our dismissal from the station and the Grand Ole Opry.

Now you just put yourself in our place and see how you would feel. We had gone to all the trouble of begging and getting the circuit and had all the trouble of making all the arrangements I have written about before and then we were pushed aside to the role of just a member of that fellow's band. They gave Uncle Dave twenty percent and this fellow twenty percent and the rest of us split what was left. Rabon and me refused to go on the show and would have taken it up with Mr. Stone, but Uncle Dave told us he would take his twenty percent and add it to what we got and we would split it. We didn't want him to do it, but he insisted and told us he didn't want to go without us and he said it would keep us all together. He didn't seem to think the big show would work out, and that it would not last very long. He told us to go along with it for a while, and it would bust up, and we could take up from where we left off, after playing the Princess. I talked to Mr. Parham about it, and he said it was a dirty deal, but he couldn't do anything about it, as Mr. Sudekum wanted the big show after they had offered it to him. So we were sunk, after all the effort we had put forth, and we all felt as low as we ever did any time as long as we were in the show business.

Well, anyway that is the way the ball bounced in those days for us. If we could have played that group of theaters, just Uncle Dave, Rabon, and I, with the two extras like Mr. Parham suggested, we could have gotten a very good start, financially, besides building up our reputation as drawing cards for other theater chains through the country. Yes, it was a major defeat for us, and a predatory coup for the bosses at the station. As long as we stayed at the station, we always had that kind of trouble. Someone else who "stood in" with the bosses wanted to take us for a ride. I guess it was just sheer love for the Grand Ole Opry and our listeners that kept us from leaving sooner than we did. In fact, I know it was.

I will write no more about the show they concocted, but it was a mess from start to finish. Uncle Dave was not allowed to play any song with us and we weren't allowed to play with him, although sometimes he would forget, and ask us to help him on some number we did so well together. There was constant bickering and a dictatorial atmosphere throughout the ill-fated tour.

CHAPTER FIFTEEN

WE MEET THE JIMMIE RODGERS KINFOLKS IN MERIDIAN

THE TRIP TO NEW ORLEANS— MAKING RECORDS, A HARD TASK

We were always thrilled to get a letter from the company telling us to report to some city or town to make records, and yet it is the hardest one thing I think I ever did do. I often tried to analyze the cause when I was making so many records but I never could come up with anything that would seem to justify my feelings. I don't think Rabon ever had the dread that I did over the sessions. If he did, he could keep it mighty well concealed because he was always cool as a cucumber when we were in the studio.

I remember one session we had in Charlotte, North Carolina.* It was a tragic one, as far as I was concerned. We had just come in from a long, weary trip from that same state. We knew well in advance when the date was, and I tried to get the station not to book us on that week but they went on and booked us anyway, because they said some of the ones playing with us had to make a living. They got real mean about it and we agreed to take the dates, knowing we should have stayed

*The date of this session was Thursday, Feb. 17, 1938. (For further details, see discography.)—Ed.

WE MEET THE JIMMIE RODGERS KINFOLKS

in Nashville and practiced for the records we had to make. So we made the trip and played the shows and along toward the end of the week, the weather turned bad and it snowed and rained some and sleeted and just about everything you can think of. I guess it would have come a tornado if it had not been in the winter time. And I don't think we made much money on the trip. Anyway, one of the guys who was for making the trip the strongest promised me he would drive all the way there and back if we would agree to go. So that was one deciding factor in our making the trip in the first place. I knew if I didn't have to go through the strain of driving much, I would retain some of my physical fitness and still be able to go through the session in Charlotte.

When we headed back for Nashville on Friday night after the last show, the weather was still very bad and road warnings were out to keep from traveling unless it was absolutely necessary. There was ice and snow in patches and you had to keep a sharp lookout. In addition, when we got into the mountains west of Asheville, there were signs telling of falling rocks and landslides and when you traveled over that, you can imagine the danger we were in. Those mountains are pretty high, between three and four thousand feet, and if a rock had hit us it would have been certain disaster.

And the guy who had wanted to make the trip so badly, and who had agreed to do all the driving, went to sleep when we got in the car. He said he would sleep about fifty miles to get a fresh start and then he would relieve me and bring us on into Nashville, and I knew he had made a logical suggestion. So I took the wheel and drove about one hundred miles before I stopped to wake him up. But we could not get him to wake up. We tried everything (there were three of us besides him on the trip), but he just wouldn't budge. I knew we had to get in, so I just kept driving. About every fifty or seventy-five miles the others would insist that I would stop and try to wake him up again, but we never did get that guy awake till long after daylight and we were about fifty or seventy-five miles east of Knoxville. I had driven the whole way back except about a hundred and fifty miles. When he finally did take the wheel, I crumbled up to sleep in the front seat of the car, and my neck got twisted and I woke up in pain when we got to Nashville. I didn't worry about it much, till I tried to sing. Then I became panic stricken. I could not sing high at all, and we had to tune the guitars way down low to sing on the Grand Ole Opry that night. I kept wondering what was going to happen on the record session in Charlotte. We had to catch the train immediately after we got through with our last program and I thought the rest on the train ride would give me some relief from my condition. I braced myself for the best and didn't get down in the dumps. But the train ride didn't help me a bit. When we got to Charlotte I still could not sing high like I always did. I was plenty worried.

I went to a doctor and he ordered me not to speak or talk to anyone till I got better. We had to make records that afternoon. When I told that doctor that, his eyes got big as door knobs. He said if I went on through that recording session, it might very well do permanent injury to my vocal cords. He was so upset he thought of forcing me into a hospital to keep me from making records. I had never seen that doctor before, but he was true to his profession. When you have to make a living a certain way, it alters things and that is what I told him. He could not agree with me, but he saw my point and wished me well and gave me his telephone number. He told me to call him if I needed him. I thanked him and left for my hotel.

We had some of our best songs to record on that session, we thought, and there I was with a throat condition. I was not worried about myself or about the records.

When we got to the studio, which was in a hotel room with heavy drapes all around it, I told Mr. Oberstein about my throat. He didn't seem upset at all. He just old us to get our instruments out and we would see what I sounded like. Of course, we had the guitars tuned real low to help me out. So we went into one of the new songs we had to record. He came back and told us I sounded fine and we would get on with the session. I tried to get him to put it off, but he couldn't be moved and we made a whole session of records there in Charlotte when I couldn't even holler. Some muscle would stop my vocal cords when it got up that high. And you know one thing? I still can't sing as high now as I could before that happened to me. I felt crippled all the way through those records, like a puppy when it has a splint on its leg and tries to walk like other dogs. But you never really know what you can do until you go through a strain like that. I remember one of the songs we did on that record date was one of my most popular called "Southern Moon."

The foregoing reminds me of the first time Arthur Smith, the Dixie Line fiddle player, made his first real session of records. Arthur helped to start the Grand Ole Opry back in ·1925.*

It was 1934 and we had a record session coming up down in New Orleans.** I wrote the company and got Arthur Smith a try-out. I knew he would make good. He paid his own way down there and his expenses, as was agreed when we first inquired. He had a free pass on the railroad trains becaus he worked for the NC&St.L railway as a lineman. But when he got down to New Orleans, and Mr. Oberstein heard him play, the RCA Company paid all his expenses both ways. He made eight breakdowns, all very well played. Mr. Oberstein liked his playing very much but he didn't do any singing and his records didn't sell well enough to bring him back again.

*There is no evidence to show that Smith was playing on the Opry as early as 1925, but he and his cousin Homer Smith were appearing as a fiddle-guitar duo as early as 1927.—Ed.

**The recording session and trip south took place in late January 1935, though quite possibly Alton's correspondence with Oberstein began in late 1934.—Ed.

WE MEET THE JIMMIE RODGERS KINFOLKS

When I told Arthur what Mr. Oberstein had written me, he nearly broke down and cried. I told him I would try to think of something that would make the company and Mr. Oberstein change their mind and give him another chance. He brightened up and said he would surely appreciate anything I could do to help him. He was a sentimental person, like most musicians, including myself, and he hated to be turned away when he had done his best.

So I got to thinking about him and I came up with an idea. You know, that's a strange thing I have found to be about 100 percent true. If you sincerely try to think your way out of a difficult situation, nine times out of ten you will better yourself and nearly that same odds applies that you will help yourself or someone else tremendously.

So when I saw Arthur and told him about the idea I had, he was tickled to death about it, and it saved the day for him in the recording business. I had heard Arthur and Sam and Kirk McGee on the Opry, years before Rabon and me went up there, and I knew they would sing and play some songs sometimes on their program. That is what gave me the idea. I would write Mr. Oberstein and see if he would let Arthur come in if he would bring some songs to sing.

I wrote to find out about it, and Mr. Oberstein liked the idea fine. He said he didn't want to let Arthur go in the first place, but the sales didn't justify bringing him in again without something different. Mr. Oberstein had a boss, too, and he had to take orders same as we did. So I gave the good news to Arthur when I saw him and we agreed to get together on some songs suitable for records. He had some songs about finished and I helped him finish them and I wrote some for him and we wrote some together, and Rabon helped out on the songs too, and together we got a good batch of material for the session.

In this first session, with us all singing, there were several good sellers and one hit record: "There's More Pretty Girls Than One."* Arthur began to make some money on his records and we did, too, for helping in the writing. But Arthur and me wrote most of them; Rabon being single, he done a lot of running around and didn't have the time to put on the songs like Arthur and myself. While we were working like this together, we wrote a big one that is better known than any of the others. The name of it is "Beautiful Brown Eyes."

I also was influential in obtaining Uncle Dave Macon a contract on the RCA label. As I have written before, he worked with Rabon and me and he did a lot for us, and when I could return the favor for him, I was only too glad to try.

Now Uncle Dave had made records before I ever thought about being in the same business, but he had had his day, or so thought most of the major companies. He would not beg them to put him on records but down in his heart he always yearned to make records again. In the old days he had made some real good money with his songs and his own records. He was still good too, I thought.

So I wrote Mr. Eli Oberstein about him and he said right away to bring him in with us for a session. Rabon and me also sang with Uncle Dave and we had a neat little trio and we knew all the songs he intended to make, because we had done them so much together on personals. Uncle Dave was easy to work with, if you just halfway tried to get together with him. Some musicians thought he was lots of trouble, but they just didn't understand the old gentleman.

Anyway, when we made the trip to New Orleans, Uncle Dave went along, too, and it was the first records he had made in many years.* So we carried two new acts into New Orleans with us that time. Uncle Dave rode with us in the car but Arthur

---

*This second session of the Delmores with Arthur Smith, the session that included the vocal numbers, was on February 17, 1936, in Charlotte, N.C. (See discography for complete details.) Here four of the eight numbers recorded were vocals, with Smith and the Delmores singing (even though the records were released as "Arthur Smith Trio"). "There's More Pretty Girls Than One" was indeed cut at the second session, but "Beautiful Brown Eyes" was not recorded until Smith's fourth Bluebird session in August 1937.—Ed.

rode the train. We had planned it all out and he was to meet us when we got there. We stayed at the Monteleone Hotel.

When we left, we took off from our dad's home in Athens and the weather was rough. It had been coming winter for some time, and it looked like it really arrived when we left for New Orleans. We moved on down through Birmingham and headed for Tuscaloosa. We intended to spend the night somewhere in Mississippi, but we didn't know how far, because we were not on a personal appearance trip and we didn't have to kill ourselves in a rush to get there. The recording sessions were always a rest from the rush and bustle of trips on the road with a strict time schedule to make.

So we just breezed along the road thinking of our records and talking about various things that just happened to cross our minds. I said something about spending the night in Meridian, Mississippi, and Rabon and Uncle Dave agreed that it would be a good place to stay, as it is not too far from New Orleans. We three could always agree on places to stay almost instantly. But others we worked with were not that easy to get along with.

There was always some guy who wanted to go on to a place where he had a cousin or for some other ridiculous reason. But I never did know Uncle Dave to insist on making an extra trip or travel extra miles for his own benefit. He was a real trooper.

When we got to Meridian, it was close to eight o'clock at night and we checked in at a hotel and didn't have anything particularly to do. We had already had supper and we didn't usually go to bed that early, so we had some time on our hands we

---

*In fact, Uncle Dave had recorded only six months prior to the New Orleans trip and the Bluebird session. In August 1934, he and the McGee Brothers recorded a number of sides for the Gennett company in Richmond, Indiana. These records did not sell especially well, however, and Uncle Dave might not have considered it a serious session. Victor's Bluebird label was a major label, and the New Orleans session did mark the beginning of a series of Bluebird recordings for Uncle Dave. They were among his last commercial recordings, but some of the most technically satisfying. If Uncle Dave was grateful to the Delmores for helping set up the association, Macon fans should be even more so.—Ed.

didn't know what to do with. Then, all at once I happened to think of something.

Meridian was the home of Jimmie Rodgers, America's Great Blue Yodeler, so famous on record. We had heard him sing so much, and had heard so many tales about him. So it was in my bones to find out something about him.* I didn't say anything to Rabon or Uncle Dave but told them I was going down to get a newspaper. When I got down in the lobby I asked were the nearest taxi stand was. The clerk said it was not far, about a couple of blocks. So I walked the distance in no time at all and found several cabbies waiting around for a call. I began to talk to one of them and finally got around to asking about Jimmie Rodgers. The cabbie was about middle aged.

"Jimmie Rodgers?" he asked, "the fellow who done all the singing? I reckon I did know him. He used to be one of my best old buddies, and still was till the day he died. Jimmie Rodgers," he mused out loud, "yes, I sure do miss him a lot. Why?" he asked, "Do you want to find out something about him?"

I told him what my interest was, and he was tickled pink. I told him my name and he had heard Rabon and me on the air. He also had heard Uncle Dave plenty of times. He was a lot of help.

I asked him did Jimmie have any folks who lived around close? He told me Jimmie had a brother who was a plain-clothes detective and he knew just where he lived. It was getting kind of late, about nine o'clock by now, and I asked him if he reckoned it was too late to go out and see him.

"Naw," he said, "Tal will be glad to see anybody who knows and thinks a lot of Jimmie. Besides he will be glad to see all you fellows, too."

So I hired him to take us out to see Tal and his wife; I wanted to find out more about my idol, Jimmie Rodgers. I didn't know whether Uncle Dave and Rabon would want

---

*Jimmie Rodgers, widely acclaimed as the first country singing star, had died in May 1933, about a year and a half before the Delmores' 1935 trip to New Orleans. In the months following his death, many songs and tributes to him became popular and succeeded in keeping his name well before the American public.—Ed.

to go out there or not, but if they didn't I had made up my mind to go by myself.

The taxi driver took me back to the hotel and waited while I went up to see if they wanted to go. I felt like Rabon wanted to go, but I didn't know for sure about Uncle Dave. Sometimes he went to bed early and this might be one of those nights. When I got to our rooms I told them of my plans and they hemmed and hawed a minute. Then I told them I was going out anyway, so they both decided to go along. And we took our guitars and Uncle Dave took his banjo, one of them. He had three he carried everywhere he went to play. I sure was glad they decided to go because I really would have felt a little cramped if they hadn't.

On the way out, the cabbie kept talking about Jimmie and the things he used to do while hanging around the taxi stand. "You know, fellows, Jimmie was broke a lot of the times, and he was not lonesome, for most of us were, too. But he was not ever in good health and he couldn't work regular at anything much, like the rest of us could. He always smoked cigarettes, but a lot of times he didn't have the money to buy a pack, so he would wait around, to get the butts from us, when we got through with one. You know that was hard times, when Jimmie was drifting around here after he had a bout with that old TB." That old cabbie boy really liked Jimmie. And he was real proud of the fact that he had known him when.

It was really too late to go to someone's house when we got out to the home of Tal Rodgers and his wife. But they both knew the old cabbie who brought us out, and that proved he was not talking through his hat about knowing Jimmie and his folks.

If you had ever seen Jimmie Rodgers's picture, you would have known that Tal was his brother by just looking at him. They both looked almost exactly alike. The cabbie introduced us to Tal, and told him all about how we wanted to see some of Jimmie's folks, if possible.

"Well, now, this is just fine. We have heard you all on the air for a long time and now, at last, we get to see you." Tal and his wife were both just beaming and I have never met two friendlier people in my life than those two people who knew the great yodeler so well.

I apologized for coming to see them so late at night but I told him the circumstances—that it was possibly the only chance we would have to see them, since we had show dates, and had to get back soon after our record session.

"Well, you all just forget about coming in a little late. We used to stay up late lots of times when Jimmie was around, just to hear him sing his new songs. He was always singing some kind of new song, blues, funny, rounder songs or sad ones. He loved to compose and he never forgot the tune or the words either. So you and Rabon and Uncle Dave are always welcome to our home, anytime you come through." His wife went into the kitchen and started fixing something for a snack, with coffee because she must have known we were going to stay a good while.

I never will forget how they treated us. They were both the kind of people who seemed to think they could never do enough to please their company. We talked a lot, nearly all about Jimmie, and what he was like and they threw in a lot of things that we never thought to ask about.

"You know what Jimmie's favorite food was?" Mrs. Tal said. "It was just plain old country fried steak and potatoes. I have cooked that for him many times when he was feeling low, and it always gave him a big lift. He also liked sweet milk and corn bread." She sighed and seemed sad at the thought of what he liked to eat.

When a person is gone it does make you feel like that. I know it does me, when I think of what Rabon liked to eat. It just seems to make you miss them so much more.

Tal asked us would we play some for him and we told him we would surely like to. But we didn't feel like playing where there had been a genius like his brother.

"Oh, gosh, I know you can't play just like Jimmie did, or sing like him either, but neither could he play and sing like any of you. It's just different ways of playing. Now you take Uncle Dave. I have never heard anyone who could sing and play like he does. He has that comedy in his voice on some of his songs, and in others he sings sadly just like Jimmie did and you two boys are just the same way. I'm a policeman, but I have picked up some of that myself. So don't stand back on account of Jimmie. He would not want you to. If he was just here he would be the happiest guy you ever saw. He always liked to be with people, especially other musicians."

That made us all feel much better and we got the guitars and banjos out and started in to play. We played with Uncle Dave first, like we did on our shows, and they liked it fine. Then, Uncle Dave played some by himself and he really went over big with them. After he played several songs, he stopped and we played several songs. There was one song I had written for Jimmie. Mr. Peer* accepted it for his next session of records but there was no next session. Jimmie passed away before that session came up. Rabon and I both knew this, but we had never told anyone about it for we thought they might think we were brag ging. So we started in to sing this particular song. We got about halfway through it, and Tal and his wife both left the room. We didn't think it would upset them so much, or we would not have done it. We had already made a record of it on RCA Bluebird and had sung it on the Opry many times, so I didn't think it would make these fine people so sad. We went through the verse we were singing and stopped. We didn't know just what to do. But they came back into the room almost immediately. Both of them had been crying. But you know what? They wanted us to sing that song again. They didn't cry this time but I nearly did myself, and I barely made it through. Rabon was not so mirthful, and Uncle Dave looked sad. The song was

*Ralph Peer was the Victor "talent scout" who discovered Rodgers on a recording field trip to Bristol, Tennessee, in 1927. Peer helped build Rodgers's reputation and served as his manager for a time, selecting the songs he was to record and helping to merchandise the music. He later founded the Peer-Southern music publishing complex.—Ed.

WE MEET THE JIMMIE RODGERS KINFOLKS

"Blue Railroad Train."

That is how people felt about Jimmie Rodgers, the Great Blue Yodeler! I can say one thing, and tell you how I feel about Jimmie Rodgers. He was simply the greatest. There has never been one man in the whole history of entertainment that packed the wallop he did by himself. There have been good singers, good players and performers that have made great hits with the public and made millions of dollars. But there has never been one man with a single instrument that could sing and play like he did. I say there never has been, and I don't believe there ever will be another just like Jimmie Rodgers. And I'm not meaning just style, either.

We talked and talked. Tal told us about the great Will Rogers, and how he would come to see Jimmie, when he had a chance. There was a picture on the wall of both of them together. Tal said that Will made a vast research into the Rodgers family history, just to find out if Jimmie and he were any kin. It took him quite a long time, but he came up with some important information and proof. Tal said Will was greatly disappointed, and so was Jimmie, because Will's efforts proved they were just about fifth cousins. He said they both got over it quickly, though, and began laughing about the whole thing and how ridiculous it was. But Tal said they were so much alike in their ways that he knew, or thought, they would turn out to be more related than that. They spelled their names Rodgers and Rogers, but Tal said some of his people had changed the name and added the "d" just to make it different. He didn't know who. He also told us that Will wanted Jimmie to make a movie with him, but when they took the screen tests, and they came back for them to see, they decided that Jimmie's slender and bony look showed up in a bad way for him, and they talked it over and Jimmie and Will both thought it would hurt Jimmie's popularity to make a movie at the time. They decided to wait till he gained a few pounds to make him look better. But he never did gain the weight and never did make the movie.*

Tal told us how Jimmie would rehearse before a record date. He said he would play a little while and decide it was too much trouble to practice, and just quit and walk downtown to be with some of his cronies.

"Why there was one time when he had a session down in New Orleans, like you fellows have now. He had a lot of original songs, ready to put on record and he told us he would try them out with us listening, to see what we thought of them. He got out his songs and his guitar and began to play. But he never did get through a single song. He would start one and then he would give up in disgust.

"This time the company wanted him to make ten sides, his records were going so good. He had the songs, all right, but he just couldn't play them. Me and my wife were worried so much we could hardly sleep that night. Jimmie had to leave the next day on the train and I decided to go with him. I was so worried about his performance. I told him I was going with him and he was really tickled to have me go along. He always traveled in style, and he had a compartment reserved on the train. I was glad he did, because I thought he could do some practicing on the way down."

He paused for a moment before he finished. None of us said a word. We wanted to know how Jimmie made out on his session.

"When we got on the train, there were some people he knew, and all the way down to New Orleans we didn't use that compartment much at all. Jimmie wanted to talk to those people. He always wanted to talk to someone when he was feeling good, and he musta been that day because he really had a time on that

---

*Rodgers did make one short film titled *The Singing Brakeman* in Camden in 1929. Rodgers toured with Will Rogers in January 1931 when they did a series of benefit appearances to aid drought victims in Arkansas.—Ed.

train. I kept wondering how he would ever get those records cut when he didn't know the songs. When we got to town we went straight to the hotel, and still he didn't practice any. I kept after him but he would just grin at me and tell me to take it easy.

"We got up the next morning and went to the studio. All those recording people were waiting for him, and they had everything set up and ready to go. I don't know how I did feel, but there was a funny feeling in the pit of my stomach. Jimmie didn't have a worry in the world. He said hello to all the record people and introduced me around, and then he got out his old guitar and began to strum it softly. They got him a music stand and he put some on it, and told them he was ready. Now, I know you will find this hard to believe, but Jimmie stood there and recorded song after song, with just a little break in between, and he didn't make one single mistake. He did that session in record time, the fastest he had ever done before, the director told me."

"What were some of the songs he did on that session?" I asked Tal.

"One of them was 'My Little Old Home Down in New Orleans' and some of the blue yodels, I just can't remember all of them, I was so surprised. But I do know one thing. We had a time that night at the hotel. There were all kinds of people up there to see Jimmie, but more hobos than anything else. Now, I don't know how they knew he was down there, but they found out some way, and Jimmie sure treated them to the best in everything to eat and drink. But he was making plenty of money and those people had helped him in his leaner days, and that was his way of appreciating them. I never said another word about him not practicing anymore, for he had something that I simply didn't understand then . . . and I don't to this day."*

When we left Tal's house, it was nearly midnight and we had to get up pretty early and head on down to New Orleans. But I'll never forget that night at Tal and

WE MEET THE JIMMIE RODGERS KINFOLKS

Mrs. Rodgers's home. It seemed like I had visited some of my long lost relatives. And I think Rabon and Uncle Dave felt the same way because they had really enjoyed that visit.

The trip down to New Orleans was really interesting. Down through southern Mississippi and on into Louisiana, the storied land of Jimmie Rodgers. He had sung about this land throughout the world by way of his records. It seemed like everywhere we looked there would be some reminder of him and his songs.

The bridge across Lake Pontchartrain was a sight to see, for all of us. It was the longest bridge we had ever crossed. It seemed like you were on a ship, it was so long. I thought of Huey Long when we crossed that bridge. I had heard Walter Winchell talk about him so much that I thought surely he must be some kind of a devil. And the newspapers and magazines did their part to add to the bad reputation they were building up for Huey Long. I decided to ask a few people down there in his own neck of the woods what they thought about him. I had been given the one part, or side, of his character and I wanted to get the impression of the people who knew him, and voted for him. I asked questions at filling stations, cafes, grocery stores, lunch counters, service stations, garages and hotels. That was about all the time I had. And you know what? I didn't get one single bad remark about the "Kingfish." I studied these people's faces and watched for something other than sincerity, but they were all frank, honest folks who just believed in their leader with heart, mind, and soul. I had been led to believe that they were a bunch of enslaved people, frightened to throw off a yoke of tyranny,

*Victor files indicate that Rodgers recorded only once in New Orleans, on November 13, 1929. Brian Rust's *Victor Master Book Vol. 2* shows only one side, "Hobo Bill's Last Ride," recorded at that time. The tune Tal remembered, "My Little Old Home Down in New Orleans," was recorded in Camden, New Jersey, June 12, 1928, one of nine titles cut that day. Since the Camden version of the song had been released before Rodgers's New Orleans session, there would have been no reason for him to re-record it. Perhaps Tal's memory slipped, or perhaps Alton misunderstood what Tal had said.—Ed.

but it was exactly opposite from that. Most of the people who didn't like Huey Long were in Washington and other far-off places who didn't know what they were talking or writing about. Down there in the bayou country they will still fight you if you say too much the wrong way about him. But you have to make a trip down there to see what he did for his flock. It isn't any wonder that they liked him so much.

When we got to New Orleans we checked in at the hotel and went about things as usual, eating and looking around generally. It is a big old city, and you can't see much when you're just gonna be there about two days, so we didn't plan on any sight-seeing tours while we were there. We contacted Mr. Oberstein and found that he was there all right and ready to make records the next day.

Rabon and me decided we would do some brushing up on our songs. We were already familiar with them, but the more you practice, the better you get, and sometimes just a dull-sounding song will present something you didn't know it had, till you do a lot of work on it. And we had several songs we thought were on the dull side. We didn't want to rehearse in our room because we might disturb someone who was sleeping, so I called the clerk and he gave us permission to use the big ball room for a while. It was really something sumptuous. We got in some good practice, and then went up to our room and went to bed.

When we woke up the next morning, it was snowing in New Orleans. It was the first snow they had had in years. It didn't accumulate very much, but the weather was freezing and had a keen penetration about it that you don't feel in many other places. They say it is on account of New Orleans being so close to the river and ocean, and I guess that's right. We went on over to the recording place when we had finished breakfast, and then we were in for a shock. The RCA company had rented an old, abandoned building that didn't have any heat in it, and it was just about as cold in that building as it was on the outside. Mr. Oberstein had got hold of a little old coal oil heater and it would not burn, just smoked a lot, and that was the only heat we had, if you can call that heat. You see, the company didn't even dream of that kind of weather in usually balmy New Orleans. But that didn't help us any at all, and we had to make records in that set-up.

When we got started recording, we didn't mind the lack of heat but the thing we did mind was the alley directly running by the window. We were on about the second floor of the building. Big trucks used that alley and I don't know how many records we had to make over, on account of that alley. We would have one just about completed, and then there would come a truck and ruin it. That got on our nerves so bad that we forgot about the heat. But we made it all right.

In those days we recorded on wax. And when you made a few mistakes on that wax, you couldn't use it any more. It was too thin or something. One of the technicians told me how it was, but I didn't ever understand it like he told me. If they used it nowadays, some of the artists never would get on record because it would take too much wax. And the recording director watched that wax like it was gold. If you missed one, two, or three times, he would come in with a blank look on his face and tell you to rehearse some more before another take. And that would only make everybody nervous.

Rabon and me recorded first. We made ten sides and it didn't take too long, but our fingers would get numb and we would have to stop and rub them to get the feeling back. Just like I said, all that old oil stove would do was smoke. If it had worked like it ought to, it could have been a lot of help.

After we got through, Arthur Smith was next on Mr. Oberstein's list.* We played with him on his records. He got through in a hurry. He didn't do any singing and I don't think he made but one or two little errors. And the trucks didn't seem to hurt his records. He played a lot louder than we did, and with our two guitars we could compete with the trucks pretty good. I don't think he had to make a single one over on account of the trucks. He made eight breakdowns and he had composed all of them. They are still being played by fiddle players all over the country. He has composed some very good ones indeed.**

After Arthur got through, it was time for Uncle Dave, and we had a time with him. He made a lot of jokes about the little old heater. There was a Negro quartet there to try out for singing spirituals, and they stayed in the back of the big room where we recorded. Uncle Dave had been telling them jokes outside the studio, and they really thought a lot of him and they would laugh even if he just looked at them. So that was the situation when it came his time to make records. He was all primed and ready to go. He had his songs all rehearsed with us, and we knew we shouldn't have any trouble at all when we started the session.† But it was not quite that easy.

We started the first record all right till we got about halfway through it, and then it happened. Uncle Dave had been looking back at the Negro quartet when he was playing and that didn't hurt anything, but when he was singing, he never looked back at them till we got about halfway through. Then, right in the middle of a verse, he turned around and looked at them and the buzzer sounded. We couldn't see the technicians and Mr. Oberstein because there was a wall between us, and they were in another room, but if something went wrong, they would buzz us and the record

---

*Actually, the original Victor session sheets show that the Delmores recorded sixteen sides instead of ten. They worked from 9:00 A.M. to 3:00 P.M. (on January 22, 1935), Smith recorded his eight sides from 4:00 to 6:00 P.M., and Uncle Dave recorded his six sides that night. Even later the "Negro quartet," the Southern University Quartet, did six more sides.—Ed.

**While all eight of Smith's titles from this session were instrumentals, they were not all breakdowns, nor were they all original. The selections included traditional standards like "Mocking Bird" and "Blackberry Blossom," as well as a couple of waltzes and a blues. (See discography.)—Ed.

†The Delmores recorded four songs with Uncle Dave at this session: "Over the Mountain," "When the Harvest Days Are Over," "One More River to Cross," and "Just One Way to the Pearly Gates." Macon also recorded two by himself. All the original labels, however, credited only Macon.—Ed.

was no good. When the buzzer sounded we all quit playing, and in a moment Mr. Oberstein came walking in real slow-like. He was not looking at anybody, but I could tell he was not pleased. He had seen Uncle Dave having fun with the quartet and he knew exactly what had happened.

"Now, Uncle Dave, you are not here to sing for those boys back there, so come on now and let's get something going." He was right, but he didn't know Uncle Dave. The record would have been just as good if he had kept on the mike. That's the way he had always made records, from the beginning.

"Now, Cap," Uncle Dave said, "I can sing anyway I want to, and still be heard. I've got a lot of git up and go." He meant volume. "And I've got a smokehouse full of country hams and all kinds of meat to eat up there in Readyyille. I've got plenty of wood hauled up, and I don't have to be bossed around by some New York sharpshooter just to make a few records, 'cause I've done done my part of the record making anyway."

Mr. Oberstein didn't know what half he said meant, but Rabon and I did. Uncle Dave was not mad but he felt like he should save a little face. Mr. Oberstein was not mad either, but he had a job to do. And he wanted to do it like he wanted it done. I did a little talking and so did Rabon and also Arthur, and we got them together and went on with the record making. After that, everything ran smoothly. Uncle Dave would still look back at the Negro quartet and laugh, but he always waited until he was just playing, to do it again. He knew what Mr. Oberstein meant, when he said "sing on the mike," and he did just that, after he was told. But he didn't lose face.

Entertainers are peculiar people. They all have their whims and they all have their fancies. Uncle Dave recorded for RCA for several years after that first little "run in" and there was never any more misunderstandings.

Since it was cold weather, Uncle Dave decided to ride back on the train with Arthur, and Rabon and I rode back in the car, by ourselves. When we got back to

WE MEET THE JIMMIE RODGERS KINFOLKS

Meridian, there was snow on the ground. We stopped by to see Tal Rodgers again, and he had been down with pneumonia, but he was better. I knew he was a police man, a plain-clothes detective, but I told him I had brought him something from New Orleans. I told him he better not arrest me and he said he wouldn't. He knew I was joking. So I went out to the car and brought him a fifth of Four Roses and handed it to him. He said he could use a little of that. Then he got a faraway look in his eyes. I wondered why. He said: "That's the kind Jimmie used to drink."

CHAPTER SIXTEEN

BEHIND THE SCENES—NO. 2*

We played the dates we had been committed to play and then we went on to Nashville to resume our regular schedule of personals and radio programs.

Nashville is a fine old town. It has its extremes in temperature, like real cold winters, and real hot summers. But it still seems like home to me. I sometimes wish I could relive those days up there and feel the same as I did then, but you know how it is when you get too old to do those kind of things. It's amazing to me how some of the old timers seem to go on and on, and keep broadcasting every Saturday night on the Grand Ole Opry. Sam & Kirk McGee are fine examples of this, and so is Herman Crook and his band. They were there when we went there, and they are still there. You can tune them in every Saturday night. You know what I think? If the Grand Ole Opry should stop for any reason at all, they would stop, and I don't believe they would live very long. The Grand Ole Opry gets in your blood. You may think you won't miss it, but wait till you leave it. And then you will find out how much you miss it from a purely personal standpoint. But you have to stay there for several years before it gets in your blood.

That brings me up to one of the famous entertainers who came to the Opry and didn't stay very long. His name is well-known throughout the musical world, but you

---

*This chapter was left untitled in Alton Delmore's manuscript. —Ed.

may be one of those who never heard of him. Maybe you were too young to remember him when he was in his heyday. The man is Clayton McMichen.* He was one of the very first real recognized old-time fiddle players who recorded. His records sold tremendously when he was in the going. I have written about him before in an earlier chapter. He discovered a lot of hidden talent. One of his discoveries was Merle Travis, the famous composer, guitarist, and singer. When Clayton came to town, the boys he brought with him were just youngsters. They all longed for company and companionship and they usually wound up out at our house. We were friendly to them. They didn't make much money in those days, and young boys have to have somewhere to go. They would usually come over every day they didn't work and would eat and play and drink beer with Rabon and me, if we had the money to buy it.

I remember Carl Cotner was one of them, and Merle, and a boy called Blackie. I don't think Blackie stayed in the business very long after his job with Clayton, but Merle Travis is a great name known all around the world and Carl Cotner wound up with Gene Autry, as Gene's musical arranger. Rabon and me really enjoyed those boys coming out and we hated to learn they were going to leave. Clayton never did hit it off with the bosses on the station and he was in the same position we were in all the time we were there. But he was a real "pro" and they couldn't push him around like they did us. He just wouldn't stand for it. Clayton McMichen was a high-tempered person when anybody tried to put something over on him and he didn't mind fighting for what he thought was right. If you fooled around with him he would knock the hell out of you with his bare hands. They learned that at the station and they didn't fool with him, but they still would not give him any breaks and they didn't give him a fair deal, either. So he left and found him another landing place.

*McMichen's Georgia Wildcats spent only one year on the Opry, 1936. The band subsequently moved on to WLW in Cincinnati.—Ed.

BEHIND THE SCENES—NO. 2

That's the way it is in the show business. There may be some guy you meet who is relatively unimportant when you meet him, but someday he may be the star, the big deal on radio and records. So I can't see passing up anyone with a mere shrug and thinking—he's just a little shot and giving him the high hat. I have known this to happen many times in my career. In fact, I have had it happen to me. And it is something you will never forget. You are inclined to forget the kind words and compliments, but you never forget those digs and you never forget who gave them to you, either.

We just couldn't seem to get along at WSM in those days. Everybody was trying to tell us what to do. And we were always nervous and tired from the long, hard road trips trying to make a living. Judge George D. Hay stopped Uncle Dave and Rabon and I from playing together altogether. He was the Artist Service manager and what he said had to go pertaining to personal appearances. So, as much as we liked Uncle Dave, we were not allowed to play together. Judge Hay would tell us he didn't want to put all his eggs in one basket when we would say anything to him. We kept drawing crowds real well and did until the day we left the station. But they would put someone with us just to fill in. And we had to make a show around them. And just about the time we got them where they would fit in pretty good they would change them to some other act. They did that way with Arthur Smith. We used Arthur on several appearances and got a real good little show started, and then they took him and put him with another act and wouldn't let us use him anymore.

We always had the top billing, Rabon and I, and the other names would be on the ads, too, but they were more or less insignificant. The people would think everybody in the show were the Delmore Brothers. So some of those people would get blind drunk and we got the credit for it. And some of them just plain didn't care what the hell they did. They seemed to think they were on a picnic or vacation, and would not take their work seriously. Sometimes I would say to them: "Now I don't mind you taking a little nip, or a bottle of beer or two, but please, fellow, we have a show to put on so slow down a little so you can make the show, and then you can get drunk and do anything else you want to, but now please slow down, please." The person would give me a baleful look and say something like this: "By god, I was playing on the Grand Ole Opry when you and your brother were just plain cotton pickers. I ain't gonna let no goddamn cotton picker tell me what to do."

Now those fellows didn't have anything at all against Rabon and me, but that was old John Barley Corn talking. But you know, sometimes when a person is drunk or pretty loaded, they reveal their inner personality as at no other time. When they would talk to me like that, I would get blue as hell. I was not trying to boss them but just trying to protect our reputation. We needed it, because Rabon and I were no angels, ourselves. Like Hank Williams used to tell me: He said if they would only tell the truth it would be bad enough, but if they added a little venom to it, it would be almost horrible.

Thelma and I decided to move away from Grove Avenue, and we started looking around for a better place to stay. There were a few chinches [bed bugs] at the Grove Avenue house and we didn't like that a bit, so that is the reason for our moving. We found a fine house on Allison Place, still in south Nashville. We lived in south Nashville all the time we were playing on the Opry. The house on Allison was away ahead of the Grove Avenue place. It was something to be proud of. We were not ashamed to have company at that house, because it rated like the houses the staff musicians lived in. Of course the rent was a little higher. This time we paid thirty-seven fifty a month. But now, in 1963, that house would cost at least one hundred a month. It was the best house we had ever lived in. There were two bedrooms downstairs and one or two upstairs. That was where Rabon lived. Over on Grove he had slept in a little room that was so small about all you could do was lay down on the bed.

Rabon and I played several show dates for Larry Sunbrock while we lived on Grove and also Allison Place. He would book us in a place and then advertise us in five or six more before he would book us again. I didn't know he did that way till he booked us in Memphis, or rather advertised us in Memphis. We had a lot of loyal listeners down that way, and when we didn't appear, they raised plenty of hell. We got at least two or three hundred letters and some of them sent telegrams to the station. It was a bad mess and we couldn't help it. Some of the letters of protest accused us of being drunk and just not showing up, and other things just as bad or worse. What caused all this was the way Sunbrock made the announcement about our not being there. Some of our friends that played on the show said he just walked out and told the audience we hadn't shown up, and he didn't understand what was the matter with us. He told them he had not heard from us and maybe we would show up pretty soon. So you can see he just left the door wide open to speculation on the part of the audience.

This man Sunbrock would advertise anybody he could think of just to draw a good crowd. He was a good promoter and he always had good crowds and he always had a very good show so the people would forget the ones he advertised and didn't have booked. He always carried a good show with him and put on fiddle players, like Curly Fox, Clayton McMichen, Clark Kessinger, Red Herron, and of course he always had Natchee the Apache Indian fiddler with him, and any of these other fiddlers that he hired had to play against Natchee. Arthur Smith was one of the best old-time fiddlers and he would hire Arthur when he could get him. But he would do them just like he did us. He would hire them and book them for maybe one job, and then he'd advertise them on five or six others without contacting them. He also did the same thing with Gene Autry, Roy Rogers, and many other stars so popular in those days. But Gene and Roy caught on to his tricks and they told him they would sue him if he didn't make some plausible excuse for their absence when he had them advertised. You know old Larry came up with a good one. He would go out after the show was rolling good, and read a telegram from whichever one he had booked. He would have a real telegram blank in his hands but he would read the message he had written on it himself. It would tell how Gene, or Roy, or some other artist who had got on to him, was sick and couldn't make it or a mix up in schedules of their plane or train, and how sorry they were, that they couldn't be there, for the biggest show ever in their favorite city. He knew exactly how to do it, to smooth things over for the good people there. But then there was a man named Barnum once who could do the same thing. But he could do it smoother and better than Larry. They usually would swallow his line of baloney hook, line, and sinker, but sometimes they would take his line for granted. Then there was hell to pay. The Memphis thing got so big that Harry Stone called us into his office. He had had letters and calls protesting our not showing up for the Memphis date. He was not mad at us.

"Now I'm not mad at you fellows for all this hell we are catching, but there's one thing I *do* want to tell you guys. That fellow will book you and play you on one date, and sell you falsely on about seven or eight others. Now, I'm not telling you what to do but personally I just don't think it does your reputation any good to do business with a guy like that."

Sunbrock always paid us very good and we needed the money, so we promised Mr. Stone if he threw us another curve, we would not play anymore for him. He said well and good and good luck to us.

We met many people on the Sunbrock show that we would have not met otherwise. He put those fiddling contests on from coast to coast and always made money. I remember the first time I ever met Cowboy Copas was on one of those shows, the first one we ever played. Cowboy Copas, Rusty Gabbard, and Natchee traveled with him and played all the contests with him. Those three fellows could put on a good enough show for anyone who was in the crowd. They could sing, play, and tell jokes and among them, they could just about play any instrument that it took to please the most particular music lover.

There is a lot said and done these days about integration. There is much hatred on account of it just because a few people are arbitrary about it and want only their way. They don't want to see the other side, which is our side, the Southerner's side. I am going to cite one instance where the dictatorial people are absolutely wrong in their methods to try to make somebody do something they want us to do, but don't do it themselves. Little DeFord Bailey was a Negro and he was crippled, but he could play the harmonica real well and was a pioneer in the field of playing the harmonica. When we joined the Opry we saw a lot of DeFord and he was a real friendly fellow and we liked him very much. So did the rest of the entertainers on the Opry. But there weren't any United States soldiers standing with bayonets drawn to make us like and respect him. We all just did it because it was the right thing to do, and we all thought just as much of DeFord as we did our white friends. He was a little fellow who commanded our admiration and respect. But he still had his little eccentricities.

Rabon and I used DeFord on a lot of our personal appearances. There was one time we booked him on a show we were playing for Larry Sunbrock. It was in Birmingham and we also had Arthur Smith with us. We all rode down in my car. Arthur and Rabon and I split the expenses as we always did on such show dates. We didn't take out mileage because we had never thought of that in those days. So the one who drove the car usually lost his shirt.

When an act booked DeFord, the usual price was five dollars an appearance, whether the act lost money on the date or not. That was the way Mr. Hay of the Artist Service had it set up and he wouldn't let DeFord go out unless the act agreed to pay DeFord in that agreement. DeFord was happy with the situation and back in those days five dollars was not bad for a fellow when he knew he was getting paid regardless. In other words if there was a big show like I have written about in Memphis, or Louisville, and we all lost money, Mr. Hay would see that DeFord got his money just the same. In times like that, I have thought I would like to have had an arrangement like DeFord had.

Now on this trip to Birmingham, we all had a substantial guarantee, but we were to pay DeFord only the five dollars for each appearance. That would have made him due ten dollars and no more. So Rabon and Arthur and I decided we would pay him more but take part of his for car expenses. I checked up, and when I took out his part on the car he had about thirty-nine dollars.

That was nearly eight times as much as he would have gotten under the Hay agreement. I paid him off and he didn't say a thing about being dissatisfied, but there was a catch to it. I was not to hear the last of that.

It was late when we got back to Nashville, and when I had taken everybody home I went straight to bed, intending to catch up on some rest. But about nine o'clock, the phone rang and when I answered it there was an angry Judge Hay on the other end of the line. "Alton, I didn't think you'd ever do such a thing to a little helpless fellow like DeFord." He was panting and breathing hard, he was so mad. I got mad, too, and told him I could not explain it to him on the phone and that I would come up there immediately, if he had the time. He said he would look for me and that I had better have a good excuse, if I expected to stay on the Grand Ole Opry. That remark made me furious. I had heard that damn remark so much when I wasn't to blame, that I was nearly crazy. I hung up the phone and got dressed and went up there as fast as I could. I felt just like taking a swing at someone. I didn't know what on earth could be wrong.

I went straight to Hay's office and he was waiting for me. "Now this better be good," were the first words he said. I bit my lip to keep from cussing him out. But I told him the whole story and how much we had paid DeFord and all the details.

He was alarmed. But he didn't ever apologize for the way he had suspected me of being a son of a bitch. He told me that DeFord never told him how much money we had paid him, but he complained that we had taken car expenses out on him. Of course, if we had done that, and not paid him like we did, it *would* have been a dirty deal. DeFord had already gone, Mr. Hay said. He said DeFord felt sick and had to go home when he called and bawled me out. Hay said: "Don't you ever pay that boy any more than I have set out in his agreement, or I won't let him go out with you fellows ever again." But Hay didn't say boy. He used a word the NAACP would not like.*

I didn't get mad at DeFord at all but I did get sore at Hay. But I stayed sore at that man as long as I was on the Opry. He did a lot for country and western music but he gave me plenty of hell while I was on the Opry. I was always a bastard, in his estimation, until proven otherwise.

We would take people out who had never been on the road before and sometimes it was a mistake. We only saw them on Saturday nights and that was not much of a criterion for knowing how trustworthy they were. Some of the men we took out would keep begging till we took them out, and then they would try to run the whole show. For instance, there was one fellow who we took out on some personals and he was a Master Mason. There was a little trouble on the trip, and he came in and told a bunch of lies and tried to get Harry Stone to fire us and he gave Stone the Mason

---

*DeFord himself has on several occasions told interviewers that he felt the Delmores were more honest in general with him than were most of the other Opry members. DeFord told folklorist Dick Hulan, in an unpublished interview, one anecdote to illustrate this. A certain promoter, who was booking DeFord, the Delmores, and other acts, learned that DeFord was a teetotaler. After tour shows, this promoter would say that he was paying everybody off in fifths of whiskey; he knew that DeFord would refuse the whiskey, and thus he was off the hook for paying DeFord, since DeFord's "five dollar" fee was usually eaten up in a couple of bottles. Alton and Rabon earned DeFord's respect when they revealed to him that the promoter was doing this on purpose in order to avoid paying DeFord his performance fee.—Ed.

pledge, whatever that is, that he was telling the truth. He had begged us for months to give him a chance on the road. That is how he paid us back. When Mr. Stone found out the facts, he just laughed at the guy, and told him not to be so excited next time he went on the road. Stone knew what we had to face on the long trips, and he was about the only one who had any consideration for a road trip.

CHAPTER SEVENTEEN

JOE FRANK, PEE WEE KING, TROUBLE STALKS

Rabon and I had both decided we would never get a fair break on the Opry, moneywise, and we had been in a desperate shape ever since we had been there. There just simply was not any luck for us there, as much as we loved that program. Somebody was always putting the pressure on us and we were just like little worms in a bed of ants. We stayed there for nearly seven years, hoping the situation would change, but we didn't know much of the facts of life in those days. We were always hoping that the bosses would accept us for what we were worth, but that never happens in real life. That is the reason so many great athletes and entertainers go broke and die of a broken heart, when they could be happy and healthy, if someone would have given them the break they deserved. People like that are too trusting, and you can't be trusting too much, if you don't want to get behind the eight ball. I have seen some of the needy big names who went down the drain of too much trusting. One notable case was the all time great baseball pitcher, the one and only "Old Pete," Grover Cleveland Alexander. I will have more to write about him later in another page but now I will go on with the outline I have made of the events previously, but I will say this much. His story is one of the most touching in all my career.

The Golden West Cowboys came to WSM from Louisville, and their manager

JOE FRANK, PEE WEE KING, TROUBLE STALKS

was Joe Frank, a great man in the entertainment field, who goes I think as one of the most neglected persons in the entire field of country and western music. Joe was an understanding person who could prod out real talent when he saw it. He was not a "high hat" person but just a down-to-earth businessman who knew what would seem to go in the game. He was like Colonel Tom Parker, Elvis Presley's manager, just an ordinary person who talked and acted like a plowboy but who had a tremendous knowledge of the entertainment world, hard to beat. Joe had been Gene Autry's manager in Chicago, and he had also managed Fibber McGee and Molly in their personal appearances and other fields where they needed an expert like him.

When he first came to the Opry, he brought Pee Wee King and the Golden West Cowboys, and he made a good go of it from the very first. They had a good band, but nothing spectacular, but Old Joe knew the score and he drained every drop of goodness out of them. He wanted, and demanded, the best they had and he got it. They were soon one of the most popular acts on the Opry.

Joe was a clean-cut, neat fellow, handsome, with a little mustache and a big Texas hat. He didn't wear the hat till he got pretty well established around WSM, but when he did, he wore it with a perfect abandon. He knew what it took to put on a show and he was always trying to find new ways to present new ways in the field of country and western music, that would make for variety. At first, Rabon and I were suspicious of him, but the more we were around him, the more we liked the man. He always had his heart in his work and he always had a good word for the down and out musician and also a handout, if they asked for it—and lots of times when they didn't ask for it. He was a truly charitable.person. And I give Joe Frank the credit for putting the Grand Ole Opry in the big-time class and prestige and also the big-time money. He was an excellent promoter and he knew just what he wanted and he always got it. He didn't use force or prestige to put over his idea. He went to the little people. For instance, he would book a big city like

JOE FRANK, PEE WEE KING, TROUBLE STALKS

Cincinnati, Ohio, and he would take his own sweet time to start promoting his show. He first would go to· the places where they hired bands in the honky tonks. He would make friends with all the musicians in the band and then he would give them tickets to the show and also tickets for their friends. Then they would go through hell for him. He would stay in the best hotels, naturally, but he didn't "high hat" those people when they came in to see him. I will write more about Joe Frank in the rest of this book, but now I will digress a little to let you know how our folks back home appreciated us, our mother and father, and our brothers and sisters and friends. They liked us very much and were indeed glad that we had climbed so far up the ladder to be just two ignorant farm boys.

Mama and Papa and Thelma's folks would make short visits to our house, and it always was a pleasure to have them. They seemed to bring us back to our realistic way of life, before we came to Nashville and the Grand Ole Opry. If anyone of us ever got a little sick they would come and stay with us till we got better. They were a lot of help. Thelma and our two little girls, Norma Gail and Billie Anne, had the measles while we were living on Allison Place, and "Miss Elsie," as I called Thelma's mother, came up and helped out a whole lot. They were all pretty sick but Thelma was the sickest of all and "Miss Elsie" helped with the cooking and waited on them all. We had an old Negro woman, Aunt Emma, who worked for us and she was a mighty good one, too. She dearly loved the children and they loved her, too. She was old, but she still knew what to do when someone was ill.

We had a telephone all the time we were in Nashville, and it was listed "Delmore Brothers." That was one of the worst mistakes we ever made. There would be people, just curiosity seekers, who would call, and we always took up time with them. We never did get a chance to get any rest, for there was always someone calling and wanting to come out and take our picture, or hear us play some. And you know what? The worst pests were not fans at all, but were just floaters who wanted to see what made a radio entertainer tick. Now when I go to Nashville, I seldom call anyone at all. I don't want to disturb them in the first place, and in the next place, I usually forget and leave their phone numbers at home. But it does not worry me at all. The Grand Ole Opry gives them enough to do, with their traveling, to keep them mighty busy.

It's been a long, long time since we played on the Opry, but lots of people still remember us, good people, and a few "worry warts." But if you don't watch out the "worry warts" will get you, so I don't even list my name in the telephone book. Now, what I refer to as the "worry warts" are people who get too high in a tavern and want other people to know they know someone who has been a radio entertainer. So, with the years, all entertainers have learned a lesson and don't list their phone numbers just on this account.

But when our folks were visiting us, they would take care of the phone calls and sometimes save us from a lot of unnecessary worry by telling the party calling that we were asleep or give some other good excuse. We felt like they could do it better than Thelma or me or Rabon. We didn't want to make anyone mad at us, and we all felt that way about it, and consequently we would take it on the chin just to satisfy the whims of the curious. Now, I'm not saying we didn't appreciate the interest of our fans, but it just wore us down till we were all just a bundle of nerves. We just didn't know how to cope with a problem like that, in those days. But we knew we could not take it very much longer and that was just one more reason why we knew we had to leave the Opry. There was no peace for us there at that time!

In the meantime, we had stopped playing personal appearances. The station would not allow us to bring in any outside talent to play with us and we could not get the good ones at the Opry. We had to take the drunkards and the troublemakers with us, and that nearly drove us nuts. We had pulled for David Stone to take Judge Hay's place as the Artist Service manager when Mr. Hay got sick and had to go to the hospital. We thought David would help us to get someone to play with we could depend on. He did, in a way, but it was not as easy with David as we thought it would be, for he strictly drove a hard bargain, and he seemed to forget that we had pulled for him to get the Artist Service job at WSM.

We had pulled for him to get the job and we had some influence around the station with the officials, but when he got in, he forgot about us, and I learned another lesson in human personality. He was Harry Stone's brother and Harry was the general manager of the station. He could have been a big help to us, but he continually gave us a rough time. One time he prohibited us from playing a date in Birmingham that promised us a shot in the arm financially. We were supposed to play it on a Sunday and he held us in the palm of his hand. He didn't have any particular grievance against us, but he just was going to prove to us who was the big boss. And that guy had ridden in the same car with us and had played many personals with us and we had got along real well together until he got the big job, he thought, of being our big boss. I begged and pleaded with him, but he remained obstinate right up until the time we had our last program on the Opry, the Saturday night before we were to play the date. We began our program and played just like we always did, thinking the date was off. But along toward the end of the program he made the announcement that we could play the date. He gave us a baleful look after he made the announcement, just like he was the king of the world. It was a concession of grudge and he couldn't conceal it. It was just like a damn cat playing with a mouse that he had already caught, but let him think he would give him one more chance. I know that sounds like tough language but that is exactly what happened and I wouldn't be very fair if I didn't write it like it was.

After that, we knew exactly where we stood at the WSM Grand Ole Opry. And I knew I could not stand it any longer. It was not long after that, that we completely quit playing personals. There had been so much trouble and my nerves were so bad that I had rather went home to share-cropping than played them. I never thought there could be so much dissension in the whole world, but I learned it over the years. It was not very long till I told David Stone not to book us anymore. But the dates kept coming in. He didn't want us to quit, because he needed the money to help run the Artist Service. But I was firm, and I told him we were not going out on another show date until we could pick the ones we wanted to play with, and who wanted to play with us. He kind of began to see our side of the situation and agreed there had been a lot of trouble. And you know when you have a lot of trouble that keeps cropping up, you get sensitive and impatient with everything and everyone concerned. That is the way it is with every business or situation that you go through in life. And little troubles take on the symbol of big troubles, many times beyond their actual meaning. David knew we were making enough money from our record and our meager salary at the station to barely make ends meet, but he didn't argue with me and promised me he would come up with a plan to allow us to start playing the road again under pleasant circumstances. He could be a nice fellow when he wanted to be. And he was trying now to make a go of the Artist Service. He began bringing in other acts, and Rabon and I both thought that was a very good move in the direction of personal appearances.

After a long absence from playing on the road, Rabon and I wanted to get back in the groove and reconsidered and told Dave Stone we would be willing to accept some of the dates when he had a big jamboree booked. He was glad to hear that, and that put him responsible for the acts of the others on the show who failed to behave like they should. And David was a good driver. He was not hard to work for, but he would not tolerate any undue foolishness on the part of anyone. And he always went along and emceed the show, which took another burden off me. He enjoyed that kind of work, and they could recognize his voice from hearing him on the Grand Ole Opry talking every Saturday night. That gave him a great kick and it was also good business. David had been a theater manager before he came to the Opry, and he had a lot better insight into the show business than the other Artist Managers before him. He was a lot younger than the other guys and that helped a lot.

I remember the first time the Grand Ole Opry was broadcasted outside of Nashville. It was a show that David promoted in Jackson, Tennessee. All of the guys and gals on the Opry went down. And it was a great success. We played a show in the afternoon and it was not broadcast, but that night, which of course was a Saturday night, we were on the air for about two hours. I said almost the whole Opry went down there, but David left enough of the gang in Nashville to keep the Opry going when our show was over. David promoted the show but there was a sponsor in Jackson who gave it the personal touch that it needed. When we got to town the sponsor was a little high but we didn't pay too much attention to that until later. He kept nipping on the bottle and he was just about past going when our night show was due. So he left and went home for a nap, he told David. He took the money with him. So we went on right ahead and put on the show, confident that the guy would be all right when it came time to check up. But when we got through with the show, he didn't show up and David was real worried. He had the guy's telephone number and he called, and his wife told David that the guy had not been home since that morning. Now when you travel on a trip like that, you usually take only enough money to get there, and then depend on your part of the proceeds to get you by till you play another date. If you take too much money, you will spend it on something foolish and never save anything. So we were all depending on our share of that show to get us back to Nashville. So David Stone was just about the most worried person I have ever seen that night when he couldn't find the sponsor. We knew we would finally get our money, when we found the guy, because he was a very honest person and he had a very responsible job. But all that didn't help poor David worth a penny. He thought he was a miserable failure on his first jaunt out of town. And most of the fellows on the show needed their part of the money to get back home. He kept asking us guys who had played the road a lot what to do. I told him not to worry because I believed everything would turn out all right.

That seemed to help him out some. But he was still extremely worried. Each of us had taken a room at the hotel to rest in, and we had left part of our things in our rooms. So we had to go back there to pack and get ready for the trip back to Nashville. So when we left the auditorium, we all went back to our hotel rooms and talked David into doing the same. But when we got to the hotel, he wouldn't go to his room. He just paced up and down in the lobby. He had hopes that the guy would turn up at the hotel and they could then check up on the money. He had been up to David's room before the afternoon show, and David thought he might turn up again. So we all got ready to leave, and when we came back down to the lobby, poor David was still at a loss as to what to do. We all had enough money to get back to Nashville. Some of us had to lend money to the ones that didn't have the money, but we didn't mind that, because we knew we would get it back. So we didn't worry any. We had played dates before and drew a blank but David was so upset, he couldn't drum enough courage to go to his room and pack his things. I talked to him and some of the rest of the guys talked and finally he decided to go up and get his clothes and leave with us. We all liked to travel pretty close to each other on dates like that, so if somebody had car trouble, they would have help somewhere along the line.

David caught the elevator and went up to his room but in no time at all, he was back down in the lobby again. He was all excited.

"I want to show you fellows something," was all he said and he buzzed for the elevator again. I went along to see what had happened. I thought maybe somebody had stolen his clothes or something. But when we got to his room it was really something!

Our sponsor had come back to the hotel and laid down on David's bed. He was tapped out, and dead to the world, and all of the money was scattered on the floor with the receipts and everything. He was snoring very loudly and getting some of the best rest, I guess, he had ever had in his life. We all helped David get him roused up and we didn't pick up a single penny till we got him good awake. He was very apologetic and sorry for what had happened. But David had a look of relief on his face. He was off the hook. After we got him all squared away, and saw that he was straight, we helped pick up the money and then we left David and him up there to check up on the money. David wanted us to wait in the lobby till he got through, so we did. It was not long till they both came down and the sponsor apologized to each one of us that had played the show. Then he left.

David counted the money and paid everyone of us off, and then he sighed a sigh of relief. "I want to get rid of that damn stuff," he said as he paid each of us. "It sure has been a lot of trouble." Old David was really happy.

That is the way it goes when you have the responsibility for a big show like we had. An honest man always worries about things like that and David Stone was honest.

There was one other event concerning David that I will tell, and it was the cause of one of the greatest of all country and western singers and musicians to get on the Grand Ole Opry. A fiddlers' contest started it all.

A group of sponsors down in west Tennessee wrote in and said their sheriff could beat our best Grand Ole Opry fiddle player and wanted to put on a contest to prove it. It was a natural. So David decided to put on a contest and carry along a show to back it all up. It would make money. He knew it would. So he gathered a bunch of us and told us what he had done, and booked about five or six of the best drawing acts on the Opry. Rabon and I agreed to play this for David, since it looked like a smash and it was:

So David got the posters and other advertising together and sent it down to the west Tennessee people. They really did a good job advertising. Our old-time fiddler had some friends he was riding down with, and when we all got there (I forget the name of the town) the place was packed and jammed. The sheriff was there, with his bow all rosined up and his fiddle in tune, and he was raring to go. He was a politician and this thing would help him out a lot, win or lose. But our fiddler didn't show. David was worried again. He paced back and forth watching the clock get nearer and nearer to show time. We told him just to start the show and get the people in a good mood, and if our fiddler was late they would soon forget about the contest and not give him the razz. He decided to do that and we started the show. It was a good crowd to play to, and we had everything going great. But still no word or appearance of our fiddler. Something was wrong. It was after nine o'clock and still our man had not shown up. We all began to give up hope. David was nearly insane from waiting on our fiddler. So we thought it all over and came up with a plan. We would let one of the other fiddle players in our group compete against the sheriff and then if our man came in later there would be another contest. This greatly pleased the audience and we were on easy street again. We put on an extra long show and had the contest, and the sheriff won to the delight of all the people. There was no grumbling and the people seemed greatly satisfied with the show. When we got ready to close, David walked out on the stage and apologized for the missing Opry fiddler. He told the stark truth. He didn't know what had happened to the man and he made them think he was really worried and concerned about our fiddler. He got a fine ovation from the crowd, but that didn't pay for the anxiety and sweat he had gone through. He was plenty mad, and anyone would have been, under the same circumstances. That kind of sweating shortens your days and shatters your nerves.

JOE FRANK, PEE WEE KING, TROUBLE STALKS

David came up to Rabon and me, and told us he was going to lay our fiddler off the Opry for four consecutive weeks and bring in a band each week to play in his place. He told us he wanted us to listen to each band and pick out the one we would like to play personals with. He would leave it all up to us to decide, and he would let them stay on the Opry for the duration of time they played with us.

"Now you boys have about six months you can play with this band, and then they will have to go. They will never be a genuine act of the Grand Ole Opry. I will tell them that, when we hire them, but it will give them some great publicity and they should have no regrets afterwards."

That is exactly what he said and he meant every word of it.

Now this man David had laid off was a good friend to me and also to Rabon. We hated to see him in that unfortunate situation, but the boss had spoken and we considered him right. The fellow later told me that his friends who were bringing him down stopped and got them some moonshine. They got too much of it and they decided not to go to the contest, and they knew he was at their mercy. So they just laughed at him when he begged them to take him on to the town. He was given the horse laugh, and he learned a lesson not to trust a lot of people after that. He told David the same story but David would not accept it. He remained adamant. Now what I am writing is the God's truth, and that is the way fate meant it to be. Otherwise the fellow I am going to write about in the next chapter may have never been heard of, and may have been left unheard of, like a beautiful flower that blooms in the wilds of some deep wilderness, never heard of, never appreciated, and left entirely out of the strange scheme of life. I think fate has a lot more on the ball than some people will admit.

On the way back from the contest Rabon and I talked it over, and although we had long made up our minds to leave the Opry, we realized that David was giving us a very good break by bringing in a band to play with us, so we could continue our personal appearances.

We both loved the Grand Ole Opry, and hated to leave, but we knew it had to be done. We had to leave. It was inevitable. Our nerves were too wrought up to last, physically, very much longer with the status quo like it was.

CHAPTER EIGHTEEN

ROY ACUFF COMES TO NASHVILLE

It was about a year before David decided to allow us to bring in a band when it happened.

We had two fifteen-minute programs before the Opry really started. One of them was at 6:30 P.M. and the other was at about 7:45 P.M. Anyway, I know we had two programs and then we would go to the Opry and play the rest of our programs. At the time we met this little fellow, the Opry was being held in a tabernacle in East Nashville, across the Cumberland River. We usually tried to be at the station an hour before our program, and we arrived at the station between five-thirty and six o'clock.

Percy Craig was the superintendent of the whole National Life building, and he was operating the elevator that Saturday night. He would let his help go out for supper and he would take care of things till they came back. He was alone and when we started for the elevator he walked with us to take us up. I always liked Percy very much, and Rabon did too, and we kidded him a whole lot, and he would kid us too. Percy was a grand fellow.

After our usual hellos, etc., he started the elevator. But he stopped when he got to the second floor. The station is on the fifth floor.

"Boys, I promised a guy I would call him and let him meet you boys. I hope you won't think I am being presumptuous, but I made a promise and I hate to break it. Now since I know you boys are just plain old country boys, I made him that promise, but if you don't want to take up any time with him, I can go out and tell him you are too busy. He is a great fan of yours, but I will leave it all up to you."

I asked him a few questions about the fellow and I decided to go back down and see this fan from east Tennessee who liked us so much. Percy had told us he was from east Tennessee, and I could tell old Percy liked him by the way he acted and talked. Now Rabon and myself always liked the people who were our fans, because they were who had made us our success in the entertainment field. Just plain old country people. They dip snuff and chew tobacco, and wear patches on their overalls, and some of them drink moonshine whiskey, or at least they did in those days. We told Percy to take us back down so we could meet this fan of ours. Percy went out into the station parking lot and brought him in. When I first looked at him, I liked him. He was just as friendly as a puppy, and he was marked all over with pure and simple sincerity. I could tell Rabon liked him, too. He was not dressed up too good and he looked a little seedy and shabby. His hat needed blocking, and he needed a shave a little bit, but we didn't mind that, as he was just a fan, and we saw lots of others like him, who came around to see us, and I can thank God we never high-hatted a person in our whole career. He shook hands with us and shook hands with Percy again for keeping his promise.

"Boys, we listen to your program every Saturday night up in east Tennessee, and my wife and I, and my father and mother, think you are wonderful. If you would just allow me to go up with you and sit outside the studio while you are putting your program on, I can go back and tell the folks something." The way he said it was a plea, a sincere one.

"No, you can't go up with us and sit outside the studio. You can come inside the studio, and be there with us when we play, and we will dedicate a song to your folks back home, so they will know you are safe and all right." That is exactly what we told the little fellow from east Tennessee. He had told us some of the bosses upstairs at WSM had mistreated him and ordered him out of the station, and he wondered what we would do about that. I reassured him that would positively not happen to him this time.

On the way up to the fifth floor I got to talking to him and he told me he had made some records for some company. I forgot what it is now, but Gene Autry, and Cliff Carlisle, and the Callahan Brothers, and a host of others had made records for the same company. I had a lot of original songs that had been recorded in those days, and I was always browsing around the dime stores to see if any of my songs had been made by some of the artists. I ran up on quite a few and in looking through the catalog I would see names of artists and I would remember them. I had seen his name in the catalog and I remembered it—Roy Acuff. He had made about twenty songs on a single session in Chicago. He had recorded "Wabash Cannonball" and the "Great Speckled Bird" on this session, but he had not made any money from them to speak of, he told me. But his main goal then was to get on the Opry.*

When we had finished our program, he was ready to go back to east Tennessee. We tried to get him to go on out to the tabernacle with us, but he would not go.

*By this time Acuff had had a good deal of radio experience: He and his Crazy Tennesseans had been playing on Knoxville radio stations WROL and WNOX since 1934. The Chicago recording session took place in October 1936, when Acuff did a number of sides for the American Recording Company. The ARC group was an immense umbrella company of the late 1930s that issued records on a bewildering variety of labels, including Perfect, Conqueror (many of Acuff's were on this label), Melotone, Banner, Okeh, and Vocalion. Acuff did indeed record "Wabash Cannonball" and "Great Speckled Bird," but many of the sides from this session featured singing by Red Jones and Dynamite Hatcher instead of Acuff. It is noteworthy, though, that Acuff's rather considerable recording start apparently made no impression on Judge Hay and the Opry staff, reinforcing the theory that recordings were not as important to radio (or to the Opry) in the prewar years as they were to become later.—Ed.

ROY ACUFF COMES TO NASHVILLE

He said he was afraid Judge Hay would run him away again. He seemed bewildered with the whole set-up around the station. He thought everybody was as friendly as they sounded, but they were not, as we had learned it the hard way. He said some of the acts he admired were so dressed up they looked like movie stars and it made him feel disappointed. I told him we were the same way when we first came to the station, but that didn't seem to help out much. He told us he would never forget how nice we had been to him, and I told him I would help him out any way I could to get on the Opry. This is what had happened to him when he first went up to ask for an audition: He told Judge Hay he wanted to get on the Opry, and it made the Judge real mad to think a country fellow like Roy Acuff would have the audacity to ever think he was good enough for the Opry. That was the attitude in those days.

It was a lot harder to get on the show then than it is now. And poor Roy ran right smack into the middle of a barrage of hostility. I told him the old timers were friendly but he was still shy of the idea. He didn't want to take the chance of being ordered away from the Opry. Rabon and I both tried to make him believe that it would never happen as long as he was our guest. But he had already "had it" one time and he told us that was enough for one day. If he had gone out with us, no one would have bothered him and he would have enjoyed it very much, but he didn't feel like stretching his luck that far.

He thanked us again and again for being nice to him, and I hated to see him leave, but he would not have it any other way. Somehow he thought he would jeopardize us. There was a mist of water in his eyes as he vanished into the night, away from the parking lot.

It was a year before we saw him again, but we never forgot him. And the way it happened is sheer fate. It just must have been in the hands of Providence that Roy Acuff should become a star in the entertainment world.

ROY ACUFF COMES TO NASHVILLE

As I have written before, David Stone brought in the four bands to audition on the Grand Ole Opry. I don't know to this day how he arrived at the decision to bring the different ones in. But he must have had letters from them asking for a chance on the Opry. Anyway, he picked some pretty fair bands and they all performed real good but the last one. There was something wrong with the last band, and when we went over the Cumberland River to the east Nashville tabernacle, we found out why. This last band called themselves the Crazy Tennesseans, after a commercial they had been on in Knoxville. The name Roy Acuff was not mentioned, and their performance was the worst of the three. Rabon and I had no idea of bringing them in to play with us. Their performance had been too far away from good entertainment. They sounded really pitiful. When we got over to the tabernacle we met them, as we had the others before them, and we were in for one of the biggest surprises we had ever had before. Their leader was none other than Roy Acuff. He was coming out the rear entrance and fixing to leave when we got there. If we had been two more minutes later, he would have been gone. He felt that he had made a miserable failure and he told us so. He was so pale he looked like he was really sick. His hands trembled as he talked to us. There was a faraway look on his face like he had just missed heaven or something equal to it. But he didn't know about the deal David Stone had made with us, and neither did the rest of the bands that came in to audition. They all just thought that they were trying out for a regular job on the Opry.

Roy introduced us to all the members of the band, and all seemed like real friendly boys.* He had a girl singer named Tiny. We had heard her sing that night, but she didn't impress us much. She was very friendly, though, as were the others. We talked

---

*The band that came with Acuff to the Opry in February 1938 included Clell Summey (Cousin Jody), Jess Easterly (guitar), "Tiny" (vocal and guitar), Roy (fiddle, vocal), and Red Jones (bass). Summey, Jones, and "Tiny" quit in January 1939.—Ed.

to Roy and the others for a little while and he said he had to go, that he felt bad and wanted to get on the road, as they had a hard trip ahead of them. I remember the last thing he said to us.

"Boys, you have both been real friends to me, and I will never forget you and your kindness, if I never see you again." With that said, Roy and his band disappeared again into the night, and this time we could tell that he felt whipped. But Rabon and I didn't feel that way about him. We both knew the minute we saw him that night that he was the one we wanted to help us play our dates, so we could leave the Grand Ole Opry. The other bands had played better, but they didn't seem nearly as sincere as Roy did. Maybe that is the reason we picked him. We had known almost nothing but trouble since we had come to the Opry, and we thought we could get along with him better than the rest. And besides, I always thought the band would be better after they got used to the atmosphere of the Opry. And this turned out to be correct also. He had a lot better band than we heard that night.

On Monday morning, I went up to see David Stone about the band we wanted to play with us. He had told us he would let us pick out the one we wanted and would not interfere with our opinion in any way. He was really fair about this all till I went up to see him that morning. When I got to his office, he was waiting for me. He wanted us to get back on the road again. It would mean more money for the Artist Service, and David wanted to make a go of it and keep it out of the red. He was doing a very good job of it, but he could always use more money in the till.

I walked in and sat down after saying hello, etc., and he asked me:

"Have you decided who of the four bands you want to play your dates with you?"

"Yes, we want Roy Acuff."

"And if I may ask, who in hell is he?"

"He is the leader, or the head man, of the last band that played last Saturday night."

He looked at me for a moment, and then he said: "Oh."

"What did you say 'oh' for David?"

"At first I thought you meant the band that played Saturday night."

"That is exactly what I meant. Rabon and I have both decided we want Roy and his band. He's an old east Tennessee boy, and I think we can get along with him better than the others."

David looked shocked and bewildered.

"I'll be god damned if I think l will ever be able to understand you crazy hill-billies. Here you are, picking the worst band that played. And I know you know better. Is there something about this Roy Acuff that has you charmed or something?"

"No. But I remember the first time we came to this place, and how we got treated and I don't want it to happen to anyone else. That old boy will crawl to make good. I just know he will and I think he deserves a chance."

I didn't get mad at David for calling us hill-billies, because everybody called us that in those days. I have written about this before but that was the way it was in those days.

David shrugged his shoulders, like somebody giving up the ship, but he didn't say any more against Roy Acuff. Rabon was not with me. He left things like that up to me.

"Well, if you want Roy Acuff, or anybody else, I'll get in touch with them and let you know their terms, so we can get started on the road again. But there is one damn thing for sure. We don't aim to keep the act you select on the Opry. After those dates are played they will be through. We've already got too many on this show, and I don't aim to crowd it up anymore. So I will take care of everything, and call you when I get in touch with Roy Acuff or the Crazy Tennesseans. I don't ever remember his name, but I will get hold of him and find out what he thinks and tell him he is going to be on the Opry for a while."

ROY ACUFF COMES TO NASHVILLE

He began looking through his papers for Roy's name and I left.

David called me the next day and said he had talked to Acuff. He told me that Roy would bring his band in, and we could travel in his station wagon. David said Roy would take 50 percent of the receipts and we could have 50 percent, Rabon and me. I told David we would not play that way. I told him that Roy had five people in his band, and he could not make it on just 50 percent. We would play it 60-40 in his favor. David argued a little bit over the fact that Roy was an unknown, and he thought we ought to make it 50-50. I told him I didn't care if he was an unknown, he had to live and that settled it.

David got in touch with Roy and told him to come in to the station in about two weeks, or just as soon as he could get the first date advertised. He knew they could not live on the little sum they were paid each week on the Opry.

I didn't know exactly whether I had made a mistake or not; but I knew if the deal with Acuff didn't work out, I would be blamed for the whole thing. I was on the spot from a certain standpoint. Because if Acuff and his band didn't work out, we, Rabon and I both knew, were in for a pretty rough time from David and the station, since he had objected to bringing Roy in, in the first place. But I took consolation in the fact that if they didn't like it, they could lump it, since we were leaving the Opry anyway. But we needed the money we would make on the personals, and I sincerely hoped that the deal would work out.

The time came for Roy and his Crazy Tennesseans to appear with us on the early morning show and they were there promptly and ready to go. They didn't start on the Opry but had an early morning show like we did during the week, and then they would play the Opry the following Saturday night, if they worked out all right.

We started playing the show dates; the first was in Dawson Spring, Kentucky. That was the first appearance of Roy Acuff and the Crazy Tennesseans and the Delmore Brothers, together. It was on a Sunday, and we had both been plugging the date all the week, and also on the Grand Ole Opry. We had a very good crowd, and Roy and his band seemed happy. We made a little extra money and that always makes you feel better. I liked Roy and all his gang, but I could tell there was dissension all around. I couldn't put my finger on it but I could tell things were not right. We played several months together and I learned what the contention was about. Roy wanted to play real hill-billy music, but the boys he had in the band wanted to be polished and uptown. Roy couldn't play the way they did and he didn't want to, if he *could* have. It had him worried. On the stage he would only do two songs and they were "I Like Molasses" and "The Great Speckled Bird." He had sung the "Great Speckled Bird" his first night on the Opry and it drew a lot of mail. It looked good for him, just a newcomer. And he began to get a lot of telegrams for it. I know some of you reading this will not appreciate it, but I am going to be frank. I never did really care for "The Great Speckled Bird." It is mentioned only once in the Bible, and that is in the twelfth chapter of Jeremiah. You know Jeremiah was the great prophet, and he likened his heritage unto the "Great Speckled Bird" despised by the other beasts of the field. Back in those ancient days, the hyena had wings and could fly like a bird and that is what Jeremiah meant when he likened his heritage unto the bird. You see, his people had plenty of money, and Jeremiah could have lived a life of ease, had he wanted to. But he chose otherwise. No one really knows who wrote the song but some uneducated preacher happened to see it in the Bible and made an issue of it because he thought himself persecuted like the bird. I met a preacher over in North Carolina who claimed he wrote it, and he might very well have, because he did fit the picture pretty well. But Roy changed it around so the bird meant the Bible. He had to do this, so he could go on singing it, because his mail was tremendous for that one song.

Roy and myself used to sit out in his station wagon and sing hymns between shows. I had always sung the old hymns and Roy had too, so we made a natural combination. Roy could not read music, but I showed him a few little things and he finally got to where he could read the shaped notes well enough to pick out a song. And that is one reason he sings so many hymns on his programs now. He loves them, and he can really put a lot of feeling into them. I always liked all his hymns except the bird.

I really didn't have much hope for Roy to make it when he first came to the Opry. It seemed like his way of programming and putting on a stage show was a bit too unorthodox to me. In other words, when he finished a song on the stage, he would not wait for the people to give him applause, but he just went right on in to the next number and when he told a joke, he didn't wait for them to laugh, but just went right on in to the next sequence of the show. That didn't give the crowd much choice of taking part and I thought, in show business, that that was a cardinal sin. But I never told him about that. He had his own way of doing his act, and I never have been the one to tell somebody something without first being asked to. Another one of Roy's eccentricities was where he finished a tune on his fiddle, he would play the "war tax" two or three or sometimes four times before he would quit. That, again was something different. But now, most of the old-time fiddlers have taken it up, and I guess Roy started something with that little twist.

There were a lot of the guys at the Grand Ole Opry who didn't understand Roy Acuff when he first came there, and they would talk to me and ask me what I ever saw in a fellow like that. I couldn't tell them because I didn't really know myself. I just knew that he was a friendly little man who wanted to make good, and he was putting some of his east Tennessee style into his performance because it was the natural thing to do.

Roy was a hungry person. Not for food, or security, but just to make a little niche in the eternal cycle of country music. I believe Roy's carelessness for security really benefited him more than anything he ever did, because he didn't seem to ever worry if we had a good date or a bad one as far as money was concerned. He just wanted to make good as an entertainer. And he was a natural salesman. He could sell himself anytime on the stage. He just seemed not to care whether he went over or not on the stage and that is what made him so great then and also now. I can't tell why, but from the very start I considered him an artist. But I also knew that he would have a hard time presenting his own true style with the band he brought in with him. But fate played a hand again and helped him out. They didn't stay with him very long. Rabon and I always listened to Roy and the band when we had the chance. One night I was listening to him sing on the radio, and he sang a song about a train. I had never heard it the way he sang it, but I immediately liked it better than anything I had ever heard him sing before. I hurried, and got over the river soon as I could, to tell him how I liked the song. Rabon had moved out to himself then, and I had to go by and pick him up, but we got over there before Roy left. l called him aside.

"Roy, what was that song you sang tonight about a train?" "Oh—that—it was that old 'Wabash Cannonball' and I don't like it at all." I was surprised to hear him say that. I had really got a thrill at the way he sang it.

"Roy, that one song is going to draw more mail than the 'Great Speckled Bird.'" He kind of laughed and said he hoped it would, because he could use some more fan mail, to help keep him on the Opry.

"Well that old song is gonna bring it in," I told him.

After that night, he began to sing it more often on all his programs, and he told me he began to like it himself. He made the train whistle with his throat and I think it hurt his throat when he did it. That's one reason he didn't like to sing it more often. But he got many requests for it and he was forced to sing it. So he had two real mail pullers that he could depend on with the Opry audience. But they were beginning to get jealous of him and some of them would laugh at the way he did things. He was not a smart aleck, but some of them seemed to think so. I could see the shape of things to come, and I wanted to help him. So I took him around and introduced him to some of the big shots whom I knew.

I knew, in case of a clique to get rid of him, they could help him out. I knew the publicity director real well, and I introduced him to Roy, and he started to give Roy some publicity in all the trade magazines. I was doing something for myself and Rabon when I did this, too. Because if Roy got publicity, he could help us draw in some more people. It worked real well and it kept old Roy on the station after we left. He had gotten himself so entrenched that it would be hard for anyone to throw him off the show. And David Stone had begun to like him, and I didn't think anybody could spread enough dirt to displace him on the Opry. Now this all may seem to sound like entertainers are a bunch of wolves, waiting to tear some one apart, like the law of the fang and claw. But it is not exactly like that, when you have been where I have been, and know the real score. I have never in my life seen any entertainer who wouldn't throw a dart now and then. And Mister, you can't confine this way of doing things to the show business alone. It rings true in politics, public works, governmental operations, and even down to the preachers of the Bible themselves. And, living here in Huntsville, Alabama, close to the space projects, etc., I have learned a lot about the way they do things, and it is the same way. I have heard some of the scientists criticize Werner Von Braun, and say that all he wanted was publicity. It is just a thing that happens, and it is natural, almost like getting one's breath, and you have to take it or leave it. For this old world is not perfect by any means and it never will be until people are given more from God the Creator to help them overcome it. We are all that way to some certain extent, but some use more restraint than others. I don't know what I use, but I try not to hurt anyone in any way. What I have been writing is in defense of entertainers, because they are not the only ones who talk out of turn and try to knock some poor devil out of something because he is going great guns. I will conclude this little deviation with this one question: How does a man get to be president? You know the answer: it is just rotten politics.

In closing this chapter on Roy Acuff, I want to say this one thing so there will be no misunderstanding about what I have written so far. I have written the truth about how he got on the Grand Ole Opry. And I have written the truth about everything I have said. It is something I think should be told, and it never has, until now. People just believe what publicity they see, and they don't think what goes on behind the scenes.

What I started out to say is this: I have helped a lot of people get started on radio and also records. Some of them you would recognize immediately and some of the others didn't make it so good. But I have always believed in helping someone who needed a little push. Some of them appreciate it, some of them don't, so I don't worry about it much. But I do think that gratitude is a wonderful thing, and some of those whom I helped out didn't even have the slightest idea of what gratitude meant. But I know this much. People don't forget who helped them out, if they never tell you about it. At least, that is the way I feel about it. I never forgot the slightest favor in my behalf when I was having it rough.

But one way I have of rationalizing this situation is the fact that although I did help the particular artist get started, I didn't make him a success. He had to make that for himself.

Now Roy Acuff worked like a bee when he got on the Opry, and he had had considerably more experience in the show business when he came to the Opry than we did. He had been in Knoxville, and there were wolves there, too, and he knew how to cope with them. We had never been on a big station before, and we were very green in our efforts and, consequently, we got took in a lot of ways. If we had been

ROY ACUFF COMES TO NASHVILLE

as experienced as Roy when we came to the Opry first, it would have made a lot of difference. He didn't let them push him around like we did, and, he didn't take their bluff game in at all. No, they couldn't scare Roy Acuff into anything.*

*"Apparently, the fiddler whose departure from the Opry (at the end of Chapter 17) made a place for Roy Acuff in the cast was none other than Arthur Smith. Acuff's biographer, Elizabeth Schlappi, reports that J. L. Frank talked to David Stone on Roy's behalf, "and it was arranged that Roy and his band could have a short audition on the show . . . because Arthur Smith, the main Opry fiddler, was going to be away." See "Roy Acuff—A Smoky Mountain Boy," in Thurston Moore, ed. *Pictorial History of Country Music.* Volume 4 (Heather Enterprises: Denver, 1972). Schlappi's account also confirms Alton's report that George Hay had been very hostile to Acuff in earlier meetings.—Ed.

CHAPTER NINETEEN

LEAVING THE OPRY*

Both Rabon and I knew that Roy Acuff was not making enough money on the dates he played with us to live like he should have, and we got to feeling that he was in a strain to make ends meet at all. He was building up his name and he was almost starving to death. But he never complained because he knew how the deal was when he came in to the Opry and we knew he would not break his promise with us. We both felt guilty about it and when we had played the best of the dates, we decided to ask Roy if he wanted to go on his own. He was getting lots of fan mail and that was a good indication that he was fast becoming established as a regular Opry star.

I asked him about it and he was very frank with me. He was apologetic but he appreciated the idea very much. I told him I thought we were getting too much of the take and if he wanted to, we would just let him go his way on the Opry with his band and that we would pull out and maybe he could make ends meet. He took it very gratefully and thanked us. Rabon and I were both tired of the consistent traveling and we needed a rest. Our nerves were shot to pieces.

---

* At this point the second major section (see Introduction) of the manuscript begins. There is a twelve-page gap in manuscript pagination between the end of the first section (or the end of Chapter 18) and the start of this section. However, little seems to be missing in the chronology of the narrative. Starting with this chapter, we also have Alton's chapter outlines (see Editor's Postscript). This suggests that he completed the first eighteen chapters, took time to outline the remainder of the book, and then went back to write as much of it as he could. However, in these later sections, he did not follow the outline exactly; numerous subjects in the outline do not appear in the completed manuscript. —Ed.

LEAVING THE OPRY

Roy was a little bit skeptical at first, but he finally agreed to try it on his own.

"I don't know what I'll do without you boys, but I am willing to try. If I can't make it, I will try something else, maybe add another act to my show or do something." So we shook hands and he was on his own after that.

I kept calling different radio stations all over the country and trying to get a program somewhere away from Nashville. But I couldn't get the right deal so we kept playing the Grand Ole Opry, although our hearts were not in our work like it was before. They had beat us down to where we knew we had to leave to be happy. We hated to go.

In the meantime we had to make a living from somewhere besides the Opry and we started playing with Joe Frank, who managed Pee Wee King & the Golden West Cowboys. Just like I have written before, Joe Frank was one of the nicest fellows we ever worked with. Pee Wee was the leader of the band but Joe was the real boss and he kept the wolf away from the door. He was a supreme promoter and nothing seemed to stop him. He knew the angles to work out that would draw people in and make us all money. He was indefatigable.

He was always optimistic and I have ridden thousands of miles with him on show dates and he never seemed to get tired. He always had a joke or something to tell and if we didn't draw like we should have, and he lost money on the date, he didn't sull up, but he kept shooting. He did till the very day he died, so I've been told, and it is not hard for me to believe.

Joe would put on big promotions, like playing ball games in outdoor parks and just about anything where he could make some money. He liked good music and singing but he also liked the money well enough to give it priority, because he knew singers and musicians had to eat, and pay rent and their bills, just like other people who have regular jobs where you punch a clock. Rabon and I learned a lot from that man. He made friends easily and he didn't spare anything to help somebody who was down and out. I have seen him go out and round up the little ragged, dirty kids who did not have money to pay to see the show. He would bring them in and treat them like they were kings. In fact, he has sent me out to round them up when he would be busy selling tickets. And it always gave me a warm glow to do this and I will never forget it. To this day, I still meet some of the guys whom I rounded up and they never fail to tell me about it. But I always give Old Joe the credit, because we were working for him and he had the authority. I tell that, too, in his memory.

I don't know exactly how many people Joe Frank made into stars. But he always had a listening ear and when he heard something he liked, he would give the person a break. Eddy Arnold is one of the greats he picked up and started. His sense of judgment was uncanny. He started Ernest Tubb on the way to the big money. Those are two known cases where he picked up someone who only needed a chance, and have made a famous name all around the world. And Joe Frank was as common as an old shoe. He reminded me of the manager of Elvis Presley, Colonel Tom Parker. Joe had that common touch and so does Colonel Parker. A lot of people get the idea that great promoters like Joe and Tom Parker are very sophisticated people who are always brushing the least bit of dust from their clothes. But they are wrong. People like that, who are great, are just like an old plowboy you see on the farm. The only difference is that they know their business deals, and business it is with them, because they live and breathe it.

I will write this one and then I will go to further things and let Joe Frank rest for awhile.

The Texas Drifter* came to Nashville. He was riding a motorcycle and said he

---

*The Texas Drifter's real name was Goebel Reeves, and he is one of the most colorful and legendary performers in country music history. Reeves was a genuine hobo who bummed around the country in the 1920s and 1930s collecting, transmitting, and recording "hobo" songs; he introduced songs like "Hobo's Lullaby," "Railroad Boomer," and "The Hobo and the Cop," and

was broke. He went up to the station and they sent him to Joe Frank. Joe had met him at WLS in Chicago and knew the tricks the Drifter used. He was not a crook but he liked to pull tricks on people. When he came to see Joe, that was all he needed to do. Joe called up the station and got him a program. He drew tremendous mail because he had something I can't define. But he moved the people. He could recite in a passionate way, and become very emotional, and actually cry on his programs. The people felt it and they cried too. Joe knew that the Drifter didn't stay at one place very long but he gave him a job with us playing personals. He could be a drawing card with all that fan mail and Joe knew it. So the Drifter started playing show dates with us and he was a very rare character indeed.

One Sunday we were playing Hopkinsville, Kentucky. We always enjoyed playing that town because the people are so friendly and we always made money. Our schedule was for four shows—two matinees and two night shows. The crowds came in very good, and this day Joe Frank had a contest for the amateurs and that helped to draw real well.

But what I really want to tell the most, about that day, is the way the Texas Drifter acted in the cafe.

When it came lunch time we all gathered in a restaurant across the street from the theater. We usually all sat around and ate together and talked. Most of us were seated at a big table in the back of the cafe. We had given our order and were waiting and talking when we saw the Texas Drifter come in the front door. He needed a shave. We all knew that but it didn't make any difference to us because we were used

claimed that he taught Jimmie Rodgers how to yodel. He recorded widely for such companies as Okeh and Brunswick. Until recently, little had been known about his life, but researcher Fred Hoeptner has discovered the outlines of his life. See Hoeptner's article, with discography, in *Old Time Music* No. 18 (Autumn 1975).—Ed.

to his habits. Sometimes he would dress up and shave and look real classy and sharp, but most of the time he just wore anything he had on when we went by to pick him up. It didn't make any difference to the crowd, either, because he always went over just the same whatever he wore. He always got a big round from the crowd.

Anyway, he came into the cafe and sat down at one of the stools up front. He saw us back at the table and some of us waved to him, but he acted like he didn't want to be bothered, so we just left him alone. Sometimes he was like that. He was a very moody person. But this time he didn't want to be just moody. He had something else on his mind. He ordered a big steak—the best, and highest priced, they had on the menu. The waitress looked at him suspiciously and the Greek owner also gave him some curious looks. But they went on ahead and served him just the same, although he looked like a bum just off a freight train. He went about his eating and never glanced at the rest of us. We learned later that if he had, it would have interfered with his plan or rather joke.

The Greek owner and the waitress who waited on him both kept an apprehensive watch over him as if they were expecting something unusual and that is exactly what they got.

The Drifter ate all the food in front of him and got him a toothpick and seemed to be basking in the fullness of a very good meal, well received. The waitress made out his ticket and asked him if he wanted anything else. He shook his head but he didn't pay the ticket. He just kept sitting there like he just had a view of heaven. I never saw any one person look so serene and happy as he did. But the Greek proprietor and the waitress were becoming more alarmed as the time passed.

Finally he called the owner over and said something in a low voice that we could not hear. The Greek stiffened and began to pound the counter, shouting and fuming in a mixture of the Greek and English languages. We could make out what he said in English.

LEAVING THE OPRY

"If you broke, vy do you haf to get the bestest out of my kitchen?"

He was almost in tears. "Yas, ve can let you wash dishes but it will take a whole week."

The Drifter shrugged his shoulders.

"Then you better call the cops," he said, "It won't be the first time I've ever been in jail."

"NO, no—all I want is ze money—ze money," he kept mumbling as he went to the cash drawer and took out a one dollar bill. He waved it in front of the Drifter's face and kept talking in Greek and English. The Texas Drifter could have bought the whole cafe it he had wanted to. He never drank or smoked or indulged in any kind of fast spending. But he was enjoying this incident to the extreme. The Greek would talk to his waitress and then he would hurry back to where the Drifter was calmly waiting to see what the owner would do.

The Greek got real mad and tried to call the police but he was so incoherent, the police evidently didn't know what he wanted, so he slammed the telephone up and came back to talk to his waitress. He told her to tell the police what had happened and to come down immediately. The whole restaurant was in a fit of laughter. He had a lot of customers and they were all getting a big kick out of what was happening. But the Drifter was a great actor, and he kept pretending he was just a bum. Several of the customers tried to pay his bill but the Greek wanted him locked up in jail.

Joe Frank waited till he saw the waitress start toward the telephone and then he got up and went over to talk with Tex, as we called the Drifter.

Joe paid his bill and agreed to get him out of town if the Greek would only drop the charges. Tex left and went down the street but Joe assured the Greek that he would take good care of the bum because he was an old friend of his. The Greek reluctantly took the money because he knew Joe was our promoter. He shrugged his shoulders.

"Hokay—hokay, but I hate to see one good man suffer because of the bum like that."

We had all enjoyed the act put on by the Texas Drifter but the poor Greek and the waitress were left with nothing but a bundle of nerves.

And the cafe owner and the waitress, to my knowledge, never did know that the "bum" was rich and also a great part of the show we were playing across the street from his cafe.

I finally got a place to land, as they say in show business. I called Raleigh, North Carolina, at WPTF. There was no salary offered but we figured we could make it on personals, as we had been doing at WSM anyway.

So I went by and got Rabon and we both went up to the station to give them a notice of two weeks. We first went to Harry Stone, and we both figured he would welcome the news that we were leaving, but it was an entirely different atmosphere than we expected. He begged us not to leave. We stayed in his office more than an hour and he tried every way he could to keep us there. When he finally realized we were not to be moved, he wanted us to go to see George D. Hay, the "Solemn Old Judge." I told him we had had too much trouble with Judge Hay, and it would not do any good, but he insisted and we went in to see the Judge about ten minutes. He was glad we were leaving, it appeared. He didn't beg us to stay or anything of that sort—just sort of chided us that we would miss the Grand Ole Opry. We both knew we would, because the Opry gets into your blood, but he didn't seem to give a damn whether we sunk or swam. But Harry Stone told us when we left his office that the key was always on the outside. That proved to be a big fallacy, like the Wizard of Oz legend.

But it wound up that we stayed four weeks instead of two, because we had dates booked with Joe Frank and the Golden West Cowboys, and Mr. Stone asked us to stay long enough to play those dates out. We agreed.

But that extra time only got us into more trouble. The Golden West Cowboys worked like hell putting out water. One of their main members almost had a nervous breakdown and he begged us to take him along. He actually cried, and we felt sorry for him and agreed to take him. He was just about on his last legs and he told us he was going to quit anyway.

Well, that's where our troubles began again. When he told Joe Frank he was leaving with us, it made Joe mad, and he paid him off and wouldn't let him play a notice out.

After all this happened, that fellow came to Rabon and me, and asked would it be all right for him to go up to Raleigh and make acquaintances and find places for us to live, etc., so we both had faith in him and told him to go on ahead. We were innocent, and it was a good idea and it would have been if he had done the right thing. But I am getting ahead of myself and will come back to this fellow later on in the following chapters.

We played out our dates with the Golden West Cowboys and prepared to leave the Opry Sept. 11, 1938. That seems a long, long time ago and it is, but when you love a place like we did the Grand Ole Opry it doesn't seem too long.

The Saturday night we left I was really too sick to play for any show. Rabon seemed to feel all right, though, and it seemed he was glad we were moving.

We stored all our furniture and prepared to leave after the last broadcast. It was raining and dismal but we had it planned to leave and it had to be that way.

The last song we sang on the Grand Ole Opry was the fine old gospel song "What Would You Give in Exchange for Your Soul." I don't remember the others, but I *do* remember that one.

David Stone was the announcer on the program and he seemed glad to see that we were leaving, just like Judge Hay.

LEAVING THE OPRY

So after our last program, we packed the cars—there were two of them. Thelma, my wife, who was very faithful, drove our car and our family, and George Peek, our manager, drove his car and carried Rabon and Nola, his wife. We knew we had a long way to go, and it's hard to start a trip when you are feeling like I was feeling, but it had to be done and I braced myself for it. I was all mixed up physically and mentally.

You always hate to leave something you love, and that is the way I felt about leaving Nashville and the Grand Ole Opry. But I don't think a man's a man until he can stand up to it, even though he is all broken up inside. This departure meant we would be a long, long way from home, this time on a permanent stay. It was just something hard to take.

We had been over the same roads before to and from Nashville, but this time it was different. I didn't have any misgivings about leaving the ones who did us wrong, but I hated to leave the institution itself, Nashville, Tennessee, and the Grand Ole Opry.

We had to be in Raleigh for a program on Monday morning. So we had to keep traveling. Over the mountains and down through the valleys, with all the scenic beauty and charm. But it was hard for me to get used to not being on the Grand Ole Opry. I guess if I had given it a thought I would have known that when we got to working over in North Carolina and the surrounding states, that I would partially forget about the Opry and Nashville, but I never did.

It was just like some men I know. They know that beyond any doubt the wife cheats on them, but yet they cannot seem to give her up. I have never been that way about women, but I was about the Grand Ole Opry.

At first I couldn't eat a bite. All I could do was drink whiskey, and it got to where I couldn't even drink, I was so sick. But I toughed it out with the help of the others in the party.

216

LEAVING THE OPRY

When we finally got to Raleigh we checked into a hotel and I tried to get some rest. But it took me several days to get entirely straight.

We began our program on WPTF early Monday morning and then we had another program somewhere around twelve o'clock. So you just had to brace up and take it the best you could.

Misery can hurt you. If I had had more confidence, it would have helped tremendously but I felt like a pioneer, or how I imagine the pioneers did when they started out on new frontiers to make it or not make it. I knew we had been drawing good crowds in that locality but I still felt very forlorn.

We made the first program and it went very well and the other entertainers on the station gathered around to give us the eye and cold, calculative evaluation. It seemed like they expected something superior out of us that they didn't have themselves and wanted to find out what it was they were missing. That always puts me on the spot. We were no different than they were. We were just better known from being on the Grand Ole Opry. Feeling like I was, I would have conceded any of them better than we were.

When we made the noon show, we had a meeting with some of the executives of the station, and I thought that was completely unnecessary. But I was to learn later of the significance of that meeting. The officials didn't talk directly to Rabon and me. They addressed their suggestions and plans to the man we had so graciously allowed to precede us into the station. That all seemed a little strange to me, and also to Rabon, but we didn't say anything to anyone about it but ourselves. And we wondered why. I had made the telephone calls for the job and made all arrangements for the programs, but we didn't register with them on that first meeting, and, for that matter, we never did.

We found it all out later. It was a bizarre thing to happen but the fellow we had let have so many liberties, in going ahead of us to the station had double-crossed

LEAVING THE OPRY

us. He had told so many untruths that we never could get over it.

I will tell that story in the next chapter or two. Now this is the show business for you. You've got to expect to be double-crossed.*

---

*After they left WSM and Nashville, the Delmores formed a stringband to back them up and help them do stage shows. This band, which remained intact for about two years, consisted of Joe Zinkan, string bass; Smiley O'Brien, standard guitar; Chuck Mauldin, fiddle; and Milton Estes, emcee and announcer. Joe Zinkan recalls that the Delmores had hired both him and Estes before they left Nashville, and had hired the other two members in North Carolina. Zinkan had come to Nashville in 1936 on a showboat, played a while, went to WLW in Cincinnati for a year, then returned to Nashville again. He was playing bass for the brothers on the Opry for some months before they left. Zinkan left the band during the brothers' stay at WCHS in Charleston to join Pee Wee King; later he played for a variety of well-known country artists, including Roy Acuff. He works today as a successful Nashville studio session man. Milton Estes, who acted as emcee for the Delmore shows in North Carolina, had been associated with a farm and home noon-hour show at WSM. Chuck Mauldin, the fiddler, was from Kentucky. This band backed the Delmores on a number of their later recordings (see discography).—Ed.

CHAPTER TWENTY

ON TOUR IN NORTH CAROLINA

North Carolina is a pretty big state and the part we were in now was somewhat different from the western part of the state, the mountainous country we knew so well. This was the land of the gib tobacco farmer, and it had an aloofness about it that is hard to understand at first. But all we wanted to do was to make money enough to live on, till we sort of got on our feet. We tried playing the big high schools and we had a hard time. The Monroe Brothers, Bill and Charlie, had done so well over there and had taken so much money out of the schools that the schools had raised their percentage, and we just couldn't make it if we had to pay the high percentage. Bill and Charlie Monroe are two of the finest fellows you will ever hope to know, and it was not their fault, but the schools just were jealous of seeing them make so much money and take it away with them. The principals are mostly the ones who hate to see the cash go out. They want you to play their schools, but they want to tell you also how to run your business like they do the pupils they boss around each school day. And that kind of business simply doesn't work with people who are in the entertainment field to make an honest living. The principal of a high school will put on a local play and take in about half what he would get from a good drawing country and western show but he will be better satisfied with just a little bit of money and a whole lot of satisfied ego.

ON TOUR IN NORTH CAROLINA

Our manager, George Peek, found that out soon after we started playing in North Carolina and he wanted to start booking theaters. We told him it was all right with us. So he started out and found out it was also hard to book the movie houses. Theater managers don't listen to the radio and they don't give a damn, or didn't used to, if they had not heard of you and most of them didn't know or ever had heard of the Delmore Brothers. So we had to show them something to get started. We were not exactly starving, but we were not far from it, so that is the reason Peek persuaded us to try out for the big theater chain, where we could make some real folding money. When he had been given the go-ahead move, he began to work fast. He believed in theaters.

The first man he contacted was a Mr. Hill, the district manager of the big chain circuit. Mr. Hill lived in Greensboro, and George went down several times before he got to see him. Mr. Hill had never heard of us so Peek had to do a lot of fast talking, to get us into one of their poorest paying places. It was Ashboro. Two big independent theaters had all the best movies tied up and, besides this, they were staging bank nights and all sorts of enticements to freeze the little chain house out of business there in Ashboro. George had to book us in between the two biggest nights of the independents. And that was the worst business night the chain house suffered during the entire week. We didn't know this till way, way later, but Mr. Hill thought that was one way of getting rid of a pest who was so persistent as George Peek. He had nothing to lose anyway, since he was not doing any business on that night. So—George came back into Raleigh and told us he had gotten a start with the chain. He didn't tell us how dreary he thought it was, but went about the job with considerable enthusiasm. He ordered the advertising and sent it to the theater and we had trailers made and he sent those also. He was really doing his best.

When we played that little house, there was standing room only, and we thought it was a pretty good start. We thought then we would get the whole circuit. But we thought wrong. We were re-booked into that little old theater. Mr. Hill, the district manager, thought it was some sort of a freak. We played that same theater three times on the same night each week and business increased each time we played it. Then Mr. Hill reluctantly gave us three more weak houses to play to prove to himself that we were genuine and there was nothing like a freak going. But you can't blame him. He had never heard of us, but the people had. We kept playing the high schools and other engagements on the side to help make a living. We had broken all records at the little theater in Ashboro but we didn't know it at the time.

When we played the other three houses it was the same thing. We broke the records again. Now this chain of theaters was very big but after we had broken the attendance records in all those houses we were still not accepted as genuine. Mr. Hill gave us five houses this time and he was still unconvinced. The only thing he knew was money for the company. If you make it you're a king if you don't make it you're a bum.

Well, the same old thing kept happening and finally we were about halfway accepted by the theater chain and got into some of the big houses. And all this time, shows out of New York and other parts of the country were getting big guarantees and playing the plush places without even drawing, and still they kept them on, the big ones, because they knew them, having heard them on the networks. I'll tell you one thing—show business is a toughie but if you can stand it you'll love it. But they really put you through the wringer and if you come out all right you're a winner. But if you ever slip just one little bit, it's the law of the fang and the claw.

But we were getting to make money now, without having to beg the egotistical high school principals for a place to put on a show. We practically abandoned playing schools except in rare instances. And then we stayed in the driver's seat. If they wanted our show they paid the right percentage or they didn't get it at all. Old

ON TOUR IN NORTH CAROLINA

George Peek had a smart idea when he started us to playing the theaters. And there's one very sweet thing about playing theaters. You can always repeat.

We kept breaking the attendance records till they had to agree that the people knew us, and we were making the money. So they finally gave us the circuit of theaters we had wanted for so long. We were still living in Raleigh then, and everything was going smoothly. But the radio station still seemed to think that the fellow we brought over with us from Nashville was our leader. We were willing to accept that because when we would say anything to him, he just laughed and said it was because he came over first and they knew him first. But when there was a memo sent to us, it was always addressed to him. It got pretty tiring, but we never did say anything to the officials at the station till the final day when we got really took. This guy had already put some money in the bank, had bought him a real good car, and was in better shape than he had ever been before. We had all those theaters hooked, and didn't have to worry about a thing, and shouldn't have any worries for a long time—and then up jumped the devil!

We went up one morning to put on our radio program and we didn't have one. That fellow had taken over. He tried to get our band to play with him, but George Peek saw to it that he didn't do that. But he had dealt us a lethal blow. He had put us in bad with the station and gone down to see Mr. Hill and told him a lot of crap about his being the drawing card and so forth and Mr. Hill swallowed it hook, line, and sinker. He called our manager and told us we were on trial for the rest of the dates, and one little hitch and he would take all the houses and give them to this fellow we had befriended when we took him away from Nashville. And you know what? His insidious plan almost worked.

We had to play two towns two days each and the towns were not big enough to support a show like ours, and the weather turned cold on the first one and it rained the two days we played the second one. So we flopped on those two dates and fell way below our regular drawing pull. And in the absence of the fellow, I had to do the emceeing and both the managers of the theaters sent in a bad report on my being the master of ceremonies. So when we got back to Raleigh, we had a letter from Mr. Hill. Or, I should say our manager had the letter, but he showed it to us. Mr. Hill wrote and said we had just one more chance and that was the two-day booking in Wilmington, North Carolina. Rabon and I both boiled over and told Peek to cancel the whole deal. But Peek persisted, and it took two hours of hard persuasion on his part to get us to play Wilmington at all. We finally agreed to play the engagement. And that was one of the best decisions we ever made in our lives.

When we arrived in Wilmington there was a long line of people waiting to get into the theater. That didn't impress us much because we were used to that in the days gone by in that chain of houses. I guess we were all pretty disgusted about what Mr. Hill had written our manager. We didn't hold anything back from the boys who worked with us, because we wanted them to be prepared in case of any development that would affect them in any way. They knew the story as well as we did, and they were sticking to us. They were a fine bunch of guys.

We had good crowds all day and we still didn't think much about it. Mr. Hill had hurt us very deeply when he had issued that ultimatum and still considered it just that. We thought our cause was simply futile, like it had been on the Grand Ole Opry for so long.

The crowds liked our show and we went over big on every performance. We liked them too, and I told them so.

We were playing Wilmington on a flat basis, I forget how much, but we still liked to know how well the manager was liking our show. So when we had finished our last show I went by to talk to the manager. He was a middle-aged man about fifty-five years old and he seemed very friendly to me. I had not met him before. He had stagehands to help us set up our equipment, so I didn't bother to go meet him, as we were playing under strained conditions anyway.

But I knew one thing. We were making him some money, and when I went up to see him he told me we had broken all the records of attendance and he said he had booked big shows out of New York with forty people and he couldn't understand how we did it. He didn't tell me how much money we had taken in and I didn't ask him, but he was might well pleased with it, and he liked our show, too. He said he had been warned that our show was just about all to pieces when we lost our MC. But he told me that if the show was any better then than it was now, he sure would have liked to have seen it. I will never forget that man. He was full of praise about our show and he was not a flattering man. He just said it was the best show that he had ever booked and I asked him if he would tell Mr. Hill.

"I've already told him, when he called me about thirty minutes ago. I gave you boys a good name to him and I also told him that he had been misinformed by somebody about the show being shot by the absence of one man. And I also told him that there were people who came in here today that had never been in this theater before."

He paused a moment and shook his head.

"I just can't understand it myself. I have had many shows in this house but never anything that adds up to this. Oh, by the way, Mr. Hill is coming down here tomorrow to see for himself what has happened. He is completely off balance, too, and he wants to talk to you and find out a few things he doesn't understand."

That suited me fine, for I wanted to talk to Mr. Hill and tell him a few things I thought he ought to know. A thing like that can make you feel mighty good after being let down so quickly without any cause when you are trying to do your best.

When I told the boys and Rabon about it, they all felt mighty good, too. It meant we had another lease on life.

George Peek, our manager, was not with us for this Wilmington date. He had gone to Washington, D.C. to try to book the Warner chain of theaters, which was a pretty big job.

The next day, our business was just as good, if not better than the day before. Everybody was swell to us. Even the mayor of Wilmington come to see us and we were taken out for a ride on the Wilmington River, which is sort of a bay instead of a river. It was on a special yacht. We enjoyed all this immensely. It was an about-face for our little show—from the ridiculous to the sublime.

We didn't usually go out much when we played a town. All the boys played cards for fun backstage. I didn't play because I didn't know how and still don't know much more. But when the boys needed some pop or a sandwich, I would be the one elected to go out for them.

The crowds still kept pouring in and I knew that we were still doing a terrific business. Along about five o'clock in the afternoon I went in to see the manager just for a casual, short visit. He told me we were beating our own record for the day before and were well ahead for a new attendance record. He was simply elated. It was the most business he had ever done, and he didn't mind passing along the credit to us. But not long after I visited him, it started to rain, just a slow steady rain, and the people stopped lining up, for the rain had been too much for them. Many people stayed in the stores close to the theater until they could get in the theater to see the show. I will never forget Wilmington. I can't. Although the rain had stopped our chance of making a new record, we were a happy gang. The boys were playing cards as usual. And some of them wanted a sandwich and a cold drink. So I donned my raincoat and went out to get them. I didn't usually go through the house but, since it was raining, I decided to go out through the lobby and get their sandwiches and drinks. On my way out, I had to pass close to the office and the door was open. I saw Mr. Hill in there and it made me mad. I just walked out like I had not seen him at all.

ON TOUR IN NORTH CAROLINA

When I came back with the order for the boys, I intended to go straight through the lobby and pass the office without stopping. But Mr. Hill came out and was really in a happy mood. He greeted me very warmly. Then he asked me did I know that we had broken all records with our appearance.

"Yes," I said bitterly. "And I don't see how we did it without the famous character you mentioned in your letters to our manager when you were threatening to end our playing days on your circuit."

He was a good talker, and he gave me a lot of soft soap, and finally I wound up telling him all about the guy who had tried to wreck our whole North Carolina reputation. He told me he would get all the other houses they were affiliated with, and would give us the entire circuit to play over, if we wanted it. Our manager would have jumped at all this. But I made a list of the houses I thought we could draw in, and it was exactly twelve. He looked a little disappointed. But I wanted to get out of his influence, for I have never trusted anyone who makes snap judgments without consideration. And he had believed that fellow who betrayed us, and put us in a state of confusion without a chance. I didn't feel stuck up (Thank God I never have) because we had broken those records.

There's one more town we played that I will tell about and then I will continue on, and go into other areas of people and country. The town I mean is Winston-Salem, in the same state—the fine old state of North Carolina. We were still living in Raleigh, but we were playing out of there and seldom had time to go downtown. And we were not interested in any of the radio stations anyway, since our tragic experience on the one we had been booted off. Things went nice for us after the Wilmington date. And Mr. Hill kept adding some really good places for us and slipping them in between our other dates. One was Asheville. Another Winston-Salem. That's the one I will tell about because it is the typical story of our fantastic tour throughout that part of the country.

Peek had it booked on a flat rate because they would not pay a percentage on it. That theater was one of the largest and best on the whole circuit.

We moved from Raleigh to Winston-Salem on New Year's Eve, December 31, 1938. It was a central location for a lot of engagements we had to play. On New Year's Day I went up to see the theater manager, and he was already in a bad mood because he had bet on Duke in the Rose Bowl, and Duke had lost to Southern California in the last few seconds of the game, 7 to 3. He was a very frank fellow and he said what was on his mind. Although he was not feeling too well, he welcomed me into his office.

"I don't own this theater, but I've managed it for twenty-five years," he said,"and this is the first time I have ever played an act that is as unknown as yours is." He looked at me straight in the eye when he said that. I guess he wanted to see how it would register with me. It didn't affect me one bit.

"And you are not the first theater manager who has told me that, and if you will do your part in the advertising I believe we will draw for you."

He shook his head and looked down at his desk. Then he took out a pen or pencil, I forget which. He reached for a little memo pad and looked at me. He looked like a trapped animal with still some fight left.

"All I want you to do is tell me what to do, and I will do it to the letter, but you still won't draw in this house. I don't mind telling you that I fought like hell to keep you out. But they overruled me and here you are, and since you're in, I will do everything in my power to draw a crowd, so I can laugh right in their faces down in Charlotte when you come in here and flop. You go ahead and tell me what to do." He began tapping his little memo pad.

"Well, the music on your trailer is not the kind we play, so run one of our records on your sound track to replace it. And put ads in the newspapers about two weeks before we play. Just put one or two ads at first and then the week we play put one in every day. Tell them to put cuts in the last three days and make it strictly corny as possible, with bales of hay and country bumpkins, with overalls on and so forth. And the day we play, arrange for a live, in person broadcast at the station you patronize the most. That will be all."

He had written everything I told him down on the little pad. When I left he got up and shook hands with me.

"Now don't think for one moment that I have anything personally against you, or any of your boys, because I don't know them. And I hope you draw because I have taken a liking to you, but I know you won't do any business here."

I left that man with an entirely different idea. We had been underdogs so many times that I was used to it. I had an inside feeling that he was away out in left field or away out on Cloud 9. I told my wife and Rabon what he said, but I didn't tell the boys because anything like that always made them feel depressed. The manager of an artist never tells his star what people say behind their back, because if he did he would always be the victim of having an unhappy heart to console, and no manager wants that. He has worries enough without adding more.

We played several dates prior to this engagement in Winston-Salem. But they were all miles away from that town, up in Virginia, and to some of the towns far away from Winston-Salem. The time passed pretty rapidly before we were to play Winston-Salem. So it finally came around and the fatal day was at hand. I still had high hopes, but I wondered if the manager would do like he said and advertise us like I told him. Now that advertising deal is a very important one. You wouldn't think that Coca-Cola would have to advertise at all because it is so popular. But just look at the billboards along the highways and listen to the radio programs and watch television and you will understand how those people feel about advertising. You have to keep on doing it till the people begin to think that it is the very best and the same goes with entertainers. That's why the old timers in show business always say you are slipping when you begin to believe your own publicity. And that is 100 percent correct.

But the man in Winston-Salem had done exactly what he said he would, and now it was up to us to show him up.

It was on Saturday when we played his house. We were scheduled to play five shows and we didn't have much time on our hands. He had made arrangements for the radio broadcast, and between shows we put on a thirty-minute show over that medium.

Long lines of people, our friends and customers, were waiting for the first show, and they were still in line when we played the last show. I didn't bother to go up to the manager's office because I didn't have the time in the first place and I didn't care about talking to him anyway. So we just went ahead and played his house like a bunch of field hands. We were enthusiastic because we thought we were proving him wrong. That is a great feeling to have. We didn't know or care what the attendance record was, but we knew we weren't flopping like he said we would. Although we were playing it on a flat rate, we still felt there was a challenge and we felt like we were overcoming it in a very convincing way.

It was nearly time for the last show when the manager came back with our pay.

He was the most forlorn-looking fellow I believe I have ever seen. That was the first time I had seen him since I visited him on the first of the year. As he walked backstage, he beckoned me into one of the dressing rooms, where there was no one but he and I.

I thought he would be a happy man, but he was anything but that. As he counted out the money to me, he didn't say one word. But when he got through he gave me a real hearty handshake and there were tears in his eyes.

"Your show has broken all records of any kind I have ever had in this theater, and I hope you will accept my sincerest apology for under-rating you right from the very start. I would like to meet the rest of your show. You have a fine outfit. It has pleased the crowds better than anything we have ever had before, and I have had shows out of New York, Chicago, and big time places and had some mighty good crowds, but this, today, beats any thing I have ever seen before. I can't understand why you draw so well."

I took him out to meet the rest of the boys and he congratulated each one personally. The compliments he made that day still ring in my ears.

He was a good man who could admit he was wrong and that is a hard thing to do. I hate to do it myself. But if a man can, he, to my way of thinking, has character beyond the ordinary person. Now this man could have lied to me and I would have never known the difference, because we were playing on a flat rate, and I didn't get to see the receipts, but he didn't and I admire him to this day for that. He just didn't listen to the radio and records, and he didn't bother to, for that was not part of his job. But if we had had just a slight bit of acting in some movie he would have understood better because all theater managers read those movie trade journals and watch for the credits on the screen when they see a new picture.

Anyway, we were a pretty happy bunch of guys when he came back and acted like he did. I will never forget Winston-Salem because it proved something to me.

We lived in Greenville, South Carolina, for a short while and I think it has to be mentioned to keep the trend of our sojourn around the country in the perspective that will enable the reader to keep the trend of how we had to go when we lived just like a gang of gypsies while on the road trying to make a living. It was a really hard lift and the odds seemed to be always against us, but we got through it.

It seemed that we were always the underdogs. The thought never dawned on me till I started writing this book, but you can peruse the pages of this account and you will come up with the same answer, or as I should say, conclusion. Some people get the breaks and some don't. That is the firm conclusion I have come into since I have a perspective and evaluated the things that happened. I hope you will excuse me for inserting my personal grievances and opinions, but I can't help it because it is the way I have always been. And remember I have always been superstitious and I guess I always will be.

In this account, I cannot praise George Peek, our manager, too much, because if it hadn't been for him, I guess we would have starved or been run out of the show business because you have to have a business manager.

CHAPTER TWENTY-ONE
THE GREENVILLE DAYS

Peek had been trying to get us a radio set-up ever since we had that misfortune in Raleigh. He went down to Greenville, South Carolina, and got us a sponsor on WFBC. We were following the trail of the Monroe Brothers, for they had had that same sponsor, Mrs. Gillespie of the Gillespie Tire Co. That proved to be a very good move while we were waiting for the Warner decision to accept us on their chain.

There was a lot of good playing dates in that territory. There were schools, big schools, and Peek had thought out a way to meet their excessive rates on the bookings. His plan was amazing. If he went in to book a school, he would book it just like they wanted it and on their own terms. I thought at first it was just a fraudulent figment of his mind because Peek was a high-pressure man, but I found out later that it worked good for everybody concerned. If the principal wanted to book us 50-50, Peek would book us in, but he had a stipulation. He would not argue with them. Be would just add a few of the costs of the show to the entire budget and still give them 50-50 and we would come out just the same as if he had the date on a 70-30 or 75-25 basis. The way he did it was like this: If they wanted a high percentage he would add advertising costs and traveling costs on the total and it would come out the same as if we had the date booked at our own level. It was just a matter of trading, but the principals didn't know it, and it made them happy to have their own way. That way he knocked out the percentage they originally wanted, but he satisfied their ego, and everybody was happy and naive in their conceptions, because the show business is a very strange thing, even to people who have been in it for years. There are tricks to every trade, but I don't believe there are any that can beat the show business. You have got to be resourceful when the chips are down or you won't go anywhere.

So we moved to Greenville, South Carolina, and we lived there for about three or four months. We enjoyed our stay there very much and got along real well. But we couldn't stay in one place very long because we would play the territory out. That is, we would run out of show dates to play. We met some very interesting people when we were there.

Doc Schneider & His Texans were on the station. He had a good band, and we had heard of him before. Doc was a business man and he had a good sponsor—Coca-Cola. They played show dates just like we did, but they seldom had a good crowd. But his commercial for the soft drink kept him going along very good financially. We could have used a sponsor like that, for the tire company didn't pay very much. They were a lot smaller than Coca-Cola. But they were a very good sponsor. Mrs. Gillespie was very cooperative in anything we tried.

Doc and his Texans had been broadcasting on the Mexican radio stations just over the border in Mexico just across the Rio Grande from Texas. And they had a real wonderful western swing band. They had played all over the United States in some of the biggest theaters. But they didn't have much of a following down around Greenville. They played the schools and the theaters, and when the Doc learned what we had taken in he was amazed. It was unbelievable to him. We would double and triple their take at the door and he couldn't understand it all. He was a very frank person and we learned to like him and all his band. At first, they were not so friendly but after they got to know us they were real swell folks. Doc and his wife would come to our house and visit and we always enjoyed their company. I remember my father and mother were visiting us one time when they came, and he took a great liking to my father and my father liked him very much also.

THE GREENVILLE DAYS

We were still playing the Wilby-Kinsey circuit of theaters and we had moved down to Greenville to finish out our dates down that way. We all would have liked to have stayed there a while longer but we moved on.

When you're on tour like we were, you never know what people you might meet or come in contact with. But we tried to be friendly to everybody in the business, whether they played good or bad. Some of those we met later turned into great stars in the country and western field.

I remember a group who were working for a patent medicine, and they came on the air for a whole hour. Their program lasted till it was time for our show. And they always stayed to watch us when we went on the air. They were real youngsters mostly, but two of the boys were pretty good size. These two boys were the main ones who watched our radio program. And they turned out to be two of the nation's top guitarists in the country field. They made records with some of the great names like Hank Williams, Red Foley, and lots more I can't mention here. They are known as Zeke Turner and Zeb Turner. Zeke made a lot of records with Rabon and myself. You could just tell him and show him how a run was made, and he could play it without rehearsing and be immediately ready for a record session. They were very valuable to a lot of musicians when they needed someone to play something without taking up too much time. And on record sessions there is a limit to the time you may take up. It's the union rules and laws, so you have to get up and go in a hurry if you don't want to run into overtime.

We played all the theaters and schools we thought would pay off and then we had to go on tour again. It was seldom we ever did get to stay in one place very long. Just about the time I got used to the people and began making some friends we had to leave. Our expenses were too much to linger in one place too long. Greenville is close to the North Carolina line, and there are mountains up to the north. We played Brevard, North Carolina, and it is in the mountains. We played the courthouse there, and it was a cold, snowy day and we didn't expect to take in much at the door, but the people came out of the hills and mountains in droves and we had a real good time there. Those kind of people like music.*

---

*According to one outline Alton prepared, he had at one time planned to include in this chapter the following subjects: "The Dixon Brothers—Homer Sherrill and the Indians of mysterious source." Nothing about these subjects appears here or in any other part of the manuscript. The Dixon Brothers were well known singers in the 1930s, and in the mid-1930s were broadcasting over WBT in Charlotte, North Carolina. Homer Sherrill has recently gained fame touring with banjoist Snuffy Jenkins.—Ed.

CHAPTER TWENTY-TWO
ROAMING

When we left Greenville, I was feeling worse than hell. The others had already gone ahead to Winston-Salem, where we were to live for several weeks, and that was the central headquarters we played out from.

The reason I was feeling bad was mostly worry. There we had a band to support and our families, and we had to make money. And it costs plenty to live on the road and also take your family along. We were just like a gang of gypsies, except we were always wondering if we had gone over good enough to merit more bookings. Just like I said earlier—if you draw you're a king and if you don't, you're a bum. That kind of thing can get on your nerves. We played all the theaters around Winston-Salem and then we had to hit the trail again. The only person I knew there was Roy Hall. Roy composed the song, "Please Come Back Little Pal" that Roy Acuff made such a big hit with. Roy and his band were working out of Winston-Salem at the time, and anytime we needed to go on the air, all we had to do was go up and play on his program. We didn't even have to tell him. But that was the way it was in those days. You were lucky if you weren't starving and people still hadn't really accepted hill-billy music like they do today. Roy Hall was a nice fellow and a good business-man, too.

While we were in Winston-Salem we played Roanoke, Virginia, and that was another cold day. We like to have frozen while we were going on that trip. And after that, we all had colds. But we liked Roanoke very much and decided to make that our headquarters for a while. Peek had booked our show in some of the Warner Brothers theaters on a tryout. That is the way it always was—tryouts, tryouts, and then more tryouts. Peek showed the Warner people what we had done down in North and South Carolina and Georgia, but they still had to be shown again. That's what kept us on pins and needles. But we always seemed to make good on long chances.

So after Winston-Salem, we headed for Roanoke to continue our dates in the Shenandoah Valley. When we left for Roanoke it was the beginning of a wonderful experience. Those were the best days of our, entire road trip. We didn't know it then, but we found out as we traveled along that we liked it better every day. It was truly wonderful country, and we were more relaxed than at any other time since we had started out from Nashville.

When we left Roanoke we settled down in Harrisonburg, Virginia, and we also enjoyed that town a whole lot. The people were really nice to us and we had shows almost every night.

One engagement was at Elkins, West Virginia, and we had to cross the George Washington National Forest. It was mountainous country, with beautiful forests. We didn't have much time to look at things like that, but they were so impressive we just had to do some looking. I guess it was the country coming out of us, for we were all country boys. As we were going to Elkins, the weather was fine but after we had played the theater the weather turned cold and it started to snow and sleet. We were warned about crossing the mountains but we were all young, and we didn't mind it so bad till we got to it. The windshield began to freeze up and Joe Zinkan, who was riding up front with me, had to keep clearing the windshield and he was a great help. But it was a rough go and it was something that you get tired of if you were driving. And I was tired. But there was one thing I will never forget about that trip. I saw my first real wild bear. I had seen them in cages and in zoos but this was the real thing. There he stood, about the size of a calf, out in the snow-covered forest, and he gave me the impression that he was the king, because we didn't excite him a bit. But I would have hated to have had to stop there in his domain. Fortunately we kept on going and he didn't seem to worry about following us, and that made us all very happy. But he did give us a big thrill.

After we left Harrisonburg we went to Frederick, Maryland, still playing the Warner chain of houses. We had already played many of them and they were watching us with careful eyes. There was a lot in store for us if we kept on drawing. We had broken several records on their circuit, and they seemed very much more impressed than the circuit down in the Carolinas.

There was a movie in store for us if we kept on going. This was the big time and we did all we could to keep up with it. We topped such big time acts as Milton Berle and the Mills Brothers and several more that I have now forgotten. We were a puzzle to the Warner officials, just like we were down in the Wilby-Kinsey chain, but they didn't have to be so convinced as they were down there. They had never heard of us either, but they kept on giving us some of their best houses and that was good for everybody concerned.

Those chain circuits really give you the bang and inch you up like a worm crawling to get out of a tight place. Warners gave us Frederick as our initial boost for the big finale. If we drew there, we would be eligible for the competition on up the line and so forth. And we had so much confidence in our show that we moved to Frederick before we played it.

They booked us two days there and we drew real good crowds. We broke a record for door attendance and we were rolling on toward the good things in the Warner chest of treasures.

We had rented a hotel suite for ourselves and the boys didn't have any trouble getting apartments for themselves so we settled down in Frederick for a good and happy stay. It was a quaint place and very historical. Francis Scott Key, the composer of the "Star Spangled Banner," was the chief interest to us, as we surveyed the old historical town from end to end. And Barbara Fritchie was another famous person whose home was there in Frederick. It was some town.

My wife, Thelma, and our two children, Billie Anne and Norma Gail, stayed in the hotel all the time we were in Frederick. We couldn't find an apartment as good as the hotel suite for anything like the price we were paying for the place we had. We only had to pay fifty dollars a month for it and the apartments with children allowed were higher in price and not near as good. That shows how prices change. But it was the nicest place we were able to find while we were on tour.

George Peek, our manager, was always trying to get us ahead and he made frequent trips to Washington, trying to get us an audition on some of the network programs. We thought it would be nice if we got a program on the networks, as it would have helped our drawing power. They had one NBC station and one CBS station there, but Peek couldn't get us an audition because the men wouldn't even see him. But he was so persistent that he finally got us an audition on the NBC station, WRC. We didn't take it too seriously, because we didn't think we would be good enough for the networks. He planned the audition on a Saturday morning, when we didn't have a show date. So we all loaded up in my car and took off to Washington, which is not far from Frederick. We were not in an enthusiastic mood at all, for we hadn't been on a regular radio program since we left WSM. But, mostly to please Peek, we went on anyhow. He had left a couple hours before we had to be there, so he could talk to the manager of the station. When we got to the station, we found a parking lot and unloaded our instruments and headed for the audition. When we got there, the girl receptionist looked like she was seeing someone from outer space. She didn't know anything about the audition or much of anything else it seemed to us. So we all got madder than a wet hen. When we asked her if there was a manager for the station she looked even more surprised.

"Oh, yes," she said very sweetly, with a touch of sarcasm, "but he's up in his suite of offices with some fellow talking business."

When she said that I almost blew my top. She just shrugged her shoulders and looked like a little dumbbell. She was trying to be nice to some hicks who had just drifted in without an engagement. At least that was our impression. We didn't know what to do, so we started to leave. But she stopped us.

"I'm sorry but I think there has been a terrible mix-up, but if you want to wait in one of our studios, I will take you back and you can relax there."

Although she had us all hopping mad, I told the boys we just as well go on back and wait for the manager and give him a good cussing, and then we would let Peek have it when we saw him back in Frederick. So we waited about an hour before we heard from anyone at all. We were beginning really to get into a stew when the most rewarding thing happened. It was a great opportunity and we almost blew it.

There was absolutely no one else around that radio station but the girl and we were simply bewildered. It looked like to us there ought to be something going on, even on Saturday, at a network outlet like that. But there wasn't. We waited with a smoldering anger that had us all upset. The boys in the band were as anxious as we were, and we kept them posted on things when they didn't go right as we thought they would. I believe we were the first ones that made this a practice. They didn't get as much of the till as we did, but they knew what they could expect regularly, each week, and they had no responsibility except to play the shows we had booked.

I began to think I could not hold them anymore when suddenly we heard a commotion outside and then things began to happen.

Peek was the first to come into the studio and he was all excited. There were several men with him, and he brought each one into the studio and introduced them to us. They were all officials—the station manager, the program director, the publicity director, and the whole works all thrown in together. Peek had done a great selling job, we thought.

We all felt a whole lot better but we hadn't prepared a program for the audition. I felt a little silly about that, for usually I was way ahead of anything like that. I always believed in punctuality, especially in our professional work. So I thought I had been caught with my pants down in this case. But all the fellows were so friendly that I somehow felt at home. That is the way it always is. You think someone is a big shot till you get to know him. Then you don't feel like that about him at all.

I asked them what they wanted us to do on the audition, and Peek had told them so much about our show, which was thirty-three minutes long, and they wanted us to do exactly what we did on the stage. The idea didn't appeal to me but I consented to do it anyway, since we all knew the routine so well and then all we had to do was tune up our musical instruments. That didn't take too long and we went into the show routine. We told the jokes we used and every bit of the show we did just like we were putting it on, on the stage. I didn't know whether they would like it or not but from what I could see on the outside, they liked it very much. They had left us alone in the studio and were listening on the loud speakers outside the studio. We finally got through with the audition and the manager of the station was the first one through the door. He was all excited and I could tell he was sincere.

"You boys have the best band of this kind I have ever listened to. You are even better than the Sons of the Pioneers"—which was conceded to be tops in the country and western field—"I could listen to that show over and over and never get tired."

Those words brought joy to my heart and also to the hearts of the rest of the boys. At last we were to have our own network program! I didn't know hardly how to answer him but I blurted out some kind of thanks and the rest of the boys did likewise. All the guys gathered around to congratulate us. I was surprised to see the girl we had first met at the reception desk in the crowd. She came up and complimented me and all the boys, but now she looked very sweet and her professionality had gone down the drain. She knew we had made it because she told us as much.

"I am sure glad that I will be seeing you boys more, and thrilled to get to listen to your wonderful music and singing."

All of us were flabbergasted. What had started out to be an annoying nightmare had suddenly turned out the other way. We gathered up our instruments and hurried out to our car. George Peek knew what to do the rest of the way. On our way back to Frederick, we all were very delighted. We could not believe what had happened but we all knew we were in.

When Peek came back from Washington he had good news. It was Saturday, and they didn't have time to sign any contracts, but he had talked to the manager and they had made a tentative agreement. We would be on the network for thirty minutes, four days a week, at a good salary for all of us. Our troubles seemed to be over and good times were knocking at our door. Peek said the manager of the networks and the station was very jubilant over being able to get us. He seemed to think it was a big honor for him and we were to get the best of publicity he could possible give to any act. That made us all very happy and we celebrated the event to the hilt. But I thought of something we should do. I decided that we should join the musicians union. We found that there was a little union at Hagerstown, Maryland. It would only cost us five dollars each and then we would be in good shape to go on the network. We all felt that it would be absurd to go on a show like that without being in proper proportion. So we decided to get down to Hagerstown Sunday morning and see if we could join before Peek went in to Washington Monday to sign the contract with the manager. So we drove down to Hagerstown the next morning, which was Sunday, and didn't have a bit of trouble joining our first musicians union. We were all musicians except Peek, and he got a booker's card to prove he was union also. Then we thought everything was wrapped up in a nice package with a blue ribbon on it. We had joined the union, we had a network program and could play anywhere we liked.

We were still playing the Warner Brothers' theaters and the next day, being Monday, we had an engagement at the Warner house in Orange, Virginia. But we felt like playing the one-night stands would soon be over for us, for we expected to be booked at least a week at a time in some of the biggest theaters in the country after we got known on the network programs. It was really a glorious feeling. For we never did feel like we were big time, although we consistently broke the records in attendance at theaters easily recognized as big time.

We had a record attendance at Orange, but that didn't thrill us too much, for we were waiting for Peek to show up. He had gone to Washington to sign the contracts with the authorities at the NBC headquarters. We never faltered in our show. We put it on just like we always had, and with a little more enthusiasm than usual. We were booked for four shows in Orange—two afternoon matinees and two night shows. We put on the first show and then we waited for Peek, but he didn't show up. We put on the second matinee and began to have the jitters. What was the matter with George Peek, our manager? That is what we were all thinking. I was out reading in my car when I saw Peek park up the street. He got out of his car real slowly, like a sick man. He was about a half a block away but I could see the expression on his face and I thought he was ill. He started down toward the theater and it seemed like his face was a mile long. I knew that something was wrong. But I didn't expect to hear what he said when he came up to my car. I waited. When he got to my car, he didn't say one word but climbed slowly into the front seat beside me. Then he sighed.

"Where are the other boys?" he said, but he was not looking at me. He seemed like someone in a trance.

"I don't know. They are somewhere around here pretty close, but I don't know where. Now, George, tell me what's wrong."

He sighed again. And when he started to talk, his voice was very thin and there was a note of despair that was very apparent. He still didn't look at me as he began to tell me what had happened.

"Well, in the first place we should not have joined that union yesterday over in Hagerstown. The whole deal is off with the network. I don't believe I have ever seen anyone so upset as that manager was when I told him what we had done. He said he wished he had told me not to join the union, because the union didn't recognize us as musicians, and he could have got by with them all right if we just had not joined. But he said now, we would have to wait at least six months before we could play and then it would be rough. The union recognizes us as legitimate members now, but before they did not, and that is where we cut our own throats."

I could not believe what he was telling me was true at all. I wanted to think it some kind of a bad dream that would soon vanish and we would resume our original status of having a bright future. But it would not pass. Peek didn't want Rabon and the other boys to know what had happened till we had finished our last show. But I told him that they could tell something was wrong, just by the way he looked.

"I know I could tell by the way you looked, and they have as much or more sense than I have. Some way I think they all have more judgment than I do because they wouldn't be out of a program if it hadn't have been my bright idea." With that I guess I began to look like Peek and I knew they would know. When we told the boys, they took it in stride lots more than Peek and myself. In a way, they didn't have as much at stake as we did, because they left all the thinking up to us. They were disappointed, of course, but they had more reserve at the moment than we did. They just seemed to depend on Peek and myself and that everything would turn out all right anyhow. It sure made both of us feel better when they took it like that without any "I told you so" remarks.

Peek went back to Washington in a few days and got some more Warner time for us. That is, he booked several more houses. The Warner people were still very much impressed with us and they had one house that was to determine whether we got the whole circuit and made a movie or would be out of the Warner chain for good. And you know what? That town was Hagerstown, Maryland, where we had joined the union.

When we were to play Hagerstown, Peek went in to inspect the theater, as he always did, and didn't get along with the manager. We had it booked for two days and it was to be the final tryout. But there was something Peek didn't know. The manager of that theater was a son-in-law of one of the big shots in the Warner chain and had been deposed because he got out of line. He resented managing the Hagerstown house after he had been one of the wheels in Washington. And he still had influence with his wife's dad. When we played the date we had good crowds but it was below our standard and Peek was not satisfied. We were supposed to beat the record of the Mills Brothers if we got any more Warner work, and Peek went to the newspapers and found out that this manager had advertised the Mills Brothers two weeks more than he did us. They didn't beat us much but that was enough and Peek went back to Washington with the evidence he had accumulated but it didn't do any good. The other big boys went along with the manager's father-in-law and we got the gate. There are heartbreaks to bear in the show business. You have them but you don't give up. That's standard.

CHAPTER TWENTY-THREE
WASHINGTON DAYS

After we got kicked off the Warner circuit, we moved to Washington and played some independent houses there. We still drew real good and kept breaking records. Mostly, though, we played the suburban houses owned by a man named Sydney Lusk or Lust, I forget which, but we did real good business and he liked our act very much. We played Bethesda, Arlington, Silver Spring, and all around the District of Columbia. Peek kept trying to do something about radio that we missed by joining the union, but the man at NBC couldn't do anything, so after trying for a long time, he finally gave up and contacted CBS. It was the same thing over again for an audition. But Peek didn't give up easily. He finally got their manager in need of someone to drive him somewhere and George agreed to drive him. That got us the audition and we made good with CBS. I remember his name. It was Lloyd Dennis and he was a great guy. We told him what our trouble was with the union, but after he heard us play and sing he said he would take a chance on getting us on anyway. And he did. But he couldn't do any good. He got real firm with Mr. Hayden, the head of the union there in Washington. He called Mr. Hayden on the phone and we heard what he said.

"Now I want these fellows on my station and also the network. And they won't knock your boys out of any work at all." He waited a moment and then he said: "If you can send me five guys who can play and sing like these fellows, I will gladly employ them. Just send them up here, for I need something like this. If you can, I'll tell these fellows to leave and hire your men. Now I think that's a fair proposition, don't you?" He waited a moment to listen to the telephone, and then he got real angry.

"I knew you couldn't do it and you never will be able to do it. These fellows have what I want and you can't supply it and yet you dictate to me and tell me it is all out of order. If that's the way you operate, I don't want any part of it and I will do anything in my power against you." With that said, he hung up the telephone and looked down at his desk.

He was in a deep study and we didn't say a word. As busy as that man was, he took at least four or five minutes in deep concentration. He had something on his mind. Suddenly he looked up and smiled.

"I'll tell you what we'll do. We'll just make a transcription, and you boys keep on playing around here till you have played your dates out. But if you leave town, let me have your address so I can write you. Because I can sell this program, and then Mr. Hayden or anybody else can't keep you from working that way."

So we made the transcription for him, and after we finished he wanted another one so he would have a variety, and we made that one also. He announced the program and did a really fine job. It was an easy-going program with a tempo that would not irritate the worst of critics of hillbilly music. It was really a good thing but somehow we didn't have much faith that we could break the union barrier. He had our address there, but I never did go back to see him.

The union tried to make us quit playing the theaters around. They claimed we were invading their territory. But they didn't have anybody who had a show that played the houses like we did. We all felt like they were a bunch of schemers, and they sure did act like it. When we didn't have a date and I had some time on my hands, I would go down to the union and try to persuade Mr. Hayden to let us have the CBS program we had auditioned for but he was a tough person to deal with. He didn't even want to talk to me. He chewed tobacco and he used a spittoon. There was one in every room in the union headquarters just for him. When I would pin him down on something he would leave the room and go to another to get rid of me, but I would follow him. He never did insult me, but he let me know in no un-certain terms that he wanted me to leave. He knew he was wrong but he couldn't do anything about it. He told me that all he could say was that what we were trying to do was against union laws. And then he would take a big chew of tobacco and quit talking. It was a case of discrimination, the worst kind, and we were the innocent victims. If we had been taking work away from anybody, I would have been the first to recognize his position and the union position, but I just didn't get it, the way they figured it. It was something absurd and incomprehensible to me and also to Peek and the boys—that old man chewing his tobacco and going from room to room just to get rid of me to keep his men from being out of work on account of us when they couldn't even do the job themselves. It made me feel limp and numb without any tangible bit of excuse on the union's part. I was raised on the farm and I have seen hogs, after they had eaten all they could possibly hold, get up in the trough and lay in the slop so the other hogs could not get anything to eat. That is the only way I can express myself about the union in Washington in those days. It may be better now. But it certainly was bad then.

I finally gave up with Mr. Hayden and we kept on playing show dates in theaters. It was a wonderful stay there in Washington, and Thelma and our two little girls got a big kick out of seeing things and places they would never had seen had we never played in Washington. And when we would be gone out of town, they would go to Baltimore to see the sights up there and attend some of the big time acts performing on the stage. We never did get the status of some of the big time acts, whom we had beaten all to pieces in attendance. We were just plain hill-billies in those days. That is how we were regarded. But if it were today it would be a lot different.

Peek got us a chance to play in the Village Barn in New York City, but they didn't offer us enough money to keep going and we didn't accept it. But, looking back now, it would have been a great thing, for we could have made some very good connections there.

We played the eastern shore of Maryland and Delaware while we were stationed in Washington. It was a great experience and we drew good business. And we went deep sea fishing while we were over there. I like that part of the country very much and it gave me always the air of freshness because it is so close to the ocean. That was one experience I'll never forget.

The eastern shore is a level land of plenty and the people there are really wonderful. They treated us better and beyond our fondest expectations. I believe I could live there and be happy ever after. But we only had a week to play there and then we had to get going again. But pleasant memories of that part of the country will always linger with me, for it is a country resembling the western plains country. The moon and the stars seem brighter there than most any other place we had traveled. We stayed at a hotel and made all of our dates out of that town. I forget what the name of the town was, but it was centrally located and that is the reason we made it our headquarters. But the people there went to bed with the chickens and we always had to have a snack to eat after we had got through with the show. So we found a cafe that would serve the kind of food we liked and we would always go to that place when we had finished a show. We all liked the owner of the cafe and, when he was not busy, he would come and sit down at our table and talk to us while we were eating. He had also been to every show that we put on, for he didn't mind spending money for what he liked, and he liked our show. He never came backstage, but we knew he was there because we could see his car parked somewhere near the theater.

We had one day without an engagement and we stopped by his cafe for a late snack. He came over as usual and sat down with us. The talk got around to what we would do the next day and some one of us mentioned a desire to go deep sea fishing. The cafe man told us he was going to take the day off, too, and he would be glad to have us go deep sea fishing with him. I don't know, but I still believe that he took the day off on our account. You meet people like that when you are in the show business. That is what makes it so wonderful. It's not that you are a moocher, but once in a while you get a glimpse of sincerity and that makes you appreciate everything you have gone through to get back to the real thing. Most people are good fans but most of them are big flatterers also. They don't mean it to be that way but it is the only way they know to get closer. Anyway, we went deep sea fishing with the restaurant owner and I'll never forget it.

He had a big yacht at Lewis, Delaware, and we were there bright and early the next morning. We left the shore at nine o'clock and stayed out till three in the afternoon. I asked the old captain how far we were from land because I couldn't see the shore anymore. He said about twelve miles and the waves were really rolling and rocking. We all took some beer with us to keep from getting seasick. We took a carton each and when we got out to the fishing area and anchored, the first thing I did was to take me out a bottle of beer and sip on it. I didn't do any good fishing, but kept sipping on the beer and it didn't worry me any at all. The rest of the boys were too busy catching fish to drink their beer and they gave most of it to me. We were out on a "loo out" anyway and it didn't make any difference but we never drank on our shows. I didn't allow it. But the boys we had in the show didn't drink much anyhow. So I didn't have to worry about them at all on the show dates.

One of the boys, Joe Zinkan, was catching more than a fish a minute. He was the champion and he didn't even think of drinking a beer. He was a sensation. But he didn't last long. He got sick and had to go lie down on the couch in the cabin. But that didn't do him any good. He was seasick. He made a fast path from the couch to the outside so he could vomit. Everybody did all they could for him but he still remained seasick. He was white as a sheet and couldn't stop regurgitating. The owner of the yacht came down and got some kind of smelling salts or something to help him but it didn't do any good. We all told Joe we would be glad to go back to the mainland so he would feel better but he wouldn't agree. He was a fellow with a lot of grit. We had been fishing only about an hour and he told us he didn't want to spoil the fun for us. So he elected to suffer it out. When we found out he was not going to be able to fish anymore, the old captain gave me his station because I hadn't caught any fish at all—not one. I tried my own line, and it didn't work and the captain gave me Joe's line to see if that would help out any. But still I could not catch anything. Everybody was having good luck but me. But I was having a wonderful time, although I hated to see Joe sick as he was. For instance: Rabon caught a flying fish and that seemed to be a rare event, for the old captain called the owner down and they anchored the elusive fish for Rabon. It had sailed over the yacht four or five times when the captain and the owner intervened. It didn't seem to fly, it just glided, but it was a sight to see! Rabon and Chuck and Smiley* caught sharks and all kinds of fish, including the crazy-looking flounders. There were all kinds of fish in that ocean but they wouldn't get on my hook. I was just a forlorn fisherman looking for a fish. When any of the boys would catch a shark, the old captain would not keep it but he would get us to help him and he would cut out its liver and throw it back to the other sharks. He told us he had seen several seamen killed by them and he had an intense hatred for them and that was his way of getting even with them. I learned later that the shark's liver is also valuable for its oil, so the old captain was getting a double reward for his hatred of the sea predators.

The day rolled on and on, and Joe was still sick and I still hadn't caught any fish. It was just a big joke to me. I had been anxious at first when I didn't have luck but it was no use, so I just settled for no fish.

The cafe man who owned the yacht was fishing for a certain species of fish and

---

*Chuck Mauldin, the band's fiddler, and Smiley O'Brien, a guitar player for the band.—Ed.

WASHINGTON DAYS

I never did learn what they were, but he had unusually good luck, for he caught fifteen of them which was more, he said, than he had ever caught before. He didn't stay down on deck with us but got out on the bow of the ship, for he had to do this in order to get his special kind of fish. But when he found out that I was the one who was not catching fish he came down and tried to help me and do something about my bad luck. You don't forget that kind of people in a year of many years to me.

I am going into detail with my bad luck because it was uncanny, and the old captain and the owner just seemed to be amazed at what was happening to me. The other boys were catching fish after fish and I was still not doing any good at all. None of these men were experienced fishermen, and they just didn't understand why I couldn't catch fish. I couldn't either, but I was not near as concerned as they were. They would let me take over at the other boys' stations and the same thing happened—no fish. And when any one of the other boys took over my station they would catch fish as usual. I don't know what was wrong and the captain and the yacht owner didn't either. But they were worried and I was not. They would bait my hook themselves and then cast it in and they would come up with fish. But they would bait my hook and I would take over and I could not get a nibble. Finally, I caught two little fish about six inches long but that was near the time we had to leave and I didn't feel very victorious about that. There were about four or five big containers or bins on the yacht and the rest of the gang had filled them to the brim. My contribution was two little ones, but I think we threw them back into the sea. But, after all the bad luck catching fish, I was really happy and I will never forget the day and the refreshing memories it gives me still. I know I am human, and to be human is to be jealous and envious of anyone who beats you at anything, but I didn't feel that way about my failure to catch fish. But I still think it is a miracle and something beyond my way of thinking that I could not catch any fish. That is the last time I have ever been fishing.

We played our engagements out on the eastern shore and then we went back to Washington. We rode the ferry to Annapolis, and we all felt great and we had about a week vacation before we had another engagement and that was down in Virginia. I stayed drunk for about half that time on apple brandy and that was the hardest drink I ever had to conquer. I was barely able to go when we took off but I gritted my teeth and my stomach and we took off. Of course, if you have been keeping up with all the ups and downs we had and the good fortune we missed, you understand how a man can be weak enough to fall for the strong drink, like I did. However, it proved to be a costly mistake, as you will learn in the next chapter or two.

I forget the name of the town we had booked to play, but I do remember the awful suffering I went through. I was not too old then. But a spree like that now would eliminate me from the face of the earth.

So we said goodbye to Washington and headed down the line to where we could make a living. I had told Peek to go to Charleston, West Virginia, and book us on that station but he made a decision for himself and made a deal with the station at Fairmont. He had a good deal, we were to find out later. But we didn't accept it then. Instead, we told him to go to Charleston as he had been directed. So he went down there and they promised us a good deal but it was not as good as the one in Fairmont. So we wound up in Charleston. And about a week later the miners went out on a strike and that was it. They weren't making any money and we didn't draw crowds. You can't get blood out of a turnip. We had to book our shows out of the Charleston territory to make any money. Cliff and Bill Carlisle were there and so was T. Texas Tyler. The Carlisles are famous for "No Help Wanted"' and Tex for his "Deck of Cards." But they didn't have anything on them then to draw those miners with empty pockets. We did fairly well or, at least we eked out a living and made enough to send our families home from there because we knew we couldn't stay in that place long with the economy all shot to hell. Oh, yes, and some more of the famous acts who starved with us there for a short while were Ace Richmond, of quartet fame now, and the Smith Brothers, who sang the famous hymn or gospel song "I Have But One Goal."

Yes, we all starved together and helped each other when we could and had a lot of fun—fun without any money. We just couldn't seem to make it at all in that West Virginia mining country. It got to where we had to team up and play Sunday outdoor dates in parks and cow pastures to make a go of it. One other famous act there was Cowboy Copas and Natchee the Indian. Sometimes we would all team up together and then we would draw well enough to make it pay. Cowboy Copas was not making any records then, but he later turned out to be one of the best sellers in the country. I will tell more of him in a later chapter.

It was there where George Peek and us parted company. He left us and went to Washington, D.C. for a job, he hoped, with Asher & Little Jimmie Sizemore. But it didn't work out and he quit the business for a while till he caught on with Johnnie & Jack.

We were looking and thinking of a place to go when we hit Charleston. But I will tell one story of that country before I get to where we left. I think it is very unique.

There was a fellow who lived there in Charleston. And he played the old time fiddle, as we called it. He was the best I have ever seen up to that time but he didn't have a nationally wide name. He had been on record, and was tremendously popular in that part of the country, so we used him when we could to help out on a show, if it was a big special. He always drew good and the people liked him very much, for he could deliver the goods. I had heard some of his records several years before but I didn't ever dream of meeting him.

Ken Hackley booked us on a tour that paid off and we had to have five people on the show. One of our men had quit and our regular fiddler was not feeling too well, so we hired this fellow to go along with us on the tour. He was glad to go and pick up the extra money, and we knew he was worth the price we were paying him. The tour was for over a week and we told him and he still said he was ready to go.

We all packed up and left one night heading for Bluefield, where we played a real early morning program to help advertise our appearances. I think the program was at five-thirty in the morning. But it didn't bother us, for we were used to getting up that early. We would get up and have coffee and then after the program we would eat breakfast and get ready for the trip, as we always had a matinee show and the roads are crooked in that part of West Virginia and we knew we had to leave early to make it on time.

The night before we had to leave, we all drank some beer and some of them drank a few shots of whiskey, but when we got up to make the program we didn't touch it. The fiddler drank whiskey that night. He said he didn't get a buzz out of the beer. So we all thought it was all right.

So bright and early the next morning we got up and headed for the radio station. We didn't pay much attention to the fiddler, for he seemed to be like the rest of us, sleepy and tired, but he went on and played the program like we did. But when we headed for the cafe to eat breakfast, he didn't want anything to eat at all but he didn't ask for a drink. I noticed he was somewhat nervous but I didn't dream he was in a bad condition like he was. We were to play War, West Virginia, and we headed out soon after we had had breakfast. He didn't say anything much to anybody but became strangely silent and didn't talk like he usually did. He was older than we were but we allowed for that. We didn't worry, for he still didn't ask for anything to drink. We didn't have anything, anyway, so we just kept on going till we got to War.

When we arrived at the theater we had work to do, putting up the public address system, etc., but the fiddler was becoming more nervous all the time and he went in and watched the picture, which had already started and we were due on after the first run of the picture. It was about ten minutes till our show and he still hadn't got backstage. I went back and found him just staring at the picture. He seemed to be in some kind of a trance. When he saw me, he got up and followed me backstage like he had forgotten we had an appearance to make in a very few minutes. When we got backstage, I helped him find his fiddle and gave him his hat and his clothes he was to wear during the show. He looked horrified.

"I just can't go on," he stammered, and he looked real blue and in a state of shock. He put his hand against the wall to help him stand up. He was in a bad shape. I didn't say anything more to him because I knew the man was sick. So we left him off the first show and told the people he was ill and didn't feel like showing and they seemed satisfied.

We went ahead and put on the show, and he just sat around looking depressed and not saying a word to anyone of us. But I could tell he was getting more nervous and sicker all the time. When we had finished the show, we put our instruments in their cases and he still sat just staring straight ahead, not saying a word.

When we got outside, he was a miserable sight to see and he couldn't talk coherently. One of the boys thought we ought to take him to the hospital but I didn't think so. I asked him a few questions about his drinking and he would nod but that is about all he could do. I knew he needed a drink and he would be all right. I told him so and he nodded vigorously. War was a dry town, so we had to find a bootlegger. Fortunately, there was a miner there with us who had been fired from the mine the week before for drinking too much. He knew where the bootleggers were, so I didn't waste any time but got him in the car and we all took off to find him a drink. That seemed to help his feelings some and he began to try to talk to us but he was still in a sad shape. On our way to the first bootlegger we had to go around a bend in the road and there was a meadow when we got around the curve and there was only one animal in it—a sheep. It had white and black markings on it, and the way it was marked it looked like something a person sees in a very ghastly, horrible nightmare—unreal. He was sitting in the front seat between one of the boys and myself. The other boys in the band had been kidding him and scaring him some. I didn't believe in that but they kept on anyway. They didn't know what a terrible shape this man was in or they wouldn't have done it. For instance: the boy riding up front with us had a little tack hammer in his hand that we used to tack up posters with when we promoted a park job and had to depend on our own to advertise it. Thi old boy would hit the back part of the front seat and the fiddler would nearly jump out of the car—just little things like that, that wouldn't amount to a thing to a normal person.

When the fiddle player saw this old scary-looking sheep, I saw him blink his eyes in disbelief. He blurted out: "Just look at that old sheep. He sure is ugly."

We were driving pretty slow and he had a good look at the monstrous looking animal. Then I did something I shouldn't have done, but I couldn't resist the temptation. I looked around and gave the boys in the back seat a wink.

"What sheep?" I asked innocently.

He pointed a trembling finger at the animal and said: "Right over there. Don't you see him?"

I shook my head and the boys joined me and said they didn't see the sheep either.

He put his hand to his forehead and groaned. He thought he was seeing things that were not real and he was but he had heard of people drinking too much and having delirium tremens and he was really scared. I speeded up the car and this seemed to ease him somewhat.

When we got to the bootlegger he was not home. He had gone to town and nobody could tell us where he kept his liquor and nobody had a drink, for they were all sober. It was then that the miner told that he knew of a place down the road about eleven more miles and he was sure we could get a drink there. I was then sorry I had gone along with the boys about the old sheep, but I didn't say anything. I just turned the car around as soon as I could and drove a lot faster than I had before. Fortunately, the road was not as full of curves and I made good time.

The miner was right. The second bootlegger had plenty to drink—almost any kind you could ask for. So I bought a pint and the fiddle player was so nervous, he couldn't pour it out for himself. So I poured it into the glass till he said or nodded it was enough. I poured about a third of the bottle in that one drink. I had to hold it to his lips and I had a soft drink in my other hand for a chaser. He downed it all in one big swallow and then he had to walk around, beating himself on the chest like Tarzan before he could get his breath. Then he took the chaser I had in my other hand. The boys knew then just how sick he was and they sympathized with him. And in about ten or maybe fifteen minutes, he was feeling much better. He could talk and laugh but he wasn't drunk. He just needed a drink. If we had taken him to a hospital, I firmly believe he would have died.

We waited around till he got him another drink and he poured this one himself. He was back on his way to a fast recovery. I bought him two more pints and told the boys it was for him only and they let it alone. He wanted everybody to drink with him but none of us did, not even the miner. He still couldn't eat anything but he played the next show and did very good. But I knew we would have to get him to eat something while he was drinking. He had been in a terrible shape. After he got better, he told me he had had a birthday about two months before and all the gifts that he received was bottles and he had been drinking about two months and not eating anything much at all. That is what had him almost down for the count. He had to play with us for a whole week and we all worked together and got him straightened out. But it took the whole week to do it. I remember the last date was at a fair or little carnival, and they always have the little food stands around those places. And our fiddle player hung around those food joints devoutly. He had tapered off on his drinking and had completely quit by the time we had played the last date. He told us we had saved his life and we probably had. It makes you feel good when you can help someone like that. And I hope you won't mind my taking up your time to tell you about it.

CHAPTER TWENTY-FOUR
BACK TO BIRMINGHAM

After we played that date, which I think was Huntington, West Virginia, we headed for Birmingham, Alabama, where we had a job on WAPI and the network of stations for the Chattanooga Medicine Company. I had written them for a program and they were very kind. They gave us a good early morning radio program of thirty minutes. We didn't have the network to start off with but we finally were sold on it and it surely was a shot in the arm for us. There were several stations on the network and we could play any of the stations in person and make our radio broadcast from the nearest one. We would usually schedule appearances around, say, Mobile and play out from WALA. It was a very good arrangement and we didn't have to travel so far to get back and get some rest. We met a number of nice people while we were on this show and we kept it till the Japs attacked Pearl Harbor.

But there is a lot of mileage before we got that program and I will tell of a few outstanding things that happened to us at the beginning.

We started off making a good living just on WAPI itself. We had been on that station on the NBC network, and also the Grand Ole Opry helped us a lot by being a good build-up. People knew us mainly from that program and they would come out in droves just to see what we looked like. And we got a lot of mail each day from the listeners on the one station.

The first year we were there we were making real good. We had about six weeks of show dates booked for that territory and were just getting on our feet from the move

BACK TO BIRMINGHAM

we had made from West Virginia and the coal strike. We had not saved any money and we were figuring on the show dates to get us by but something happened—a big snow. It set a record for Birmingham and it stopped us cold. We didn't have any groceries and no coal and the water and gas froze. And Thelma and I were expecting our third baby. I had bought a ton of coal and when the Negro came to deliver it, it was raining and he had to drive up a bank to get it in our yard. He tried very much to get the truck up the bank but I told him to carry it back and bring it the next day, as we already had some coal and it would do till then. So he took the coal back. We lived on a hill on Twenty-First Avenue real close to the Vulcan statue, and there are hills and banks all around that part of Birmingham.

The next morning, when the boy was to deliver the coal, there was about ten inches of snow on the ground and then we knew we had had it. Nobody could drive in that kind of weather. And to cap it all off, sleet started falling on top of the snow and all traffic stopped and the stores closed their doors and Birmingham was a silent city. As I have written before, we already were the parents of two sweet little girls and they behaved like a couple of little angels when we went through that crisis. They didn't complain, but stayed in bed all day to keep warm. I had not been in Birmingham long enough to get any credit from anybody, and the grocery stores would not give me any credit at all and we had to just exist some way. One of our aunts had given us some canned goods and we rationed it out to last till we could get over this bad spell of weather and have something to eat again. I remember there were some canned blackberries, several cans of them, and they tasted like some kind of heavenly food to us because we knew that we had to eat to survive. We didn't call on our parents for anything. We never did that. We just tightened our belts and kept up our lowly condition because we felt it was our problem and not theirs.

I had to get out of bed real early in the freezing weather and walk to the station to put our program on. And all the personnel of the station who made it at all had to do the same thing. It was rough. One morning I started to the station, and I slipped and fell and my guitar went down the bank ahead of me. When it got to the street, it was like a sled. It slid about two blocks before it came to a stop. But I was not worried because I had a good case for it and I knew there would be no kind of traffic to bother it. I just took my time and when I got to where it was I picked it up and kept on going up Twenty-First Avenue till I got to the station. And several times when we would get to the station, some of the other stations would be frozen up and could carry our program and we had to wait till they thawed out to get the program over to them.

Maury Farrell, now of sports announcing fame, lived out my way, and we would walk out together and have fun on the way home. Once in a while, one of us would have a bottle and we would stop at my house and have a drink to pass the weather away. Weather like that makes everybody stick together. I have seen cities paralyzed, many of the big ones besides Birmingham and it is the same in each case. I'm not trying to impress you with religion but when the hand of God takes over, there is not much that artificiality can do but try in their feeble way to combat it. And the people become more used to the old ways of the pioneers of our civilization and then they can come up with the answer—just wait it out. There is nothing else to do. But when it is all over, they revert back to their same old ways of thinking and then they are in the rut again. Pardon my philosophy, but if we had more of the same kind of reasoning all the time that we have in a crisis, we would all be far better off than we are now. I think we are too quick to forget that the future of our nation and our civilization lies in the capable hands of the force we call God, and we are quick to forget when the situation comes back to normal and we are prone to revert back to the status quo. In other words, I think we take too much for granted. I know I do.

Thelma and I didn't know what to do about things, for we had no money and the baby was due any day. We had already had one baby born early and we were just hoping it would not happen again. If it had, I can't imagine what would have happened, for we didn't have any transportation and we didn't have any money to pay for anything. But we kept hoping. We were still under contract to RCA, and when the snow and sleet all melted away they called us to Atlanta for a recording session. Then we knew, barring any unforeseen mishaps, that we at least had that part of the problem solved, for we always made advance money on the recording sessions. But we still kept our fingers crossed just in case.

All the dates we had booked had to be canceled, of course, and we had to start from scratch again, but we had the recording session coming up and we had a lot more confidence. If a man can have confidence without any promise or security, I would like to look into his face and see what makes him tick. Some have more than others but I don't think any mortal human being can hold out too long in the face of great odds.

Rabon and myself had to go through with that many times, but we always had some little fortitude left to instill the faith that we needed. It sounds incredible to you who have never known our troubles and trials, but we had plenty of them even though we sounded like we didn't have a worry in the world. And that goes for just about 99 percent of the people you are listening to right now when you turn your radio, record player, or television on, for I know most of them and they don't get by with a magic delivery into prominence or by the waft of a magician's wand. You have to dig and dig and keep on digging to get just a teeny weeny break and then you are sifted through hands, often inexperienced, to get a tiny break into the field of the glamorous business called entertainment. You have to cling like a leech till you feel like you are ready to fall, but you love it when it pays off.

That bad spell of weather came in the month of February 1940. Our baby was due sometime in March. As I have written before, our oldest child, a little girl we called Billie Anne, was born over two weeks earlier than she was supposed to be and we almost lost her, she was so fragile. And if this baby had come earlier we might have had the same thing happen again because of the terrible weather.

We went over to Atlanta and made the records. I think we made ten sides.* The weather was still pretty and cold and there was still some snow on the ground, but we made it all right and then we had some money to help out. When we got back to Birmingham, one of the first things we did was to pay the hospital bill in advance. We had worried long enough about that and it was quite a relief to know we had it paid up before the baby was born. It turned out to be a boy, our first and only one, and I named him Lionel. His mother put the Alton to his name. But I didn't want anybody named after me. But there were a lot of babies named after Rabon and me when we were going good on the radio, especially the Grand Ole Opry. I named the boy Lionel after Lionel Barrymore, the great movie actor. I always thought he was one of the best and it seemed he could play any role and make it convincing, even if he was the hero or the villain.

For two more years we played out of Birmingham. In the summer we played out of town, going all over the country because we could make more money that way. In all, we played for three seasons in and around Birmingham and we kept drawing better and better as the people got used to us hanging around.

One summer we went up to Pennsylvania and spent the whole season playing the parks. We met a lot of the famous people we had heard and seen on records and also the moving pictures. Tex Ritter was one of the greats we met up there. We had played the same circuit of theaters down in the Carolinas. But we had never met him in person. Sometimes he would play two weeks ahead of us and sometimes it

---

*The date of this Atlanta session—the Delmores' last for Victor-Bluebird—was February 6, 1940. For further details, see discography.—Ed.

was the other way around.

Tex had made over three hundred movies and was a real favorite with the fans. He would announce us and we would in turn announce him. One time I felt a little mean and I announced that Tex would get every kid a nickel or an ice cream and for them to meet him at the backstage door. After I made the announcement, the manager of the theatre was a little concerned about it and I told him it was just a big joke and I felt it coming on and just had to get it out of my system. He laughed about it and then he said: "I feel sorry for poor old Tex. It will take every cent he makes to buy ice cream for those kids." We had a good crowd there. But I told him I thought it was good business. And I never did know how it came out till I saw Tex up there in Pennsylvania. I was eating a hot dog and when he was introduced to me he took my hot dog and put his fingers all over it. He was laughing when he did it and I knew he was making a big joke out of it for some reason.

"Now I'm even with you for having to buy all that ice cream for those kids. It came near breaking me up." He laughed. I don't even remember the town but he did. I mumbled out some kind of an apology but he slapped me on the back and said: "That was the best time I ever had with those kids and one of my best crowds on the whole circuit. I wish you'd have done every place I played."

So it paid off for him after all and it made me feel pretty darn swell. Tex Ritter is one of the finest fellows I have ever met in the show business. He is known as America's best beloved cowboy, and if you have ever had the pleasure of meeting him you will know the reason without a doubt. Both Rabon and me had our picture taken with him, and whoever took it sent us one of them and here is how it paid off for us. When we went back to Birmingham, I couldn't get anyone to book for us, so I had to do the job myself for a while. And brother, I'm telling you that is one of the hardest things that can happen to an entertainer. You can't do any bragging and you can't even tell the prospect that you have a good show.

BACK TO BIRMINGHAM

He will always get the idea that you are egotistical or stuck up and then your well-known goose is cooked. The way I got around all that and did a good job was by booking with cash receipts and showing the way we advertised and also a few pictures of our act and others with whom we had performed. That worked especially well with theatre managers. All the guys around Birmingham knew the good places from the bad ones and the ones you could book and couldn't book. They all agreed that Montevallo was one of the places you couldn't book at all. They knew by experience. I was down that way one day and I had not had much luck. It was time for lunch so I went on into Montevallo to eat. The cafe was not far from the theatre and I decided to try my luck there after I had finished eating. The theatre was the one that had never booked any of the Birmingham gang and didn't believe in stage shows, anyway, so it was quite a challenge. That is where the college is and it was an all-girl school then and they turned out so good that the owner-manager didn't have a thing to worry about. That is the reason he would not book any of the gang in there. He didn't need them.

I was lucky when I got to the theatre, for the owner was there checking up on some pictures or something. Anyway, he turned out to be a very friendly person. I introduced myself and he was cordial enough, but I could tell by the way he looked at me that I didn't register with him.

But he told me to go ahead and show him the posters and receipts and pictures I had brought in. "Now, I have a great business here every day in the week. I wish I could use some good shows once in a while, but I would just be giving away some of my money." I agreed with him, for I knew he was right.

I put on my display and I could tell he liked it by the way he received it. He was really a nice fellow. And I knew I didn't have a chance to play his house. But I was enjoying my demonstration very much. I was taking up his time and also mine, but neither of us was bored.

BACK TO BIRMINGHAM

I realized I had to get moving on down the line to make any progress, so I was finishing up when I thought I would show him some of our snapshots. I went through them real fast, showing him this one and that one, then I came to the picture of Tex Ritter and Rabon and myself. I told him where it was taken and he stopped me.

"Are you sure you know this man?" He looked at me in a serious way. He kept looking at the picture and then back at me. I felt kind of like a goldfish.

"Sure, I know him. He's a swell guy. Just as common as an old shoe. He's made a lot of pictures—yes, Old Tex Ritter and our show have played a lot of theaters over in the Carolinas and all around. We were playing a party together up in Pennsylvania when that one was taken."

The manager-owner held the picture up in disbelief. "Yes, that's Tex Ritter all right," he said, more to himself than to me. He looked me over again.

"If you've played with guys like Tex Ritter, you're good for my theater, and I'll book you on a flat rate any day you want to come in." I was thunderstruck. He was booking our show any day we wanted to play it just because we knew Tex Ritter!

We decided to play it on a Saturday, his biggest day and he paid us well and he said he liked our show. After we had played it the first time he came around and told me we could play his theatre any Saturday we didn't have another date. So we played his theatre several times before we left Birmingham. His brother owned a theatre over in Columbia and he got us booked in that one also. So that one little snapshot of Tex Ritter got us a good business proposition, and we made some real good money. Just like I have said before, theatre men don't listen to the radio and records. They are movie minded.

It was on a Sunday, but this Sunday held tragedy for everybody in the United States and also the world. It was December 7, 1941.

Thelma and the kids and myself were out riding around in Birmingham. It was a beautiful day and we had the desire to ride around from the monotony of our apartment. We had the radio turned on, not too loud, but just loud enough for us to hear the program. People used to listen to the radio much more than they do now. I forget what program we were listening to but suddenly we heard it! It was an awful interruption.

The Japs had bombed Pearl Harbor!

We were at first numbed into silence, for we knew it meant war. But we didn't know how it would bear on us and what influence it would have. One thing we didn't know then that we learned later. We could not stay in Birmingham!

The next day was Monday and President Franklin D. Roosevelt made a talk on the radio, declaring war on the Japanese Empire. It was hell all the way around. Everybody's future was affected by the sneak Japanese attack. We waited to see what the consequences would be but we were apprehensive. Everybody was. The war had been going on over in Europe for several years but we all thought somehow we would not get involved in this one. But now the Japs had spat in our face and we had to do something about it. All at once you hated Japs and all they stood for. I remember there was a Japanese wrestler there in Birmingham and he had to quit his profession. There was a story in the newspaper about him. He was a Japanese-American, but he still was a Jap and he had to quit. I would not have minded seeing him wrestle but a lot of people look at things like that in a different way. So, for his own safety, the promoters told him he had to go. I don't know what happened to him. But a lot of those kind of Japs joined the United States forces in different branches, and he might have joined too.

We were still doing very good on WAPI and the medicine network, and we intended to stay till there was something to change our situation. It was not long in coming. The government announced they were going to ration automobile tires and gas and that was it. The big stations didn't appeal to us because they always have a boss who tries to be a dictator and we got our belly full of that at WSM. But we

BACK TO BIRMINGHAM

knew we had to go somewhere. But we didn't think of the Opry. We would have quit before we would have gone back there.

One of the boys who used to work for us was working on WLW in Cincinnati. He was working with Curly and Ruby, and he came home not long after Pearl Harbor and told us we would like working on the Nation's Station, as they called it in those days and I think they still do. It is a good sub-title.

It was not long after he came down to Birmingham that we had arranged for an audition in Cincinnati. They demanded that, although they knew we had made many records and played on the networks and they knew what we could do. We first resented the idea, but we couldn't think of any alternative. So we wound up auditioning for the big wigs at WLW.

We thought they would be a bunch of big shots but they were not. They just wanted to know by the audition where they could fit us in. They gave us a job and then our worries were over, we thought, for the time being for gas and tires. They had a big bus they traveled in on their personal appearances and besides they paid us a regular salary for our radio programs and extra for commercials we were on. It was the best job we had ever had on any radio station before that. We never did like to be bossed around and they didn't do that much with very few exceptions. And the entertainers were the best we have worked with, where they paid a good salary. Of course, there was politics but it never did get as bad as it did on most of the stations we had worked on. The artists didn't carry tales like they did on most stations. They just didn't.

There were many artists of WLW and some of them became very popular later, and are still popular today on records, television, and the movies. Some of them I will name now and then tell a little more about them later: Merle Travis, whom I have mentioned before; Chet Atkins, the wonderful guitarist; Andy Williams of the Williams Brothers; Doris Day, the beautiful movie star; Ralph Moody, of television fame, a character actor; the Clooney Sisters, Rosemary and Betty, who sang on the Moon River show; and many others.

There was a very good atmosphere of association on the Nation's Station. Nobody thought they were better than you because you played country and western music. Some of the fellows in the symphony orchestra were very good friends of mine and they considered as long as you could make your living playing music, you were as professional as they were. It was a very, very rare experience indeed for us and also very enjoyable.

That is the way it is today most anywhere you play, but if you doubt what I am writing, just ask some of the old timers in the game who have been snubbed like we were several times by the demagogues.

When we auditioned for WLW, we still retained our program on WAPI and the network. We had it understood in talks with the officials at the station. And they realized how it was, and they were very co-operative with us for they were all a fine group of gentlemen and they knew that we had to make a living mostly on our personals. So they held the program open till we knew whether we got the WLW job or not.

I may be digressing somewhat, but we passed the audition and got the job. But the station program director had to have us come in for an interview the next day. He sat behind his desk and gave us the long look, like some officials can, while he puffed on a pipe. He liked our act and told us so. But he told us he would have to let some other act go if he hired us. He was nonchalant in his statement and that disturbed us.

He told us the station was as full as the budget would allow and that was the reason he had to make room for us. He kept looking at us, straight in the eye. I guess he thought we were desperate and we were, but I didn't let him know it. I thought for a moment and cleared my throat.

BACK TO BIRMINGHAM

"Now, listen, mister, we didn't come up here to take anyone's job and we can go back to Birmingham and our same program is still waiting for us. If you think for a moment we will knock somebody else out of a job, you are 100 percent wrong. Where would they go? They can't go to Birmingham like we can and you can just forget about us, if that is the way it has to be." We got up to leave, but he stopped us with a wave of his hand.

He smiled. "Now come on, boys, can't you take a joke?"

"Yes sir, we can take a joke but not one like that." I was madder than hell and I guess he saw it. He kept toying around with us, making us think we weren't taking anyone's job but it didn't impress us one bit. Finally I was fed up with the whole thing and I told him:

"We need this job. I'm being frank with you. But we don't have to take someone else's job to promote ourselves. We never have, and we are not going to start it now. If you want us to play on this station, we will, but we are going to keep watch and if you lay off anyone for the next six months, we will quit ourselves because we can take it and we know it, and some of these poor guys on your station couldn't get a job anywhere and you know it."

So he agreed with us and he gave us the job. But he had a strange look on his face as he said: "This is the first time I have ever seen this happen. Most of them only look out for themselves."*

---

*Alton's outline for the Birmingham chapter includes the following topics not covered in his final draft: "Organizing the hillbilly union for our own protection—A letter from Mr. Lloyd Dennis telling of the good job we missed—Hank Williams when he lived in Montgomery, a sad boy."—Ed.

CHAPTER TWENTY-FIVE
OUR DAYS AT WLW

It was far different at WLW than it was at WSM. We always did like the gang at WSM, but we couldn't make any money there, just barely a living. But at WLW they paid us a good salary and we also got paid for all personal appearances. It was the best job we ever had, where we had to work for a boss.

We had to get up real early, for the kind of music we played had that kind of an audience. And the station made more money on us early morning entertainers than they did on the other programs they had during the later part of the day. The way we got by was a natural for us. We would stay up late as we wanted and make the programs real early and then we would go back home and sleep for a long while till it was time to get up in the afternoon. Everybody on the station did that, for it was an altered schedule and you have to get used to those things. I couldn't begin to do it now, but then it was just another thing to be done. Pa McCormick was the oldest one of the early morning entertainers and he always seemed cheerful unless something happened to his harp [harmonica] while he was on the air. Then he would get excited and throw the harp against the wall of the studio and several times he barely missed hitting another artist who happened to be in the way. He was a generous soul and he didn't mean any harm to anyone and when he almost hit someone, he would come to them after his show with tears in his eyes and beg their apologies. Everybody loved Pa and Ma McCormick. We all called her Ma, and she played the piano and helped Pa put on his radio show.

OUR DAYS AT WLW

Pa McCormick and his wife started the hillbilly part of the Nation's Station's broadcast. I know you sport-minded people will remember Mr. Powell Crosley Jr., who owned the station, for he also owned the Cincinnati Reds baseball team.

When Pa and Ma McCormick first auditioned at the station, the manager turned them down, thinking they were too corny to play on a station like WLW. So Pa went over the station manager's head and got an appointment with Mr. Crosley himself. When Mr. Crosley heard Pa and Ma play, he told his manager to hire them. They were what the American people wanted, he told the manager, and so they started the whole *Top of the Morning Show*.

Several years later, when they were both getting older, Mr. Crosley gave them a lifetime job on the station and told them he didn't want them to make their programs anymore because they had done enough to enjoy themselves the rest of their days on earth. But they told him they had rather make the programs and he told them it was all right if they felt like it, so they continued to make their programs, like the rest of us did, till Pa McCormick died, and then Ma continued to make the programs by herself after she got used to the absence of her life mate.

So that gives you somewhat of a picture of what the so-called big shots are like. I met Mr. Crosley only once and he impressed me as anything but a big shot. He was dignified but he didn't ever give me the idea that he was anything or anybody that thought they were important. I knew of many cases where he helped some announcer or someone working on the station. He was just a plain person who had a lot of business sense. And I believe that was one reason the station, although maintaining a lofty level in the broadcasting industry, was always down to earth in a lot of ways that one would never know, unless they worked on the station like we did. We had many happy days while on WLW, and I could tell without asking that all the other entertainers felt the same way we did. The bosses who ran the business end of the station didn't feel puffed up about working on a station of that caliber and everybody felt at home. When they got on the air they felt the same way, and I can truthfully say that there were no big shots working and throwing their weight around. It just didn't happen there. And it was a big surprise to us, for we had felt the huff and puff of many bosses on other stations.

Merle Travis, Grandpa Jones, Rabon, and myself formed a quartet and Merle named it "The Brown's Ferry Four" after the song I had written by that title. Merle had worked with the Brown Brothers and they had a real fine sounding group and he had always enjoyed singing that kind of music and so had Grandpa and Rabon and I. We worked together fine and I taught some of them how to read music. Grandpa and Rabon learned to read pretty well and neither of them could pick out a song, but Merle used to come over to my house and we would talk nothing but music and how it was written and so forth, till away past midnight. He was determined to learn how to read and also write music, and he did. It took him about two weeks to learn to read and about that long to learn how to write it. And when he learned to write, he could beat me, and I had been writing music since I was about eleven years old.

One case in point is the Williams Brothers. They had a program and it was a quartet but they sang all four parts, by adding a sixth all through the song. The Andy Williams you hear now was one of that group then, but all of the Williams boys were younger than me or Merle. I would say that their ages approximately were twelve, fourteen, sixteen, and eighteen when they were singing on WLW. Their father was a very nice man, and I learned to know him real well. He knew I could write music and he asked me to listen to the boys and see if I could work out some arrangements for them as they were short on material. I listened but I couldn't hear that sixth well enough to write it down, but I kept trying. But now here is what I have been coming around to. About one month after I taught Merle Travis how to write music, I told him about the Williams boys and in no time at all he was doing some writing and arranging for them and they all liked it very much. So that is the kind of talent Merle Travis possesses. I don't believe I have ever seen one person with so much talent. But he worked hard to gain it from the start. Unless he had listened to what I taught him about music, he couldn't have possibly have done it. I could write a whole book about what happened on WLW but I guess I had better settle for just a few more little items.

I was the oldest of our quartet and thought I would be the last one to have to go into the war. I had three children and Rabon didn't have any and Grandpa had two but Merle only had one. And it was in the newspapers that they were not taking married men with children. But they changed me from 4-A to 1-A in less than a week and called me up for an examination. I had been turned down for too much sugar by many insurance companies on account of it, including the National Life & Accident Insurance Company while I was working on their station, WSM, but I went through that examination for the service like a greased pig. In a week I was on my way to Great Lakes for training. They call it "boot camp" in the Navy. Rabon had been turned down because of his eyes and Merle joined the Marines. He didn't last long in the Marines. Before I got through "boot camp," Merle had a medical discharge and was out for good. He had made them a good man but they found something and let him go. I didn't last long, either. But it was an experience I can never forget. I saw more absolute, wanton waste in the service than I have ever seen before or since, anywhere. I guess I had better quit writing things like that, because the different branches of the services think the sun rises and sets in their particular branch, so I might start a revolution.

Oh, I learned to like it pretty good after so long a time but it was a sickening thing, it was so unjust. Most every guy in my company had kids and one guy, a little Catholic Italian from Chicago had nine. One morning I bought a copy of a Chicago newspaper, and I was shocked when I read the headlines. I thought of the little guy who was sleeping on the front berth of my bunk and carried it back for him to read. He was a devout Catholic and he was saying his prayers from a little book he carried with him when he could, and I had to wait for him to get through before I approached him. I just held the paper up to him and he read it. The headline said: FATHERS MAY HAVE TO BE DRAFTED SOON.

That is exactly the way it was, and I am no better than anyone else to have to go to the service of my country, but I'll admit that such things like that were a little hard to take. Because I knew of guys who kept out in some way who had no kids and had no physical impairments. How come? The answer to that one is blowing in the wind.

Before I was drafted into the Navy, just broadcasting on WLW, with a good job, I helped to start a recording company there in Cincinnati. This is the way it happened:

Rabon and me had been under contract with Decca Records, but Boss Petrillo called a musician's strike and no one was allowed to play any music on a record.* We had made several records for Decca and they sold real well. I have failed to mention it, but we had a publisher for songs now. We made contact with him while in Washington, D.C., and had been under contract with him ever since. He was Sylvester L. Cross of American Music, Inc., of Hollywood, California. We had already put out one folio of our songs with him, and he wanted another one, which was number two.** I wrote the music for the folio, but he said he could get a better version from the records of the songs. I had sent him only a lead sheet of each song, and the arranger couldn't capture our way of playing the songs as well as he could from a lead sheet. Back in those days, there was no such thing as a tape recorder,

---

*The Petrillo ban on recording began August 1, 1942, and was enforced until September 1943 (for Decca) and November 1944 (for Columbia and Victor).—Ed.

**American Music published the second folio as *Delmore Brothers Folio of Native American Melodies No. 2* (American Music: Portland, Oregon, 1942). The same publisher had issued an earlier folio in 1940.—Ed.

so I had to browse around and find the old records that we made, as we didn't have them anymore. We tried saving our records and tried to keep one of each and every one we made, but somebody would come and borrow it and never bring it back.

So I got in touch with a young man who was the distributor for Decca in Cincinnati. I thought he might have some way of getting the records for me but he tried and they had gone out of print. That was pretty soon after Petdllo had lifted the record ban, and none of the companies had done much during that period. I only needed about four or five songs because I had sent all the rest of them in to the publisher. That is how I got acquainted with Paul Cohen, and he was a nice young man then.* But still I didn't know what to do about the records. I used to go over to the Decca place, and Paul and I would listen to the newest releases and each of us would try to pick the good sellers or the hits. It was a lot of fun. One day Paul snapped his finger and said:

"Alton, I know where you can go and maybe pick up those old records you need for your folio. Go over to Syd's Record Shop. He handles only old and used records and he has a lot of them. He is located down in the Negro section of town. But you might do some good there." He told me how to get there, and I went over immediately.

When I first found the place, it looked like a dump. It was old and when I went inside, I found out that the floors were littered and dusty and filthy. I thought I had come to the wrong place because no one answered when I called out. I waited for a moment, and then I saw the old records stacked in a rack along the wall. He didn't have as many records as Paul thought he had, but I began looking and found exactly the ones I needed to send to the publisher. I knew there was someone around somewhere, so I called out again and then Syd Nathan came out. He was all stained with the dyes of different colors of the pictures that he had been developing. He had

---

*Paul Cohen went on to become head of Decca's country division in 1945, a post he held until 1958. He was elected to the Country Music Hall of Fame in 1976.—Ed.

on double lens glasses. He was fat and short, and with all that coloring he looked like someone from another planet. His hands were held up to keep the color from getting on his clothes, and he really looked like a groundhog, just emerging from its hole in the ground. But he had a smile on his face and he asked me what he could do for me. I told him I wanted the records I had picked out, and he looked at them and then he asked: "Who are you?"

I told him and he began shaking his head.

"I don't want any money for these records. I used to use your records on my juke-box route down in Florida, and you have made me plenty of money, so I guess it's about time for me to pay back for some of those things you did for me while I was working for a living." He was very jolly and he began to talk about forming a record company. He was smart and up to date.

"I don't know how you and Rabon are fixed, but I want you to help me with the company. I can't start it by myself, but if you boys will sign up with me and the new company, I can give you most anything you want, that is, in royalties." I was very dubious about this fellow, although he showed me a lot of intelligence. He certainly did belie his appearance. I understood right off the bat that he was a thinking man and nobody's dumbbell.

"But how will you get the money to start a record company unless you have it already? You know, Syd, it takes money to do all this."

I had been approached by many phonies before but I didn't recognize this guy as one. He seemed like the real thing to me. We had been making records for many years, and after I talked to him a little while I could tell he knew what he was talking about. I forgot about his appearance, the dyes he was stained with, and his general appearance when I talked to him and heard his ideas. But I didn't think it was possible for him to start a record company without any money. All of this flashed through my mind as I waited for him to answer my question.

"Well, I don't have a penny of money, and that's why I'm making these pictures, for just a little meat and bread for my wife and boy." He smiled and looked very seriously at me. And then he said: "Although I don't have the money, I can get it if I can produce some abstract results. By that, I mean, if I can get someone like you to go along with me, I can jar the 'sugar daddies' loose from some money and we can start operating right away."

I asked him what he wanted me to do to help out, and he told me that he wanted me mostly as a recruiter for talent. He wanted some of the talent on WLW and he thought I could pull the deal for him. He told me that if we would agree to work with him we never would have to worry again about working on a radio station. It sounded like a very great deal for Rabon and myself, if we could get something going for ourselves for once. He mentioned the names of some of the ones he wanted to record for him and our company. It was supposed to be our mutual deal, with me getting the talent and leaving the money part up to him. He wanted Grandpa Jones, Cowboy Copas, and the Carlisles, Bill and Cliff to start with and then he said we could get going nicely. All of them were real close friends of mine, and I knew I could get them and they would believe me, if I told them that Syd was on the level. I promised to talk with them and then I left with the records he had given me. It seemed incredible to me that a guy like that could start a record company, but I respected his intelligence and knowledge, but I thought it just as impossible as the verse in the Bible about turning a mustard seed into a mountain, or turning a mountain into a mole hill.

Back in those days everybody wanted to get on record. It helped tremendously, as it does now, to establish a reputation. I told Rabon about the deal and he was skeptical of the idea at first, but when he met Syd, he changed his mind, for old Syd has a personality that won't quit. I contacted the fellows he wanted, and none of them had contracts, it being just after the Petrillo ban, and most of us guys who had made records were free to sign with any company we liked and would give us the best proposition. I even tried to get Bob Wills and Roy Acuff, who had been sensational sellers, but they were under long time contract and it lasted out the record ban.

I worked along with Syd, writing songs for the talent and helping out any way that I could. I recommended, and got a lot of the boys on record, but when the company began to get bigger and bigger, the talk about my contract for the 10 percent of the company began to take a semblance of a legend or something that happened in the long lost past, but was obsolete for the present.

Rabon and I even signed a contract that was not half as good as we had with Decca and RCA. When we kicked, Syd had the answer. "Are you guys idiots? If the rest of the guys know what you sign for, they will sign for less, too, and you will benefit, because you are a stockholder yourself."

We both signed. But we were not stockholders then and never have been and never will be. It was not our idea to beat the other artists out of anything but since I was helping start the company, I signed at his own terms. And here is something that will amaze you.

All the rest of the artists that signed got better contracts than we did! And we were known coast to coast and had been making records for years. Bill and Cliff Carlisle were also known, but they didn't sign at first like we did, and Sydney Nathan got his start from our name. Grandpa Jones made the first record and we made the second and Syd got his start from the sale of those two records.* The records were released simultaneously. And then we made more. But our contract ought to have been better. No wonder Syd could convince those guys putting up the money, when he could get someone to make records for him for practically nothing at all, and, besides this, people with names in the record field. When I think of the way I fell for that line he shot at us, I get sick—real sick inside me. But I know it has happened to other people in various kinds of business, and I don't feel so stupid, after all. I just miss the money. But I wonder what Syd will do with it when he faces the Great Beyond. That seems like a sentimental statement, but it is the only consolation I have left. I guess you wonder what the name of the record company is. It is the King Record Company, and they have been tremendously successful. And that's the reason, today, I think it is a sin to be too trusting in the line of any kind of business.

***

When I first came back to WLW, the program director would not give me back my job, although the government plainly stated that they would compel them to take all of us veterans back to the same old job. I didn't argue with him but I asked him why and he told me that when I came to the station I was working with my brother and that there was no stipulation that he had to take me back alone. They wouldn't take Rabon back, for he had a defense job at Wright Aircraft there in Cincinnati and they could not move him without the company's consent. So I was left out. I stalked out of the station without a word and I was bitter because of the change in events. If you have ever been in the service, you know how it is when you first get discharged. I was just a bundle of nerves and I had to have time to get over my time and find myself again, so I didn't give a damn whether he took me back or not. I had my mustering out pay and I could get along for a while with out doing much worrying. So I just took it with a grain of salt, and then one day I was walking around up town and I met the fellow who had hired us in the first place. I had not seen him since I came out of the service. He was real friendly with me. We shook

---

*The King files show that the first two records released by the label were from the Sheppard Brothers (Merle Travis and Grandpa Jones) and Bob McCarthy (Merle Travis), released on King 500 and King 501, respectively. The Delmores' first recordings for the company were made in Cincinnati in 1944. They were "Prisoner's Farewell" and "Sweet Sweet Thing," released on King 503.—Ed.

hands and he asked me what I was doing, I told him I was doing nothing.

"Did you go over and see Howard about coming back with us?"

"Yes sir, but he said I was not eligible and I just let it go at that."

He frowned.

"If you want to start back for us we need you to take charge of the quartet. I'll tell Howard what to do and you may start back anytime you wish."

Then I told him what Howard had said and that I hated to go back and ask him to take me back again. He looked me straight in the eye. He was serious.

"You just make it over there tomorrow and Howard will take care of you because I have a little talking I've got to do with him. You just be there any time tomorrow. He will be glad to see you. I want you and we need you."

That man was Mr. George C. Biggar. I have never in my life, met a finer man or gentleman.

So I started out on WLW by myself. I knew I could make it with the quartet, but I wasn't sure how I would fare otherwise. It really surprised me how I got along all alone. I had never done much without Rabon and I missed him tremendously but I didn't let any one know how I felt. I still had the nervous adjustment to get over like everybody does when they first are discharged from the service. I well remember it was old Pa McCormick who put his arm around my shoulders and told me that he appreciated me being back at WLW. He did me more good than anyone except George C. Biggar, who hired me back after Howard had turned me down. Pa said:

"Now, boy, don't you feel like you're not wanted around here. You have done as much as you could in the Navy and I, for one, am glad to see you back here with us." He was, too, and he always made me feel good when he talked to me. The other guys took me for what I was, or had been on the station before I left, but that was not enough. I just simply never will forget Pa McCormick. And here is something else I will never forget. Grandpa Jones, Buddy Ross, and myself were considered the most nervous persons on the station, yet the service took us in without a glance and turned the others down, most of them on account of their nerves. I just don't get it and never will. But then if I were as smart as those policy makers for the services, I'd be a rich man, like some of them are. You don't get rich by working. You get rich by scheming, and I never have been a schemer.

So I got along great on WLW after I had regained my bearings. And I made more money and got more publicity than I did when Rabon and I were playing together. But still I was not satisfied. I wanted Rabon back but the bosses said that I was doing better and suited them better than both of us together. So I let it go at that. I had to make a living and I couldn't quit and go rambling around like Rabon and me were used to doing. I was older than Rabon and I felt responsible for him more than I ought to, I guess.

Hank Penny and his band were on WLW, and they would back me up on my singing. We had been friends for a long time and Hank really did a lot to help me get straightened out when I came back to WLW. Hank had a very good band indeed, and his band consisted of fellows like Chet Atkins, Louis Innis, Zed Tennis, and several others I can't recall offhand. But they all went on to do something great in their own field. You have heard from them in various ways, and they deserve everything they get in the way of plaudits from the public. Merle Travis had left and gone to California. There, in Hollywood, he got a real good start. But he told me it was rough at first, and I would be the last one to doubt what he said.

I had several unique experiences while at WLW that seem somewhat unbelievable now in the light of what has happened since then. So I will relate several of those and then go on with the story in chronological fashion.

The first one is about an all-time great in the field of baseball. His name was Grover Cleveland Alexander and I know if you are a baseball fan at all you have heard of him. He drifted into Cincinnati and I never did ask him why, but he was just a drifter when I knew him. But he still was a great man and gentleman. Jim Hardwick, who ran a bookstore, introduced him to me. Jim was a great friend of mine and also a great sports fan. He had been a coach at a Midwestern university at one time in his career, and that is how he had learned to respect athletes so much. When he heard that "Old Pete" was in town, he looked him up and offered to help him any way he could. "Old Pete" is what all of Grover Cleveland Alexander's real friends and associates called him, for that is what he wanted to be called. He was a very modest man.

EDITOR'S POSTSCRIPT
THE DELMORES' LAST YEARS, 1945–1964

Alton Delmore's manuscript breaks off at this point, and it now seems unlikely that he completed any further sections of it. To complete the Delmore story, which in Alton's case extended almost twenty years beyond the final date in the manuscript, I have appended this final chapter in which I attempt to sketch the Delmore career from 1945 to 1964. It is by no means as full or colorful as Alton would have made it, but it does cover some events crucial to understanding the Delmores' role in American popular music. I have been guided by an outline of the unwritten chapters that Alton prepared about midway through his writing of the manuscript. As a prelude to this final chapter, we reproduce Alton's chapter outlines.—Ed.

ALTON'S ORIGINAL CHAPTER OUTLINES

25—Indianapolis and the fine people up there—Friends from WLW—The Bosses—We become dissatisfied.

26—Memphis and the best place we ever worked and the country I love—Roaming again—Wayne Raney—Lonnie Glosson—Chattanooga—Jackson—Back to Alabama for a short while—Fort Smith, Arkansas—Our Hit Records—We always seem to come back again, with something new—the way it is with a record artist.

27—Del Rio, Texas—I learn to love that country—the desert country they call the

THE DELMORES' LAST YEARS

last frontier—A heart attack in San Antonio; Texas—Leaving Del Rio.

28—Houston, Texas and the way we landed there—An old friend comes through for us, Jack Harris—KPRC—Curly and Ruby—My adventures running a beer tavern—My daddy dies—"Blues Stay Away from Me"—We lose our little Susan—Rod Cameron and other stars like Tommy Sands and Tennessee Ernie.

29—Bartender at the Pick-Adilly—Rabon in Detroit—I join him—He is critically ill—Our last record session in Cincinnati—Rabon's last days—the unreality of death—readjusting myself.

30—One can do better even if they are handicapped—How people laugh with their silence and attitudes—Politics—Teaching and false teaching.

When World War II ended, both brothers were still in Cincinnati, but only Alton was playing on WLW's *Boone County Jamboree*. Even after his defense job ended, the station refused to rehire Rabon. Rabon had continued to play as a solo act on the station for a time after Alton had been drafted but had run into difficulty with the management of the station and had been asked to leave. Thus, for a time toward the end of the war each brother was, for the first time in his career, working as a solo act. Alton was quite successfully managing a quartet on WLW, but Rabon, unused to working alone, was having serious problems. For some months Alton tried to help Rabon, loaning him money and giving him advice, but it finally became evident that the brothers would have to get back together again. Alton asked if both could rejoin WLW but was told that under no circumstances would Rabon be hired back at the station. Alton was then faced with a decision: he could continue as a single act at WLW, or the brothers could reunite and leave Cincinnati. He chose the latter.

After a brief but unsuccessful stint at Indianapolis, the brothers went to Memphis, where, in 1945, they began appearing regularly on WMC. Alton referred to Memphis as "the pest place we ever worked," and it was here the Delmores experienced a remarkable resurgence in their career. They once again had a successful early morning radio show, and their Memphis location gave them access to a relatively new audience in Arkansas, Missouri, Tennessee, and Mississippi. Furthermore, they continued to record for King Records, and in 1945 had their first successful King hit, "Hillbilly Boogie.'" "Hillbilly Boogie" was Rabon's composition, and it was one of the first successful attempts to translate into a country idiom the boogie-woogie blues fad, which had swept the country in the mid-1940s. The blues element of the Delmores' music, which had not always been always fully reflected on the brothers' Bluebird records, now came to the fore, and the brothers began producing a string of King records which had a strong blues content. The brothers also became more willing to deviate from their classic tenor guitar–standard guitar instrumental format, and to experiment with amplification. On the session that produced "Hillbilly Boogie," Louis Innis played rhythm guitar. Memphis, which had been the center for Southern blues since the 1920s, responded enthusiastically to the Delmores' more bluesy sound.

It was also in Memphis during that time (late 1945) that Alton and Rabon met harmonica player Wayne Raney, who was to have considerable impact on their music. Raney was from the small Arkansas hamlet of Wolf Bayou; as a young man he had learned to play choke style harmonica under the influence of an older Arkansas musician named Lonnie Glosson. Raney in fact teamed with Glosson in 1938 to work a unique twin-harmonica act at KARK in Little Rock, Arkansas, and throughout the 1940s the two men often played together. Raney journeyed north in 1941 to Cincinnati, where he played on WCKY and sold hundreds of his "talking harmonicas" by mail.* But oddly enough, he apparently did not meet the Delmores until after he had returned to Arkansas and they were broadcasting from Memphis.

THE DELMORES' LAST YEARS

Alton's son Lionel recalls that Raney just appeared at their home in West Memphis, Arkansas, one day asking to meet the famous Delmore Brothers. Alton was immediately impressed with Raney's talent, and before long Raney was playing on the Delmores' WMC radio show. Glosson was a frequent guest as well.

Alton's son Lionel recalls what a typical Delmore stage show was like in 1946: "You'd have the Delmore Brothers, Wayne Raney, and Lonnie Glosson. Lonnie could play a guitar and a harmonica at the same time in a holder—Wayne could mainly play the harmonica. They put on a typical show like this. The Delmore Brothers would come out and do their part. Then Wayne would come out and do his specialties, numbers like the old 'Fox Chase' or 'Race with Model T Ford,' he'd do his part. Then the Brown's Ferry Four might come out, all of them singing the different parts. Then Lonnie might do his bit with his 'talking harmonica' bit. Wayne and Lonnie would also dress up as clowns—one of them was called Cyclone, and I can't think of the other name. They'd dress up like a hobo, maybe put white stuff on their face, black out some teeth. Then they'd all come back and have a sort of grand finale. This made one heck of a fine stage show. They traveled all over. But the humor was all good clean humor. And even when they had some of these boogies as big hit records, they would never play a boogie in a church."

Raney complemented the Delmore sound so well that he began recording with them in 1946 as the brothers continued to document their country blues and boogie sound for King. Writing under the pseudonyms of Jim Scott (Alton) and Bob Nabor (Rabon), the Delmores produced a string of blues-tinged songs: "Leavin' Town," "Rounder's Blues," "Boogie Woogie Baby," and "Born to Be Blue." At the same recording sessions they continued to produce gospel records under the name

---

*For more information about Raney's background and later career, see Mike Leadbitter, "Wayne Raney and the Delmore Brothers on King," *Old Time Music* No. 10 (Autumn 1973), pp. 19–23.—Ed.

THE DELMORES' LAST YEARS

of the Brown's Ferry Four. But it was another blues song that gave them their next big hit: "Freight Train Boogie." This 1946 record, really more of an instrumental showpiece than a vocal, featured Raney's harmonica, Alton's inspired flat-top picking, and some interesting back-up rhythm work by two men who were later to become known as the comedy team of Homer & Jethro.

Though audience demographics for the time are almost certainly nonexistent, it would seem very likely that the Delmores were, in their boogie blues work, beginning to appeal to a newer, younger audience in addition to their traditional fans. While their work as the Brown's Ferry Four and their clean, close harmonies still appealed to vast numbers of fans of traditional music, their blues sound appealed to Southern youngsters who within a few years would be embracing the rockabilly sound that was to emerge from Sun Records in Memphis. The appeal of the countrified blues sound was made even more evident three years later (1949), when the Delmores and Raney had their biggest hit yet, "Blues Stay Away from Me."

Like many popular standards, "Blues Stay Away from Me" was written in a rather casual and off-hand manner. At a session on May 6, 1949, at King's Cincinnati studio, Syd Nathan approached Alton and asked him if he had heard the new dance tune, "The Hucklebuck." Alton of course had, since the tune, in various jazz and blues guises, was sweeping the country. "Alton," said Syd, "I want you to write me a hillbilly Hucklebuck. I want a beat, but I want it to be hillbilly." Alton soon formulated the outline of the song, and Rabon helped him work out some suitable words. But the song didn't have quite the beat it needed, and Alton turned for advice to Henry Glover. Glover, a Black pianist and arranger, served as sort of a house musician and producer for King's rhythm & blues series. According to Lionel Delmore, Glover would frequently help out in Delmore sessions, playing on some sides and helping to write parts on others. It was Glover who finally helped Alton work out the famous background riff that opens "Blues Stay Away from Me."' (The completed song carried four composer credits: Alton, Rabon, Glover, and Raney.) Glover apparently did not actually play on the record; Wayne Raney and Lonnie Glosson played twin harmonicas to the Delmores' singing. This side and its reverse side, "Goin' Back to the Blue Ridge Mountains," became two of the Delmores' biggest hit records.

By the summer of 1949, when "Blues Stay Away from Me" began to climb best-seller charts, the Delmores were in Fort Smith, Arkansas. They had left Memphis in late 1946, primarily because they had "burned the area out." Lionel Delmore says: "They did all their own booking, remember. If you look at a map of Memphis, you can only travel so far in any direction. They would try not to go back and play a place, say, more than once every six months. They just got to where they didn't have any more places to play around Memphis. But they always said Memphis was the most successful place they played." Short radio stints followed, at Chattanooga, then at Jackson, Mississippi, then back to Alabama for a while. They finally settled for a year or so at Fort Smith, just across the river from Oklahoma, and a regional broadcasting center for western swing. (In fact, Bob Wills's father had a radio show in Forth Smith for a time.) By this time the brothers were, in the accepted practice of the day, involving their children in their radio shows, and Alton's son Lionel, then ten years old, began appearing in shows. The Delmores also began to make radio transcriptions at Fort Smith, thus easing the burden of constant live programming.

Wayne Raney was still often playing with the brothers at Fort Smith, though the success of his 1949 hit "Why Don't You Haul Off and Love Me" was soon to net him a call from the Grand Ole Opry. It was in Fort Smith that the brothers hit upon another suc cessful idea for booking live stage shows, the "all night singing." They would select a small town within listening distance of their radio show, pick a date for a show, and book the local school or auditorium about six months ahead of time. The Delmores would always head up the show themselves, but they would book five or six other acts on the radio station with them, usually paying the acts out of their own pocket a flat rate. Each act would then be allowed to do as much as a sixty-minute show apiece, and the audience would be treated to a marathon evening of country entertainment. Lionel Delmore has especially vivid memories of one such show held in Poteau, Oklahoma, in 1949.

"They would have one stage show, usually on a Friday or Saturday, at the end of the week. That would be the big deal. They would book these things up in advance, and four months before this date, they'd be saying on their radio show, 'Now don't forget, in four months we're going to be down in Poteau.' Then as the date got closer, they'd start hitting them heavier and heavier on the air with reminders and advertising. Two weeks before we were due in Poteau, we went in and put up posters, put 'em up at just the choice spots. We went into the guys that were booking us in, the school, and said, 'OK, where are you sure we can get posters in?' And they said, 'Well, we'll definitely put one in the auditorium, we'll send notes home with the kids, and all.' This was about two weeks before. Then about a week before the show was to go on, we went in and we hit every store along the main drag, say, 'Hey, man, can we put a poster in your window?' Then we'd leave, go out of town, give it about two hours, then we went back in to see who had taken our posters out of their window. I remember in Poteau, everybody we went in to said, 'Sure, give us a poster.' So we put 'em in, left town, went back two hours later, posters were still there—that was a sure sign, everything was going to be good. So the night we played Poteau, we got into town, and downtown Poteau was just deserted. There wasn't nothing there. And all these places that we'd put these posters in had taken them out. And my dad was fit to be tied. They were playing a high school auditorium there. We got to the auditorium there, and they had Oklahoma State Patrolmen about a mile from the school. Traffic backed up. And Dad thought that they had scheduled it on a football night, and he said, 'My gosh, have we goofed up.' So traffic keeps piling up and piling up, and it's time for them to go on. So he finally pulls out of line and goes up to this patrolman and says, 'Buddy, I got to get to the auditorium.' He says, 'Well, so have the rest of these people.' And dad says, 'What?' He says, 'These people, they're here to see the Delmore Brothers.' And Dad says, 'Well, if you don't let me through, they're not going to see one of them.' And they gave him an escort. But they actually turned people away—people filled the aisles, standing along the side, hanging in the windows. It was the biggest crowd they ever had, and that's the first night they ever played 'Blues Stay Away from Me' and 'Why Don't You Haul Off and Love Me' in public."

By 1950, the brothers had moved on to Del Rio, Texas, where they broadcast over XERF. This station was one of a number of powerful stations located just across the U.S. border in Mexico; out of the jurisdiction of the Federal Radio Commission and U.S. authorities, these stations blanketed the South and Southwest in the 1930s, 1940s, and early 1950s with strong signals carrying country music and sales pitches for every variety of mail order merchandise. Artists like the Carter Family, J. E. Mainer, and Cowboy Slim Rinehart had successfully boosted faltering careers by going on border radio, and the prospect at Del Rio looked good to the brothers. Like most entertainers on border radio, the Delmores worked via electrical transcription, recording entire programs, complete with announcer's introductions and studio patter, on sixteen-inch aluminum discs. These transcriptions were then sent to five or six other stations along the border network and replayed in each one. But the Delmores soon found that they weren't going to make any real money at Del Rio: the halcyon days of border radio were drawing to a close. Nor did they like the flat, arid country around Del Rio. They continued to do personal appearances, and at one of these, in San Antonio, Alton experienced a mild heart attack. It wasn't a severe attack, but it scared Alton. This, along with the fact that they weren't making any money in Del Rio, caused the brothers to move on after only about five months.

The next stop was Houston radio station KPRC, 1951–1952. At first it looked like the job in Houston would stabilize the brothers' career. Alton's two oldest children were well into high school and were popular and successful academically; Rabon's wife had relatives in Dallas, and their often stormy marriage showed signs of settling down. "Blues Stay Away from Me" was still popular, and the brothers were continuing to record regularly for King, often using a full country stringband to achieve a more "modern" sound. Rosemary Clooney and a number of other popular artists had discovered "Beautiful Brown Eyes" and were making it a best-selling song in 1951, and Alton looked forward to royalties that would take some of his financial pressure off. But then every thing started to go sour.

In the first place, Alton got involved in an authorship dispute over "Beautiful Brown Eyes," and, lacking funds to engage in a legal battle, had to settle his claims to the song for $1,500. Then Alton was hit by a series of personal tragedies. First, his father, to whom he had always been close, died. Then within a few months Alton's youngest daughter, Susan, died. Susan was only three when she died, and the event had a shattering effect on Alton. He began to drink heavily and to lose interest in music. To compound the problem, Rabon's marriage began to break up, and he was putting pressure on Alton to move again. Alton, however, was mindful of the roots his family was establishing in Houston and hesitated to move them again. He was also beginning to think that the days for his type of music were numbered and was looking around to find a more stable occupation. He thus didn't argue when Rabon announced that he was going to Detroit to try to make it as a single act; the break-up of the act seemed like the final blow in a devastating year.

Alton looked around for various work he could do outside the music business, and finally settled on running a tavern. He was determined to create a more stable lifestyle, both for himself and his family. But in early 1952 Rabon contacted Alton from Detroit, asking that Alton join him and hinting that he was not in good health. Alton did finally go to join Rabon, and the two played their last really professional engagement at the Roosevelt Lounge in Detroit. Alton then found what had been troubling Rabon: he had a pain in his shoulder and finally admitted to Alton that there was a lump. The lump was cancer, and doctors advised Alton to take his brother back to Alabama where they would be reasonably close to Nashville's Vanderbilt Hospital for treatment. Alton sent a word to his family in Houston that Rabon was ill and asked them to meet him and Rabon back in Athens.

There was time for a last recording session in Cincinnati. On August 28, 1952, a session by the Brown's Ferry Four produced recordings of Alton's "Praise God! He Loves Everybody" and "What Shall I Do with Jesus" and two standard hymns. The next day, August 29, saw the last recordings by the Delmore Brothers: Alton's "The Trail of Time," Rabon's "I Needed You," and two last collaborations, "Whatcha Gonna Gimme" and "That Old Train." It marked the end of a recording career that included over 200 sides.

Back home Rabon was operated on at Vanderbilt, but his illness—lung cancer—was much too far advanced to be effectively treated. Alton became even closer to his brother in his last days, and they often talked about old times and old songs, the people they had met, and the places they had played. But Rabon continued to weaken, and on December 4, 1952, he died.

Alton had a great deal of difficulty in accepting his brother's death. Not only was it a great personal loss, but it meant the end of any hope for a comeback. The Delmore Brothers were no more. Alton moved to Huntsville, near Athens, and continued to support his family by working at a variety of jobs. For some months after his brother's death, friends and relatives report that Alton was a lonely and bitter man. He worked as a salesman for a while, as a postman, and at a variety of odd jobs. Yet he couldn't completely keep his music out of his life, and as time passed began to perform some. In the early 1960s, he had an early morning radio program in Hattiesburg, Mississippi, and as his son Lionel began to show musical talent Alton seriously considered resurrecting the old act with Lionel taking Rabon's place. Nothing much came of these ventures, however, and Alton spent most of his later years teaching guitar in Huntsville.

Alton did continue his songwriting, though, and had the satisfaction of seeing, many of his songs performed by nationally known artists. Tennessee Ernie Ford chose Alton's "False Hearted Girl" as the follow-up release to his 1955 hit "Sixteen Tons." Royalties from earlier songs helped supplement Alton's income and make life a little easier. He wanted to get even more involved in songwriting, especially as he watched Nashville become a publishing and recording center in the 1950s, but he felt cut off from Nashville by being in Huntsville, some 100 miles to the south.

He channeled part of his creative urge into prose writing. For some years Alton had been toying with short stories, and now he began to write earnestly, aiming for commercial markets like the *Saturday Evening Post*. Research does not indicate that he ever placed any of his stories, but he obviously achieved some satisfaction simply in writing them, for he wrote dozens of them. The ones that have survived indicate that Alton was a competent regional writer with a strong interest in documenting the South and Alabama in particular. Most of his time, however, was spent in writing his autobiography, and evidence suggests that this was the last writing project he was working on before his death.

Alton died June 9, 1964, in Huntsville as a result of complications caused by a liver disorder. He was survived by his wife, Thelma, three daughters, and his son, Lionel. Thelma died in 1971.

In October 1971, the Delmore Brothers were elected to the Nashville

THE DELMORES' LAST YEARS

Songwriters Hall of Fame. After years of repeated nominations, they were elected to the Country Music Hall of Fame in 2001. To this day, their music and their songs continue to be heard throughout the country.

DISCOGRAPHY

The following discography attempts to list the known commercial recordings of the Delmore Brothers. A number of people helped in the compilation of this discography, and special thanks are due to Frank Driggs (who generously provided copies of the original session sheets for the Delmores' many Bluebird sides), to Tony Russell (who provided much of the King data), to Dave Freeman, Bill Vernon, and Bob Pinson (who reviewed the finished discography and helped with reissue data).

An additional note is in order regarding the complex King discography. The foundation for this discography was laid by the late Mike Leadbitter in his fine article "Wayne Raney and the Delmore Brothers on King," which appeared in *Old Time Music*, No. 10 (Autumn 1973).

Leadbitter's data was drawn from the original King session books. This has been supplemented by data from Tony Russell, from aural evidence on the records themselves, from interviews with some of the participants, and from data in the Country Music Foundation archives.

Still, it seems unlikely that the exact personnel on all these important records will ever be fully known. At various times the gospel quartet called the Brown's Ferry Four included—in addition to the Delmores—Red Foley, Grandpa Jones, Merle Travis, and Cowboy Copas, but we have been unable to determine which singers appeared on which sessions. According to Lionel Delmore, the quartet was originally composed of the Delmores, Jones, and Travis, with Red Foley (who also played string bass on some regular Delmore sessions) occasionally substituting for Travis.

After Jones and Travis left the King label, the quartet at various times included Wayne Raney, Clyde Moody, and Cowboy Copas. A similar Delmore quartet

DISCOGRAPHY

also recorded as the Harlan County Four for King, and reportedly as the Hartford Quartet on an unknown label. It now also seems very likely that Homer Haynes and Jethro Burns played on some of the duet sides, and equally likely that Travis played guitar on some of these sides; almost certainly guitarist Zeb Turner and Black pianist Henry Glover appeared on some sides as well.

Composer credits for the King sides are reflected in the following code: (AD)—Alton Delmore; (RD)—Rabon Delmore; (WR)—Wayne Raney; (LC)—Louis Clark; (LG)—Lonnie Glosson; (HG)—Henry Glover; (NK)—Norma King; (M & NL)—Mac and Norma Luna; (LM)—Lois Mann; (BN)—Bob Nabor; (PD)—Public Domain; (TN)—Tom Neely; (JS)—Jim Scott. A number of these names are Delmore pseudonyms. For example, Jim Scott is Alton, Bob Nabor is Rabon. The King release numbers for 78s and 45s were identical, with the exception of a "45" prefix; thus, here we have given only the original 78 release number and the EP or LP reissue numbers, if any.

Many of the original King masters appeared later on Starday, Starday Gusto, and Pine Mountain LPs.

CKW

RECORD LABEL ABBREVIATIONS

Bb – Bluebird

CAL/CAS – RCA Camden

Co – Columbia

Cy – County

De – Decca

El – Electradisk

HMV – His Master's Voice

MCA – MCA (Japan)

Me – Melotone (Canada)

MW – Montgomery Ward

Parlo(E) – Parlophone (England)

Pd – Polydor

PMR – Pine Mountain Records

RCA – RCA Victor

RZ – Regal Zonophone (Australia)

Su – Sunrise

Tw – Twin

DISCOGRAPHY

COLUMBIA RELEASES

DELMORE BROTHERS (Alton & Rabon): *vcl duets, acc. by own gtr, ten gtr*
Atlanta, Georgia, Wednesday, October 28, 1931

| 151976- | I've Got The Kansas City Blues | Co 15724-D |
| 151977- | Alabama Lullaby | — |

BLUEBIRD RELEASES

Chicago, December 6, 1933

7728-2	I Ain't Got Nowhere To Travel	Bb B-5467, HMV N4334
77219-1	Ramblin' Minded Blues	—, —
77220-1	Smoky Mountain Bill And His Song	Bb B-5589
77221-2	Gonna Lay Down My Old Guitar	Bb B-5299, El 2170, Cy402
		Su S-3380, MW M-4420
77222-1	Lonesome Yodel Blues	Bb 8 5299, El 2170,
		Su S-3380, MW M-4420
77223-1	I Ain't Gonna Stay Here Long	Bb B-5653, Tw FT1829
77224-1	Brown's Ferry Blues	Bb B-5403, MW M-4750,
		HMV N4324,
		RCA LPM-6015, Cy402
77225-1	I'm Mississippi Bound	Bb B-5653
77226-1	I'm Goin' Back To Alabama	Bb B-5358, Su S-3439,
		MWM4459
77227-1	I'm Leavin' You	Bb B-5358, Su S-3439,
		MWM-4459
77228-1	I've Got The Big River Blues	Bb B-5531, HMV N4349,
		Cy402
77229-1	The Girls Don't Worry My Mind	Bb B-5589, Tw FT1810

NOTE: *rev. B-5403, M-4750, N4324 by the Allen Brothers and rev. FT1810, FT1829 by Riley Puckett*

DISCOGRAPHY

Chicago, December 7, 1933

77252-1	Bury Me Out On The Prairie	Bb B-5338, Su S-3419, MW M-4458
77253-1	The Frozen Girl	Bb B-5338, Su S-3419, MW M-4458
77254-2	Lonesome Jailhouse Blues	Bb B-5741, Tw FT1862
77255-1	Blue Railroad Train	Bb B-5531, HMV N4349, CAL/CAS-898, Cy 402
77256-1	By The Banks Of The Rio Grande	Bb B-5741, Tw FT1862

New Orleans, Louisiana, January 22, 1935

87660 2	Don't Let Me Be In The Way	Bb B-6120, Tw FT8024
87661-2	When It's Summertime In A Southern Clime	Bb B-5957
87662-1	Hey Hey, I'm Memphis Bound	Bb B-5857, MW M-4553
87663-2	I Guess I've Got To Be Goin'	Bb B-6002
87664-1	Blow Yo' Whistle, Freight Train	Bb B-5925, CAL/CAS-898
87665-1	Down South	Bb 8-6034, MW M-4751, Tw FT1979
87666-1	Brown's Ferry Blues—Part 2	Bb 8-5893, MW M-4553, Tw FT1906
87667-1	I Got The Kansas City Blues	Bb B-6002
87668-2	I Know I'll Be Happy In Heaven	Bb 8-6120, Tw FT8024
87669-1	Keep The Camp Fires Burning	Bb B-6019, MW M-4752, RZ G22791
87670-1	Alabama Lullaby	Bb B-6034, MW M-4751, Tw FT1979

DISCOGRAPHY

87671-1	The Fugitive's Lament	Bb 8-6019, MW M-4752, RZ G22791, Tw FT1961, Cy 402
87672-1	I Believe It For My Mother Told Me So	Bb B-5857, MW M-4552
87673-1	I'm Going Away	Bb B-5853, Tw FT1906
87674-1	I LongTo See My Mot!ter	Bb 8-5957, MW M-4552
87675-1	Lorena, The Slave	Bb 8-5925, Tw FTl941

NOTE: *rev. FT1941 by Eddie Bell, FT1961 by Lasses & Honey*

Charlotte, North Carolina, February 17, 1936
Arthur Smith (fiddle) —1

99171-1	The Nashville Blues	Bb B-6312, MW M-4753, Tw FT 8111, Cy 402
99172-2	The Lover's Warning	Bb B-6522
99173-1	I'm Worried Now	Bb B-6349, MW M-4754
99174-2	Take Away This Lonesome Day	Bb B-6998
99175-1	Promise Me You'll Always Be Faithful	Bb B-8637, RZ G24925
99176-1	Don't You See That Train?	Bb B-6522, Cy 402
99177-2	It's Takin' Me Down	Bb B-6312, MW M-4753, Tw FT811 l
99178-1, 2	That Yodelin' Gal—Miss Julie	Bb B-8687
99179-1, 2	I'm Gonna Change My Way	Bb B-6349, MW M-4754
99180-1	Gamblin' Yodel	Bb unissued
99181-1	Happy Hickey—The Hobo	Bb B-6386, Tw FT8143
99182-1	Lonesome Yodel Blues No. 2	Bb B-6386
99183-1	Put Me On The Trail To Carolina—1	Bb B-6401, Tw FT8165
99184-1	Carry Me Back To Alabama—1	
99185-1,2	My Smokey Mountain Gal—1	Bb B-7778, MW M-7849
99186-1	Take Me Back To The Range—1	Bb B-8687

NOTE: *rev. FT8143 by Cliff Carlisle*

301

DISCOGRAPHY

Charlotte, North Carolina, February 17, 1937

Arthur Smith (fiddle)—1

07087-1	No Drunkard Can Enter There	Bb B-6915, MW M-7150; Cy 508
07088-1	Southern Moon	Bb B-6841, MW M-7151
07089-1	False Hearted Girl	Bb B-6949, MW M-7153, Tw FT8400
07090-1	The Budded Rose—1	Bb B-7262, MW M-7154
07091-1	Blind Child	Bb B-6915, MW M-7153
07092-1	Are You Marching With The Savior?	Bb B-7029, MW M-7154, RZ G23273
07093-1	I Don't Know Why I Love Her	Bb B-6841, MW M-7151
07094-1	Don't Forget Me Darling	Bb B-7029, MW M-7152, RZ G23273
07116-1	Memories Of My Carolina Girl	Bb B-6949, MW M-7152
07117-1	No One	Bb B-6998, MW M-7150

NOTE: *rev. FT8400 by the Three Tobacco Tags*

Charlotte, North Carolina, August 3, 1937

Arthur Smith (fiddle)—1

011885-1	Lead Me	Bb B-7337, MW M-7318
011886-1	I Need The Prayers Of Those I Love	Bb B-7672, —
011887-1	I've Got The Railroad Blues	Bb B-7300, MW M-7319
011888-1	The Weary Lonesome Blues	—, —
011889-1	Heavenly Light Is Shining On Me	Bb B-7337; MW M-7317
011890-1	Wonderful There	Bb B-7672, —
011891-1	The Farmer's Girl	Bb B-7383, MW M-7320
011892-1	Singing My Troubles Away	Bb B-7129, —
011893-1	They Say It Is Sinful To Flirt	—, MW M-7321; RCA LPV-548

DISCOGRAPHY

011894-1	Till The Roses Bloom Again	Bb B-7262, MW M-7321,
		Cy 402
011895-1	When We Held Our Hymn	BbB-7192, MW M-7322
	Books Together	
011896-1	Hi De Ho Baby Mine—1	Bb B-7129
011897-1	Look Up, Look Down	BbB-7383, MW M-7322
	The LonesomeRoad	

Charlotte, North Carolina, January 25, 1938

018713-1	Ain't It Hard To Love	Bb B-7560, MW M-7853
018714-1	Bury Me Under The Weeping Willow	Bb B-7741, MW M-7853
018715-1	Brother Take Warning	Bb B-7741, MW M-7475
018716-1, 2	Alcatraz Island Blues	Bb B-7778, MW M-7849
018717-1, 2	Goodbye Booze	Bb B-7436
018718-1	There's A Lonesome Road	Bb B-8052, MW M-7475

January 26, 1938

018754-1	Cause I Don't Mean To Cry	Bb B-7496, MW M-7474
	When You're Gone	
018755-1	Careless Love (Bring My Baby Back)	Bb B-7436, MW M-7473
018756-1	In That Vine Covered Chapel	Bb B-7496, —,
	In The Valley	Tw FT8571
018757-1	Big Ball In Texas	Bb B-7560, MW M-7474

NOTE: *rev. FT8571 by Wiley, Zeke & Homer*

Rock Hill, South Carolina, September 29, 1938
Acc. by own gtr and ten gtr, with Chuck Maudlin (fiddle), Smiley O'Brien (gtr/vcl—2),
Joe Zinkan (sbs)

027642-1	Leavin' On That Train	Bb B-7913, MWM-7677
.027643-1	The Cannon Ball	Bb B-7991, —,
		RCA LPV-532, RD-7870

DISCOGRAPHY

027644-1, 2	My Home's Across The Blue Ridge Mountains	Bb B-8247, MW M-7678
027645-1, 2	15 Miles From Birmingham	Bb 8 8031, —
027646-1	I'm Alabama Bound	Bb B-8264, MW M-7695
027647-1, 2	Nothing Bue The Blues	Bb B-8247, —
027648-1	Some Of These Days You're Gonna Be Sad	Bb B-7957, MW M-7696
027649-1	Where Is My Sailor Boy	—, MW M-7679
027671-1, 2	Heare Of Sorrow	Bb B-8637, MW M-7696
027672-	Quit Treacin' Me Mean	Bb B-8031, MW M-7697
027673-1, 2	Just The Same Sweet Thing To Me	Bb B-8290, MW M-7698
027674-	The Only Star	Bb B-7991, MW M-7679
027675-	A Better Range Is Home—2	Bb B-8290, MW M-7698
027676-	Git Along	Bb B-7913, MW M-7697

Rocky Hill, South Carolina, February 5, 1939

032669-1	Don't Let My Ramblin' Bother Your Mind	Bb B-8177, MW M-7852
032670-1,2	Baby You're Throwing Me Down	
032671-1	Gonna Lay Down My Old Guitar—Part 2	Bb B8215, RZ G24087
032672-1	Brown's Ferry Blues—Part 3	Bb B-8230
032673-1	I Loved You Better Than You Knew	Bb B-8215, MW M-7851, RZ G24087
032674-1	Goin' Back To Georgia	Bb B-8264, MW M-7850
032675-1	Home On The River	Bb B-8052, MW M-7851
032676-1	Gamblers Yodel	Bb B-8230
032677-1	Wabash Blues	Bb B-8204, MW M-7850
032678-1	Go Easy Mabel—2	Bb B-8204

DISCOGRAPHY

Atlanta, Georgia, February 6, 1940. Unidentified steel gtr—3

047551-1	The Wabash Cannon Ball Blues—3	Bb B-8404, MW M-8685
047552-1	Over The Hills—3	Bb B-8451, MW M-8686, RZ G24925
047553-1	The Dying Truckdriver—3	Bb B-8451, MW M-8686
047554-1	Scatterbrain Mama—3	Bb B-8404, MW M-8685
047555-1	Happy On The Mississippi Shore	Bb B-8613, MW M-8687, Cy 402
047556-1	That's How I Feel, So Goodbye	Bb B-8557, MW M-8688
047557-1	Rainin' On The Mountain	—, —
047558-1	See That Coon In A Hickory Tree	Bb B-8418, MW M-8687
047559-1	The Storms Are On The Ocean	Bb B-8613, MW 8689
047560-1	Back To Birmingham	Bb B-8418, —, Cy 402
047561-1	The Eastern Gate	Bb B-8488, MW M-8690
047562-1	God Put A Rainbow In The Clouds	Bb B-8488, —

DECCA RELEASES

New York, New York, September 11, 1940
Acc. by own gtr and ten gtr.

68069-A	There's Trouble On My Mind Today	De 5878; MCA VIM- 4017
68070-A	Silver Dollar	—, —
68071-A	Old Mountain Dew	De 5890, Me 45398; MCA VIM-4017
68072-A	In The Blue Hills Of Virginia	—, —
68073-A	Make Room In The Lifeboat For Me	De 5897, MCA VIM-4017
68074-A	When It's Time For The Whip-Poor-Will To Sing	De 5925, X2209, Me 45423
68075-A	Will You Be Lonesome Too?	De 5925, X2209, Me 45423, MCA VIM-4017
68076-A	Broken Hearted Lover	De 5907, Cy 402
68077-A	She Won't Be My Little Darling	MCA VIM-4017
68078-A	Gathering Flowers From The Hillside	De 5897, —

DISCOGRAPHY

New York, New York, July 16, 1941
Unidentified bjo — 4, poss. Zeke Phillips (sbs) added

69508-A	I Now Have A Bugle To Play	
69509-A	Last Night I Was Your Only Darling—4	De 6000; MCA VIM- 4017
69510-A	Baby Girl	De 6051, —
69511-A	New False Hearted Girl	De 6080, Me 45552
69512-A	I Wonder Where My Darling Is Tonight	De6051, MCA VIM- 4017
69513-A	Precious Jewel	De 5970, 46049, —
69514-A	Gospel Cannon Ball	—, —, —
69515-A	I'll Never Fall In Love Again-4	De 6080, Me 45552
69516-A	Honey I'm Ramblin Away	De 46043, Cy 402
69517-A	I'm Leavin' You	—
69518-A	You Ain't Got Nothin' I Can't Do Without	De unissued

KING RELEASES

Dayton, Ohio, January 1944
Acc. by own gtrs

K-1772	Prisoner's Farewell	503
K-1774	Sweet Sweet Thing (JS)	503, 5866, LP589, LP983,
NOTE: *matrix K-1773 not used*		PMR289

Cincinnati, August 1945
Acc. by own gtrs, unkn. bs

K-1928	The Fast Old Shovel	509
K-1929	Why Did You Leave Me Dear (AD-JS)	514
K-1930	I Found An Angel	525
K-1931	Lonely Moon (AD)	518
K-1932	Midnight Special (JS)	514, LP785, LP983, LP869, KS1090, STK962
K-1933	Be My Little Pet	518
K-1934	Remember I Feel Lonesome Too (AD)	509
K 1935	Fast Express	525

DISCOGRAPHY

Hollywood, January 1946

Acc. by own gtrs, Merle Travis (gtr), Louis Innis (gtr), Roy Starkey (bs)

(*) Indicates sides credited to BROWN'S FERRY FOUR

K-1971	I'm Sorry I Caused You To Cry (AD)	527, LP785
K-1972	Hillbilly Boogie (RD)	527, EP222, LP589, KS1090, STK962, PMR289
K-1973	I'm Lonesome Without You (AD)	533
K-1974	Don't Talk About Me (AD)	unissued
K-1975	I Won't Be Worried Long (AD)	1053, LP887
K-1976	Don't Forget Me (AD-RD)	548
K-1977	*Will The Circle Be Unbroken	530, EP320, LP590, LP807, LP943,
K-1978	*Just A Little Talk With Jesus (C. Derricks)	530, EP320, LP590, LP943, PMR250
K-1979	She Left Me Standing On The Mountain (AD)	533
K-1980	Somebody Else's Darling (AD)	570
K-1981	Kentucky Moutain (AD)	1005, LP785, LP920, LP983, PMR289
K-1982	Midnight Train (AD)	548, GEP8728, LP589, PMR289

Chicago, February 2, 1946

Acc. by own gtrs, Roy Starkey (bs), Wayne Raney (hca), Homer Haynes (gtr),

Jethro Burns (mand or el-gtr)

K-2092	Someday You'll Pay (JS)	873, LP785, LP983
K-2093	Goin' Back To The Blue Ridge Mountains (JS)	803, LP785, LP920, LP983
K-2094	My Heart Will Be Cryin' (JS)	873
K-2095	Take It To The Captain (JS)	718, LP785
K-2096	Leavin' Town (JS)	unissued
K-2097	Rounder's Blues (JS)	643, LP785
K-2098	The Wrath Of God (JS-WR-BN)	769, LP556, LP807

K-2099	Calling To That Other Shore (JS)	769, EP313, LP807, LP910, PMR218
K-2100	Freight Train Boogie (JS-BN)—1	570, 5866, Sd8022, SG110, EP222, GEP8728, LP589, KS1090, STK962, PMR289
K-2101	Boogie Woogie Baby (JS-BN)	599
K-2102	Shame On Me (BN)	751
K-2103	Born To Be Blue (BN)—1	599, LP589, PMR289
K-2104	Waitin' For That Train (JS)	680
K-2105	Harmonica Blues (WR)	643
K-2106	The Love I Cast Away (WR)	LP1006
K-2107	Mississippi Shore (AD)	592, LP920, Polydor(E)Pd 545029

Hollywood, September 1946
Acc. by own gtrs, Wayne Raney (hca), Merle Travis (vcl and gtr), Grandpa Jones (vcl),
Red Foley (vcl and bs). Issued as by DELMORE BROTHERS except those items marked
with (*) by BROWN'S FERRY FOUR or (**) WAYNE RANEY.

K-2124	*Rockin' On The Waves (Sebren)	577, EP320, LP551, PMR251, PMR299
K-2125	*If We Never Meet Again (Brumley)	577, EP237, LP590, PMR250
K-2126	*I'll Fly Away (Brumley)	785, EP320, LP551, PMR251
K-2127	*The Lord Is Watching (Over Me) (PD)	631, EP238, LP590, LP943, PMR220, PMR250, PMR299
K-2128	*Everybody Will Be Happy (Over There)	631, LP590, LP943, PMR220, PMR250, PMR299
K-2129	*Hallelujah Morning (AD-Lanman)	750, LP590, LP943, PMR220, PMR250, PMR299

DISCOGRAPHY

K 2130	*Old Camp Meeting (L. M. Jones)	593, EP237, LP551, PMR251
K-2131	*There's A Light Guiding Me (Newton-Foley)	593, EP238, LP551 LP943, PMR220, PMR251, Pd545029
K-2132	*Salvation Has Been Brought Down (Brumley)	662, EP238, LP551, PMR251
K-2133	*When The Good Lord Cares (AD)	662, LP590, LP943, PMR220, PMR250
K-2134	*Over ln Glory Land (Lou Ferden)	799, LP590, LP943, PMR220, PMR250, PMR299
K-2135	*On The Jericho Road (D. McCrossam)	832, LP551, LP943, PMR220, PMR251,
K-2136	Brown's Ferry Blues (Delmore)	Pd545029592, EP222, LP910, LP589, LP KS1090, PMR289, PMR218
K 2137	**Green Valley Waltz (PD)	676
K-2138	**Under The Double Eagle (PD)	856
K-2139	**Fox Chase (PD)	676

Cincinnati, September 1947
Acc. by own gtrs, Wayne Raney (hca), possibly Al Strickland (steel gtr),unidentified bs,
unidentified fiddle, sound effects added—1

K-2520	Mobile Boogie (TN-NK)	680, LP785
K-2521	Stop That Boogie (TN-NK)	751
K-2522	Weary Day (TN-NK)	784, LP785, LP910, PMR218
K-2523	Used Car Blues (TN-NK)	664, LP983
K-2524	Barnyard Boogie (LM)-1	664, LP KS1090, STK962

DISCOGRAPHY

Cincinnati, October 1947

Acc. by own gtrs

K-2592	You Can't Go Wrong And Get By (PD)	LP910, EP313, PMR218, PMR299
K-2593	Long Journey Home (PD)	LP910, EP322, Pd545029, PMR218
K-2594	'Dis Train (PD)	EP313, LP920
K-2595	Frozen Girl (PD)	EP322, LP920
K-2596	Red River Valley (PD)	EP322, LP910, LP887, PMR218
K-2597	Silver Threads Among The Gold (PD)	5407, LP910, PMR218
K-2598	Oh Susannah (S. Foster)	EP322, LP920
K-2599	Give Me Your Hand	EP313, LP910, PMR218

Cincinnati, October 1947

As BROWN'S FERRY FOUR

Acc. by own gtrs, Wayne Raney (hca), poss. Red Foley (bs, vcl)

K-2600	On The Jericho Road (McCrossam)	832
K-2601	His Boundless Love (Presley)	760, LP551, LP943, PMR220, PMR251
K-2602	Rock Of Ages Hide Thou Me (Haltsman)	700, EP238, LP551, LP943, PMR220, PMR251, PMR299
K-2603	When He Blessed My Soul (Derricks)	780, LP590, LP943, PMR220, PMR251
K-2604	I've Got The Old Time Religion In My Heart (Milsap)	760, LP551, PMR250
K-2605	I'm Naturalized For Heaven (McCoy-Pace)	832, LP590, PMR251
K-2606	When He Calls His Reapers (Presley)	933, LP590, PMR251
K-2607	I've Made A Covenant With My Lord (Arnold)	758, EP237, LP551, PMR250

DISCOGRAPHY

K-2608	Throne Eternal (Brumley)	933, LP590, PMR250
K-2609	After The Sunrise (Baxter-Wright)	799, LP551, PMR251, Pd545029
K-2610	I'll Meet You In The Morning (Brumley)	854, LP590, PMR250
K-2611	Jesus Hold My Hand (Brumley)	854, LP590, LP943, PMR220, PMR251
K-2612	Keep On The Firing Line	700, EP237, LP551, LP943, PMR220, PMR250

Cincinnati, November 1947

Acc. by own gtrs, Roy Lanham (el-gtr), Wayne Raney (hca), Grandpa Jones (vcl and bjo) on K-2567/8

K-2653	Fifty Miles To Travel (JS)	739
K-2654	Now I'm Free (JS)	739, LP785, LP983
K-2655	Lonesome Day (JS)	946
K-2656	Let Your Conscience Be Your Guide (JS)	5407, LP920
K-2657	Darby's Ram (PD)	708
K-2658	Take It On Out The Door (TN-Jones-NK)	708
K-2659	Down Home Boogie—2 (TN)	784
K-2660	Peach Tree Street Boogie (AD-RD-H. Penny)	718
K-2661	Gotta Have Some Lovin' (AD)	935
K-2662	Beale Street Boogie (Roy Lanham-AD-RD)	unissued

Cincinnati, December 1947

Acc. by own gtrs, Wayne Raney (hca & vcl), Roy Lanham (el-gtr), prob. Henry Glover (dms)

K-2833	Jack and Jill Boogie	732
K-2836	Lost John Boogie	719

DISCOGRAPHY

Cincinnati, May 6, 1949

Acc. by own gtrs, Zeke Turner (el-gtr), Lonnie Glosson (2nd hca) (—3); Wayne Raney
(vcl and hca), prob. Henry Glover(dms), unidentified sbs

K-2911	Pan American Boogie (AD-RD)—3	826, LP785, LP983, LPKI090, STK962
K-2912	Sand Mountain Blues (AD-RD)	849, LP920, Maple Leaf 25-210
K-2913	I Swear By The Stars (AD-RD)	849, LP920, Maple Leaf 25-210
K-2914	Blues Stay Away From Me (AD-RD-LG-WR)—3	803, 5675, Sd8022, EP222, LP537, LP910, KS1090, LP983, Col CS9468, Parlophone (E) LP PMD-1064, PMR291, PMR289, PMR218, Starday SLP-9-451, SLP962, Golden Classics GC1005

same location and date

Acc by own gtrs, Wayne Raney (hca), unknown el-gtr

K-2940	Fast Train Through Arkansas (AD-RD)	unissued
K-2941	Trouble Ain't Nothin' But The Blues (AD-RD-WR)	unissued

NOTE: *matrices K-2938-41 were recut at the Cincinnati studios the following month, the same master-numbers being used. It is assumed issued titles are from the second session.*

Cincinnati, October 14, 1949

DELMORE BROTHERS: *as before*

K-2940	Fast Train Through Arkansas (AD-RD)	unissued
K-2941	Trouble Ain't Nothin' But The Blues (AD-RD-WR)	826, 5675, LP697, LP785, LP983, KS1090, STK962

DISCOGRAPHY

Cincinnati, October 3, 1950

WAYNE RANEY: *vcl, acc. by own hca, Lonnie Glosson (hca), Delmore Brothers (gtrs), unknown sbs, dms*

K-3099	I've Done And Sold My Soul (LG-WR)	939
K-3100	Pardon My Whiskers (WR-LM)	910
K-3101	I Love My Little Yo Yo (WR)	939
K-3102	Old Fashioned Matrimony In Mind (WR)	910

Cincinnati, October 5, 1950

DELMORE BROTHERS: *vcl duets, acc. by unknown el-gtr, Wayne Raney (hca), unknown sbs, dms, fiddle (—1), Lonnie Glosson (hca)*

K-3107	Everybody Loves Her (AD-RD)	946, EP, Parlo(E)GEP8728, LP983, LP589, PMR289
K-3108	Life's Too Short (AD-RD)—1	911, LP910, PMR218
K-3109	Field Hand Man (AD-RD-LM)	935, LP983, LP589, STK96, KS1090, PMR289
K-3110	Blues You Never Lose (AD-RD-HG)	911, LP589, LP920, LP983, Pd545029, PMR289

Cincinnati, October 9, 1950

Delmore Brothers, *vcl duets and gtrs, Wayne Raney, (hca), prob. Al Myers (el-gtr)*

WAYNE RANEY** or DELMORE BROTHERS

K-3111	**I'm On My Way (HG-LG-Smith)	956
K-3112	I Let The Freight Train Carry Me On (AD-RD-LM)	927, LP785, LP983
K-3113	Please Be My Sunshine (AD-RD)	927, LP983, PMR289, LP589
K-3114	**The Family Tree Musta Fell On Me (WR-LM HG)	925
K-3115	**I Ain't Nothin' But A Tom Cat's Kitten (WR)	956
K-3116	**If You've Got The Money, I've Got The Time (Frizzell)	914

DISCOGRAPHY

| K-3117 | **My Annabelle Lee (WR) | 925 |
| K-3118 | **Real Hot Boogie (WR-Norman) | 914 |

Cincinnati, March 12, 1951

Acc. by el-gtr, gtr, Wayne Raney (hca), unknown pno, sbs, dms, or WAYNE RANEY**

vcl acc. by own hca, others unknown

K-3172	Who's Gonna Be Lonesome For Me (AD-RD)	966, LP785, LP983, Quality(C) K4059
K-3173	The Girl By The River (AD-RD)	981, LP785, LP910, LP983, LP871, PMR218
K-3174	**I Had My Fingers Crossed (LC-WR)	974
K-3175	**You Better Treat Your Man Right (WR)	989
K-3176	**Blues At My Door (WR-LC)	989 K-3177
K-3177	**I Want A Home In Dixie (WR-LC)	974
K-3178	There's Sumpin' About Love (AD-RD)	981, LP589, LP983, PMR289
K-3179	Tennessee Choo Choo (AD-RD)	966, LP697, LP KS1090 STK962; Quality (C) K4059

Cincinnati, October 22, 1951

Acc. by el-gtr, gtr, Wayne Raney (hca), unknown (sbs, dms), prob Henry Glover (pno)

K-3266	I'll Be There (HG)	1023, LP589, KS1090, STK962, PMR289
K-3267	Heartbreak Ridge (AD-RD-LM-HG)	1005
K-3268	Good Time Saturday Night (AD-RD-HG)	1053, GEP8728, LP589, PMR289
K-3269	Steamboat Bill Boogie (AD-RD)	1023, LP589, LP871, PMR289

DISCOGRAPHY

Cincinnati, October 28, 1951

As BROWN'S FERRY FOUR: *Alton and Rabon Delmore, (vcl and gtrs), Grandpa Jones (vcl), Ulysses "Red" Turner (vcl and gtr)*

K-3274	The Judgement Day (AD)	unissued
K-3275	There's A Page In The Bible (AD)	1059, LP590, LP943, PMR220, PMR251
K-3276	We Should Walk Together (AD)	1059, LP590, PMR250
K-3277	I Am A Weary Pilgrim (AD)	1032, LP943, PMR220
K-3278	Heaven Eternal For Me (Louis M. Jones)	1032, LP822, LP943, PMR220, PMR222
K-3279	I'm Traveling Home (AD)	unissued

Cincinnati, ca. October 28-30, 1951

As HARLAN COUNTY FOUR: *Ulysses "Red" Turner (vcl and leader), l,eke Turner (gtr and baritone vcl), Alton and Rabon Delmore (vcl and gtr)*

K-3284	Show Me The Way	1121
K-3285	God Will Guide You	1121
K-3286	The Atomic Telephone	1016
K-3287	Ten Commandments	1016
K-3288(?)	John Three Sixteen	1050
K-3289(?)	My Father's Mansion	1050
K-3290	Start To Praying	1068
K-3291	I Cried Holy	1068

Cincinnati, May 21, 1952

WAYNE RANEY** or DELMORE BROTHERS. *Wayne Raney (vcl and hca), Alton and Rabon Delmore (vcl and gtr), unidentified bs, unidentified dms*

K-3383	**I'm Really Needin' You (WR)	1087
K-3384	**Undertakin' Daddy	1116
K-3385	How You Gonna Get Your Lovin' Done (AD)	1113

DISCOGRAPHY

K-3386	**When They Let The Hammer Down (WR-AD-RD)	1116
K-3387	**Beatin' Round The Bush (WR-AD-RD)	1087
K-3388	Got No Way Of Knowing (AD)	1084
K-3389	I Said Goodnight To My Darling	1113 (AD)
K-3390	Muddy Water (AD)	1084, LP589, LPKS1090, PMR289

Cincinnati, May 23, 1952

As BROWN'S FERRY FOUR: *Alton and Rabon Delmore (vcl and gtrs), Grandpa Jones (vcl), Ulysses "Red" Turner (vcl and bs)*

K-3395	The Arm Of God (AD)	1086, LP822, LP910, LP943, PMRZZ0; PMR222, PMR218, MR299
K-3396	Bound For The Shore (Mrs. C. E. Delmore-AD)	1086, LP822, LP943, PMR220, PMR222
K-3397	Eternity Without Him (Roder-Turner-Delmore)	1114, LP822, LP943, PMR220, PMR222, PMR299
K-3398	Can't You Hear Him Calling (Turner-Delmore)	1114, LP822, LP920, LP943, PMR220, PMR222

Cincinnati, August 17, 1952

Issued as CLYDE MOODY (K-3453) or BROWN'S FERRY FOUR (K-3454) or CLYDE MOODY & BROWN'S FERRY FOUR (K-3455/56). *Alton and Rabon Delmore (vcls and gtrs), Clyde Moody (vcl and gtr), Ulysses "Red" Turner (vcl and bs)*

K-3453	I Feel Like Traveling On (Hunter-Vaughan)	1177, New American LP NA101

DISCOGRAPHY

K-3454	I Need The Prayers	1133
	(James D. Vaughan)	
K-3455	The Unclouded Day	1177
	(Rev. J.K. Alwood)	
K-3456	Through The Pearly Gate (Moody)	1133, LP943, PMR220, PMR299

Cincinnati, August 28, 1952

As BROWN'S FERRY FOUR: *Alton and Rabon Delmore (vcls and gtrs), Grandpa Jones (vcls), Ulysses "Red" Red Turner (vcl, gtr, mand)*

K-3461	When The Redeemed Are Gathering In	1209
	(Oatman-Dutton)	
K-3462	Praise God! He Loves Everybody	1153, LP822,
	(AD)	LP943, PMR220, PMR222
K-3463	You Must Be Born Again (Ulys-Turner)	1153, LP822, LP943, PMR220, PMR222
K-3464	What Shall I Do With Jesus	1209, LP822, LP943,
	(AD-Vaughan)	PMR220, PMR222

Cincinnati, August 29, 1952

Alton and Rabon Delmore, (vcls and gtrs), Red Turner, (bs or mand)

K-3465	That Old Train (AD-RD)	1141
K-3466	The Trail Of Time (AD)	1158, LP785, LP920, LP983
K-346.7	I Needed You (RD)	1141
K-3468	Whatcha Gonna Gimme (AD-RD)	1158

LONDON RELEASES

[NOTE: *While still under contract to King, Alton Delmore and Wayne Raney recorded a number of sides for the new and ill-fated London country series in 1950 and 1951. The sides were generally issued under the pseudonyms Lonesome Willie Evans (Raney) and Hank Dalton (Alton). Guitarist Roy Lanham was present on at least some of the sessions, but it is not clear if Rabon was present. Before his death, Wayne Raney confirmed the pseudonyms to the editor of* The Hillbilly Researcher.]

DISCOGRAPHY

Location uncertain, circa January 1950.

As LONESOME WILLIE EVANS. *Wayne Raney (vcl and hca), Alton Delmore (vcl and gtr), other personnel unidentified.*

50235	Hillbilly Fever (G. Vaughn)	London 16019
50236	900 Miles From Home (L. Southerland)	London 16019

Location uncertain, circa February 1950.

As LONESOME WILLIE EVANS. *As for preceding session.*

50278	The Sun Has Gone Down (On The Only One I Love) (L. Southerland)	London 16025
50279	Lonesome Railroad Blues (L. Southerland)	London 16025

As HANK DALTON AND THE BRAKEMEN. *As for preceding session.*

50294	Hummingbird Special (George Vaughn)	London 16032
50295	Little Girl, You're Mean to Me (Glossoh-Dalton)	London 16032

Location uncertain, circa July 1950

As LONESOME WILLIE EVANS. *As for preceding session.*

50401	Trouble, Then Satisfaction (Srange-Vaughn)	London 16035
50402	Whippoorwill Song (Strange-Vaughn)	London 16035

Location uncertain, circa October 1950.

As HANK DALTON (50562, 50569) *or* HANK DALTON & THE BUCKEYE BOYS. *Alton Delmore (vcl and gtr), Wayne Raney (vcl and hca), poss. Roy Lanham (el-gtr),* others unidentified

50546	If You've Got the Money (Frizzell)	London 16050
50547	Two Sweethearts (J. Van Tilzer)	London 16050
50562	It's No Secret (Hamblen)	London 16051
MX?	When The Saints Go Marching Home (Lane)	London 8587

DISCOGRAPHY

| 50568 | You Gotta Walk the Straight and Narrow (Vaughn) | London 8587 |
| 50569 | All Alone 'Neath The Blue Grass (Vaughn) | London 16051 |

ACME RELEASES

Circa 1956, possibly Bristol, Tennessee.

ALTON DELMORE & THE BROWN'S FERRY FOUR.

Alton Delmore, (gtr and vcl), other vocalists unidentified

MX?	The Devil is Mounted (AD)	Acme 1110A, PM125
MX?	Gonna Rowe [*sic*] My Boat	Acme 1110B, PM125, PM299
MX?	Peaceful Home	Acme ?, PM 125, 299
MX?	Gonna Fly Away With Christ	Acme ?, PM 125, 299

LINCO RELEASES

Fayetteville, Tennessee, ca. 1959

ALTON DELMORE. *Alton Delmore, (vcl and gtr), other unknown*

| MX? | Good Times in Memphis (AD) | Linco?, WL 8808 |
| MX? | [Unknown title] | Linco? |

INDEX

Acuff, Roy, xi, 84, 87, 196n, 207n, 218n, 236, 280
  arrival of, 194-207
  eccentricities of, 203-4
  fan mail for, 208
  Grand Ole Opry and, 203, 206-8
  problems with, 201-2, 205-6
  publicity for, 205
Alabama Courier, stories in, 83
"Alabama Lullaby," 45; 60, 66, 67n
Alexander, Grover Cleveland, 182, 284
Allen, Austin, 49
Allen Brothers, x, 48-49, 61
Allison Place, living on, 175, 176
Alloway Street, living on, 131, 134-35
American Music, Inc., 276, 276n
American Recording Company (ARC), 196n
Anderson, Sam Jones, 115, 116
Anniston, Alabama: radio program in, 70, 124
ARC. *See* American Recording Company
Arlington, Virginia: playing at, 246
Arnold, Eddy, 84, 210
Arthur Smith Trio, 157n
Artist Service, 186-87, 199
Ashboro, North Carolina: playing in, 220, 221
Asheville, North Carolina: playing in, 227
Athens, Georgia, 11, 25
  old-time fiddlers' contest at, 46-47
Athens Agricultural High School, old-time fiddlers' contest at, 39n, 47
Athens Courier, job at, 44

Athens Music Company, writing for, xii
Atkins, Chet, 72, 270, 283
Atlanta, Georgia
  recording in, 263, 264
  trip to, 51-59
Auditioning, 51, 59-60, 62, 73 80, 108, 197-98, 246, 247, 270-71
  for Grand Ole Opry, 69-80
  for network programs, 239-43
Autry, Gene, 173, 177, 183, 196

Bailey, DeFord, 94n
  performance fee for, 180, 180n
  working with, 178-79
Balliett, Whitney, ix
Baniza, Mr.: audition for, 108
Bankhead, Tallulah, 53
Banner label, 196n
Basketball, 20-21, 24
"Beautiful Brown Eyes," viii, 157, 157n
  authorship dispute over, 293
Belue, Elgar, 52
"Ben Dewberry's Final Run," 56
Berle, Milton, 238
Bethesda, Maryland: playing at, 246
Biggar, George C., 282
Bill (tramp printer), 32
Birmingham, Alabama: living in, 260-71
Bitting, Mr.: Uncle Dave and, 116-17
Bitting Chevrolet Company, dealing with, 115-16
Black, Jewel, 95
"Blackberry Blossom," 169n
Blackie (boy), 173
Bluebird label, 89n, 264n, 287
  recording on, 157n, 158n, 162

INDEX

Bluefield, West Virginia: playing in,
  255-56
"Blue Railroad Train," 163
Blue Sky Boys (Bolick Brothers), viii
"Blues Stay Away from Me," viii, 286
  playing, 292
  popularity of, 290, 293
  writing, 289
Bolick Brothers, viii
Bond, Johnny, viii
Boogie blues, 288-89
"Boogie Woogie Baby," 288
Bookings, 220, 222, 232-33, 236, 237,
  245, 253, 255
  problems with, 266, 267
Boone County Jamboree, 286
Bootlegger, finding, 257-58
Border radio, 292-93
"Born Thirty Years Too Soon," 64, 109
"Born to Be Blue," 288
Boswell papers, xiv
"Bound for the Shore," 26n
Boxing, 36-37
Brescia, Pete, 146
Brevard, North Carolina: playing in,
  235
Brock, Dwight, xii
"Brown's Ferry Blues," viii, 96
  dispute about, 129, 130n
  playing, 47, 83
  writing, 43-44
Brown's Ferry Four, x, 26n
  formation of, 274
  recording by, 288-89, 294
Brown's Ferry Road, 11, 12, 35
  living on, 49, 44-46, 52, 115
Brown, Bill, 60n

Brown Brothers, 274
Brunswick label, 21ln

Cafe, working in, 29-30
Callahan Brothers, viii, 196
Cameron, Rod, 286
Cantor, Eddie, 119
Carlisle, Bill, 254, 279, 280
Carlisle, Cliff, 196, 254, 278, 280
Cars, buying, 114-17
Carson, Fiddlin' John, vii, x, 56, 63
Carson, Martha, 122
Carter, A. P., vii
Carter Family, ix, 292
Casa Loma Orchestra, 120n
Cash, Johnny, 72
CBS network, auditioning for, 246,
  247
Charleston, West Virginia: living in,
  253-55
Charlotte, North Carolina: recording
  in, 152-55, 157n
Chattanooga, Tennessee living in, 285
  radio stint at, 290
Chattanooga Medicine Company, 260
  Church of Christ (Valley View),
  singing at, 22
Cincinnati, Ohio: living in, 286
Circuits, playing, 135, 143, 144-46,
  148-50, 151, 220, 225, 232,
  234, 238, 246, 265
Clements, Zeke, 135, 135n, 136, 143
Clements High School, old-time
  fiddlers' contest at, 41, 42-43
Cline, Mrs., 94n
Clooney, Betty, 270
Clooney, Rosemary, 270, 293

INDEX

Cobb, David, 103-4

Coca-Cola, 228, 233

Coffman, Dick, 104

Cohen, Paul, 277, 277n

Colliers, writing for, xiii

Collins family, tornado and, 9-10

Columbia Records, 49-50n, 67n, 120n
  auditioning for, 51, 59-60, 62
  Great Depression and, 64
  letters to/from, 43, 49-50, 51
  recording for, x, 46n
  strike against, 276n

"Columbus Stockade Blues," 48

Comedy songs, working on, 43-44

Compton, Merritt, 2

Conqueror label, 196n

Conventions, playing at, 41-50, 41n

Copas, Cowboy, 178, 254, 279

Cotner, Carl, 173

Cotton gin, job at, 45-46

Country Music Hall of Fame, 139,
  277n, 296

Craig, Francis, xi, 120-21, 120n, 125

Craig, Percy, 194, 195

Crazy Tennesseans, 196n, 198, 200,
  201

Crescent Amusement circuit, playing,
  135, 143

Crook, Herman, 136, 172

Crook, Lewis, 136

Crosley, Powell Jr.: Pa and Ma
  McCormick and, 273

Crosley Corporation, 97

Cross, Hugh, 49, 50, 50n, 56

Cross, Sylvester L.: contract with, 276

Cyclone (clown), 288

Dalhart, Vernon, vii, 49-50n, 66

Darby, Tom, 56

Darby & Tarlton, 49, 50n

Davis, Claude, 61

Dawson Spring, Kentucky: playing at,
  201

Day, Doris, 270

"Death of Floyd Collins, The," 56

Decatur, Alabama
  flu epidemic in, 33
  living in, 24-25, 35

Decca Records, 280
  recording with, 276, 277
  strike against, 276n

"Deck of Cards," 254

Delmore, Alton
  birth of, ix
  death of, xiii, 296
  heart attack for, 285, 293
  personal tragedies for, 293-95
  songwriting by, xii, 290
  tavern keeping by, 294
  writing by, vii-viii, xi-xvi, 295
  youth of, x

Delmore, Billie Anne, 184, 239, 264
birth of, 132
help for, 133-34

Delmore, Charlie, 14-15
  Uncle Dave and, 111

Delmore, Ed, 1, 15
  adventures with, 4-6
  ghost light and, 17
  railroad work for, 23
  typhoid fever for, 8-9

Delmore, Leonard, 1, 8, 15
  adventures with, 4-6
  ghost light and, 18

Delmore, Lionel, xiv, 26n; 295, 296
  birth of, 264
  on Glover, 289-90
  interview with, xiv
  on Poteau show, 290-91
  on Raney, 288
Delmore, Max, 2, 6, 15
  mechanical skills of, 12-13
  railroad work of, 23
Delmore, Mollie, 114
  songwriting by, xii, 26n
  Uncle Dave and, 111
Delmore, Nola, 216
Delmore, Norma Gail, 184, 239
Delmore, Rabon
  birth of, ix
  Brown's Ferry Four and, 274
  circuit and, 148, 149
  death of, 286, 294-95
  deep sea fishing and, 251
  fan mail for, 141
  Grand Ole Opry and, 72, 73, 75,
    78, 79, 83 87, 92, 93, 100, 101,
    175,182, 215, 216
  illness for, 147, 294
  marital problems for, 293
  old-time fiddlers' contests and; 42,
    46-47, 48
  personal appearances with, 108-9,
    143
  playing with, 38-40, 70, 71, 103,
    176
  popularity of, 40, 43
  recording with, 51, 55, 152, 156,
    158, 168, 170, 171, 263
  songwriting by, 290
  youth of, x, 3

Delmore, Susan: death of, 286, 293
Delmore, Thelma Neely, 86, 98, 99,
    100, 140, 145, 147, 149, 175, 184,
    185, 216, 239, 268
  dating, 40
  death of, 296
  help for, 133
  illness for, 142
  pregnancy of, 131-32, 261, 263
Delmore, Tom, 34, 35
Delmore Brothers Folio of Native
    American Melodies No. 2, 276n
Del Rio, Texas: working in, 292-93,
    295
Dennis, Lloyd, 246, 271n
Devine, Ott, 70, 124-25
Dixie Dew Drop (Uncle Dave Macon),
    136
Dixon Brothers, 235n
Dylan, Bob, viii

Early Birds, 100n
Easterly, Jess, 198n
Eastern shore (Maryland/Delaware),
    playing, 249-50, 253
Easter Sunday, memories of, 4
Electrical transcriptions, 292
Elkins, West Virginia: playing in, 237
Elkmont, Alabama
  life in, 1-2, 8, 9
  old fiddlers' contest at, 43
Elk River, fishing on, 4-6, 8
Emma, Aunt (Black woman), 184
Estes, Milton, 218n
Everly Brothers, 87

"False Hearted Girl," 295

Fan mail, 108, 121-22, 134-35, 204, 208, 211

    answering, 141

Farrell, Maury: visits with, 262

Federal Radio Commission, 82n, 292

Fibber McGee & Molly, 183

Fiddle player, problems with, 255-59

Fiddlers' contests. *See* Old-time fiddlers' contests

Fighting, 36-37

Fishing, 4-6, 250-53

Fitzgerald, Ella, ix

Florence Road: living on, 22, 26

Flu epidemic, 33

Foley, Red, 234

Ford, Tennessee Ernie, 286, 295

Fort Smith, Arkansas: radio stint at, 285, 290

Foster, Fred, 99

Foster, Stephen, 87

Foster Music Co., 99

Fox, Curly, 135n, 176, 269, 286

Fox, Texas Ruby, 135, 135n, 136, 143, 269, 286

"Fox Chase," 288

Frank, J. L. "Joe," 182-93, 207n, 214, 215

    promotions by, 209-10

    Texas Drifter and, 211, 213

Frederick, Maryland: living in, 238-39, 242

Freeman, Dave, xv

"Freight Train Boogie," 289

Fritche, Barbara, 239

Fruit Jar Drinkers, 87, 96

Gabbard, Rusty, 178

Garland, Hank "Sugarfoot," 72

Gennett company, 158n

George Washington National Forest, 237

Georgia Wildcats, 173n

Ghost light, story about, 15-18

Gillespie, Mrs., 232, 233

Gillespie Tire Co., sponsorship from, 232

"Girls Don't Worry My Mind, The," 60, 67n

    recording, 67

Glosson, Lonnie, 285, 290

    at WMC, 288

    working with, 287

Glover, Henry, 289-90

"God Put a Rainbow in the Cloud," 57

"Goin' Back to the Blue Ridge Mountains," 290

Golden West Cowboys, 182, 183, 209

    playing with; 214-15

"Gonna Lay Down My Old Guitar," viii, 130n

Gospel music, ix-x, xii

"Got the Kansas City Blues," 45, 67n-playing, 60

    recording, 66

Grand Ole Opry, viii, x, xii, 48, 94n, 99, 153, 179, 185-88

    auditioning for, 69-80

    fiddling contest and, 190-92

    leaving, 193,199, 201, 208-18

    listening to, 34, 72

    memories of, 73, 94-102, 103, 151

    performing in Memphis, 106

    money from, 86

    National Barn Dance and, 99n

personal appearances and,105
playing for, 81, 141, 172, 175, 209
problems with, 86, 92-93, 127, 128, 137
visitors from, 134
WSM and, 82
Gray, Glen, 120n
Great Depression, recording industry and, 64, 68n
"Great Speckled Bird, The," 196, 196n, 204
playing, 202
Green; Ranger Doug, xv
Greenville, South Carolina: living in, 230-31, 232-35
Grove Avenue, living on, 136, 137, 139-41, 175, 176
Guitars, buying, 35
Gully Jumpers, 100n

Hackley, Ken: bookings by, 255
Hagerstown, Maryland:, musicians union at, 242-43, 245
Hall, Roy, 236
Hardwick, Jim, 284
Harkreader; Fiddlin' Sid, 109
Harper, Richard, 94-95
Harris, Texas Jack, 125, 286
Harrison, Bill, xiv, 39n, 41n
on Alton's writing, xiii
Harrisonburg, Virginia: living in, 237
Hatcher, Dynamite, 196n
Hattiesburg, Mississippi: radio stint at, 295
Hay, George D., 96, 99n, 106, 149-50, 174, 186, 196n, 214,215
Acuff and, 196, 197, 207n

Bailey and, 179, 180
illness of, 107, 107n
Hayden, Mr., 246, 247-48
Heflin, Tom, 53
Herron, Red, 176
Hess, Jake, ii
Hill, Mr., 222
confrontation with, 224, 226
letter from, 223
working for, 220, 221
"Hillbilly Boogie," composing, 287
"Hobo and the Cop, The," 211n
"Hobo Bill's Last Ride," 166n
"Hobo's Lullaby," 211n
Hobo songs, 210-11n
Hoeptner, Fred, 211n
Homer & Jethro, 289
"Honeysuckle Rose," playing, 91
Hopkinsville, Kentucky: playing in, 211-12
Hornsby, Dan, 60, 60n, 65
Houston, Texas: living in, 286, 293
"Hucklebuck, The," 289
Hulan, Dick, 180n
Huntsville, Alabama: living in, 295
Husky, Ferlin, 87
Hutcherson, Bert, 100n
Hymns, singing, 202-3

"I Ain't Got Nowhere to Travel," 77, 139
"I'd Rather Die Young," 123
"I Have But One Goal," 254
"I Like Molasses," 202
"I'm Mississippi Bound," 77
Indianapolis, Indiana: living in, 285, 286

INDEX

"I Needed You," 294

Innis, Louis, 283, 287

"I Was Country When Country Wasn't Cool," xii

Jackson, Mississippi: radio stint at, 285,290

Japanese-Americans, prejudices against, 268

Jenkins, Andrew, 56, 63

Jenkins, Snuffy, 235n

Jim & Jesse, viii

Jim the Greek, working for, 29-30

Johnny & Jack, 90, 254

Johnson, Mr. (principal): encounters with, 25-26

Jones, Grandpa, viii, 274, 275, 279, 280, 281n, 283

Jones, Red, 196n, 198n

Journal of Country Music (CMF), xv

"Just One Way to the Pearly Gates," 169n

KARK (Little Rock, Arkansas), working at, 287

Kessinger, Clark, 176

Key, Francis Scott, 239

King, Pee Wee, 182-93, 209, 218n

King Record Company, viii, x, xiv, 281, 281n

recording for, 287, 293

Kingston Trio, 87

KPRC (Houswn, Texas), working at, 286, 293

Ladies' Home Journal, 32

Lair, John, 50n

Lang, Eddie: listening to, 33

Lanson, Snooky, xi, 120, 125

Lasses & Honey, 143

"Leavin' Town/ 288

"Left My Gal in the Mountains," 63

Lester (childhood friend), 24

Lillie, Aunt, 3

Limestone Democrat, stories in, 83

Linotype machines, fixing, 31, 33

Loew's Theatre, Uncle Dave at, 114n

Long, Huey, 166, 167

Louisville, Kentucky: playing in, 106-7

Louisville Courier Journal, 32

Louvin Brothers, viii, 87

Lucas; Nick, 84, 88

listening to, 33

"Lucky Ol Sun," 123

Lusk/Lust, Sydney: working for, 246

McCarthy, Bob, 281n

McCormick, Ma: working with, 272-73

McCormick, Pa, 282, 283

working with, 272-73

McGee, Kirk, 87, 103-17, 136, 156, 158n, 172

McGee, Sam, 87, 103-17, 136, 156, 158n, 172

McLemore, Bee, 61, 70

Atlanta trip and, 51, 54, 55

McMichen, Clayton, 49, 56; 173n, 176

talent discovery by, 173-74

Macon, Dorris, 96, 108

Macon, Uncle Dave, vii, xi, 61, 87, 96, 101, 114n, 145, 147, 174

car buying and, 114-17

circuit playing by, 148-49, 150, 151

Delmore parents and, 110-11
fan mail for, 108
personal appearances with, 143
prank on, 111-14
recording by, 157, 158, 158n, 169, 169n, 170-71
visits from, 136, 140-41
working with, 103-17, 141-42
Mad dogs, fear of, 9
Mainer, J. E., 292
Managers, 87, 101, 220
booking with, 266, 267
Mathews, Mr. and Mrs.: help from, 103, 132-34
Maudlin, Chuck, 218n, 251n
deep sea fishing and, 251
Melotone label, 196n
Melton, James, 120
Memphis, Tennessee
Grand Ole Opry performing in, 106
living in, 285, 286-87
Miller, Bob, 55, 60, 60n, 67, 67n, 69, 97
letter from, 51
meeting, 56-57, 61, 65
recording with, 66-68, 68n
Mills Brothers, 238, 245
"Mocking Bird," 169n
Monroe, Bill, 219
Monroe, Charlie, 219
Monroe Brothers, viii, 219, 232
Moody, Ralph, 270
Moon River show, 270
Music, reading, 85, 88
Musicians union, 246
joining, 242-43, 245
problems with, 243-45, 247-48

strike by, 276
Music lessons, 19-20, 27-28
"My Little Home Down in New Orleans," 165, 166n

Nabor, Bob. See Delmore, Rabon
Nashville, Tennessee: living in, 131-42, 172, 216, 218n
Nashville Songwriters' Hall of Fame, 296
Nashville Tennessean, 94n
Natchee the Apache, 176, 178, 254
Nathan, Sydney, 289
meeting, 278-79
problems with, 280-81
Nation's Station. See WLW
National Barn Dance (WLS), Grand Ole Opry and, 99n
National Life & Accident Insurance Company, 120n, 275
convention, 118, 119
NBC network
auditioning for, 239-41
working for, 260
"Near You," 120
Neely, Elsie, 184
Neely, Thelma. See Delmore, Thelma Neely
Network programs, auditioning for, 239-42, 243
New Orleans, Louisiana: recording in, 155, 157-58, 167-68
"Night Train To Memphis," 23
"Ninety-Nine Years," 97
"No Help Wanted," 254
Norris, Fate, 61
North Carolina, touring in, 219-31

Oberstein, Eli, 88, 89, 89n, 126, 127, 155n
  recording with, 155, 156, 167-71
  Uncle Dave and, 157
O'Brien, Smiley, 218n, 251n
  deep sea fishing and, 251
Odom, Tennis: playing with, 28
"Oh, Carry Me Back to the Land of My Dreams," 66
Okeh label, 196n, 211n
Old Athens Agricultural School, old fiddlers' contest at, 39n, 47
Old Cabin Co., Inc., 129n, 130n
Old Cabin Songs for the Fiddle & the Bow As Sung by the Vagabonds, 129n
Old fiddlers' contests, 190-92
  competing in, 39, 41-50, 71, 72, 74
  popularity of, 39n
"Old Master Painter, The," 123
"One More River to Cross," 169n
Orange, Virginia: playing at, 243
"Over the Mountain," 169n

Parham, Russell, 145, 147-51
  advertising by, 146
  working with, 144
Parker, Colonel Tom, 183, 210
Paul and Bert, 100, 100n
Pearl Harbor day, 268
Peek, George; 216, 225, 227, 248
  auditions and, 239, 240-41, 242, 246
  bookings by, 220, 222, 232-33, 237, 245, 253
  Hill and, 223
  parting with, 254
  praise for, 231

  publicity and, 242
  union troubles and, 243-45
Peer, Ralph, 89n
  Rodgers and, 162, 162n
Pennsylvania, playing in, 264-65
Penny, Hank, 283
Perfect label, 196n
Personal appearances, 103-17, 136, 143, 272, 293
  Grand Ole Opry and, 86
  making, 172, 192, 193
  stopping, 185-86, 187
Petrillo, Boss, 277
  musician's strike and, 276, 276n.
Pickard, Obed, 102
Pickard Family, 79, 94n, 99n, 101-2
"Please Come Back Little Pal," 236
Poe, Edgar Allan, 88
Poole, Charlie, vii
Poplin, W. E. stringband, 94n
Possum Hunters, 96
Poteau, Oklahoma: show at, 291-92
Poulton, Curt, 130n
"Praise God! He Loves Everybody," 294
Presley, Elvis, 183, 210
Princess Theatre, playing at, 144-47, 149, 150
Printing office, working at, 30-32, 34-35
Puckett, Riley, ix, 49, 50n, 56, 67n
  listening to, 33

"Race with Model T Ford," 288
"Railroad Boomer," 211n
Railroads, fascination with, 2
Raleigh, North Carolina: living in, 216, 217, 222

Rambling, songs about, 32-33

Raney, Wayne, 91, 285, 287, 289
  songwriting by, 290
  at WMC, 288

Ray, Baby, 104

RCA Victor Records, 88, 155, 280
  contract with, 263
  recording for, 168, 171
  songwriting for, 126
  See also Victor Records
  making, 46, 51-68, 152-71, 294
  selling, 126

Red Boiling Springs, Tennessee: playing
  in, 105

"Red Rose," 120, 121

Reeves, Goebel. *See* Texas Drifter

Renfro Valley Barn Dance, 50n

R. E. Winsett (company), x

Rice, Tony, viii

Richmond, Ace, 254

Riders in the Sky, xv

Rinehart, Cowboy Slim, 292

Ritter, Tex, 264-65
  playing with, 267-68

Roanoke, Virginia: playing at, 236-37

Robbins, Marty, 84

Robert (childhood friend), 24

Robison, Carson, 66, 67
  listening to, 33

Roche, Dorv, 104

Rockabilly, 289

Rodgers, Jimmie, vii, ix, xi, 162n, 211n
  death of, 159n
  family of, 152-71
  film by, 164n
  listening to, 33
  remembering, 161-66, 166n

Will Rogers and, 163-64, 164n

Rodgers, Tal, 159-60, 166, 166n, 171
  on Jimmie Rodgers, 161-65

Rodgers, Mrs. Tal, 161

Rogers, Roy, 177

Rogers, Will: Jimmie Rodgers and,
  163-64, 164n

Roosevelt, Franklin D., 268

Roosevelt Lounge, performance at,
  294

Rose, Fred, xi, 72-73
  visits from, 137-39

Ross, Buddy, 283

"Rounder's Blues," 288

Royalties, 67, 293, 295
  problems collecting, 126-27

Rust, Brian, 166n

"St. Louis Blues," playing, 48

Salt, Frank, 143, 144

Salt & Peanuts, 143, 144

"Salty Dog," 49

San Antonio, Texas: performing in,
  285, 293

Sands, Tommy, 286

Sargent, Kenny, 120n

Saturday Evening Post, xiii, 32, 295

Schlappi, Elizabeth: on Acuff, 207n

Schneider, Doc, and his Texans:
  working with, 233-34

Schooling, 6-7, 25-26, 27, 30

Schools, playing at, 146, 232, 234-35

Scott, Jim. *See* Delmore, Alton

*Sentimental Songs from the Heart of the
  Hills*, 130n

Sepia, 88

Sharecropping, 1-2, 7-8, 12-13

INDEX

Shelton Brothers, viii

Sheppard Brothers, 281n

Sherrill, Homer, 235n

Shore, Fannie Rose (Dinah), xi, 119-20

Silver Spring, Maryland: playing at, 246

Singing Brakeman, The (film), 164n

"Sixteen Tons," 295

Sizemore, Asher, 143, 254

Sizemore, Little Jimmie, 143, 254

Skaggs, Ricky, viii

Skillet Lickers, ix, 49n, 60n

Smith's Sacred Singers, 50n

Smith, Arthur, xi, 87, 155,-155n, 157n, 158, 169n, 171, 174, 176, 178
  Acuff and, 207n Bailey and, 179
  recording by, 168-69
  songwriting by, 156-57

Smith, Beasley, 122-23

Smith, George: traveling with, 71-72

Smith, Homer, 155n

Smith Brothers, 254

"Smoky Mountain Bill," 67

"Smoky Mountain Bill and His Song," 67, 67n

Songwriting, 26-27, 43-45, 48-50, 72-73, 137-38, 156, 288, 295
  advice on, 85
  collecting for, 126-27

Sons of the Pioneers, 241

"Southern Moon," 155

Southern University Quartet, recording by, 169, 169n, 170

Speer Family, xii

Stokes, Lowe, 56

Stone, David, 193, 194, 207n, 215

Acuff and, 199-200, 201, 205

artist service and, 186-87 auditions and, 197-98

fiddling contest and, 190-92

problems for, 188-90

Stone, Harry, 95, 100, 103, 127, 177, 181
  audition with, 73-80
  circuit playing and, 150
  Hay illness and, 107n
  leaving, 214, 215
  problems with: 101, 118-19, 128
  raise from, 98-99

Stone Mountain Memorial, visiting, 58

Stowe, Tiny, 96

Sudekum, Mr., 144, 148, 150

Sudekum Circuit, playing, 135, 143, 149

Summey, Clell, 198n

Sunbrock, Larry, 176, 177, 178

Sun Records, 289

"Swingin'," xv

Syd's (Nathan's) Record Shop, 277

"Talking Blues," 49

Talking harmonicas, 287, 288

Tanner, Gid, 49, 56, 61

Tarlton, Jimmie, 56

Tennessee Band, 60n

Tennis, Zed, 283

Terry, Bill, 104-5

Texas Drifter (Goebel Reeves), xi, 210-11, 210-11n
  eccentricities of, 211-14

Texas Ruby. *See* Fox, Texas Ruby

"That's Why I'm Jealous of You," 42, 138

INDEX

"That Old Train," 294

"That Silver Haired Daddy of Mine," 78

Theatres, playing at, 144-46, 221-22, 234-35, 265

"There's More Pretty Girls Than One," viii, 156-57, 157n

Tiny (Acuff singer), 198, 198n

"Top of the Morning Show," 273

Tormé, Mel, ix

Tornadoes, fear of, 9-10

"Trail of Time, The," 294

Tramp printers, 31-32

Travis, Merle, viii, 72, 125, 270, 274, 281n, 283
  discovery of, 173
  military service and, 275

Tubb, Ernest, xiii, 73
  discovery of, 210

Tucker, Bobby, 125

Turner, Grant, 107n

Turner, Zeb, 234

Turner, Zeke: recordings by, 234

"Twenty-One Years," 67, 67n
  playing, 97

Tyler, T. Texas, 254

Uncle Dave Macon and Dorris, 96
  See also Macon, Dorris; Macon, Uncle Dave

Vagabonds, The, 96; 97
  dispute with, 128-29, 129-30n

Victor Master Book Vol. 2, 166n

Victor Records, 48, 127, 129n, 158n, 264n
  letters to, 43
  recording with, 169n

  strike against, 276n
  See also RCA Victor Records

Village Barn (New York City), turning down, 249

Vocalion label, 196n

Von Braun, Werner, 205

"Wabash Cannonball," 50n, 196, 196n, 204

WALA (Mobile, Alabama), working at, 260

Walker, Frank, 60n

Wanderlust, songs about, 32-33

WAPI (Birmingham, Alabama), working at, 260, 269, 270

War, West Virginia: playing in, 256-57

Warmack, Paul, 100n

Warner Brothers' theaters, playing, 225, 232, 237, 238, 243, 245, 246

Washington, D.C. living in, 246-59
  playing in, 246, 248

Watson, Doc, viii

WCHS (Charleston, West Virginia), 218n

WCKY (Cincinnati, Ohio), 287

Weaver Brothers & Elviry, 109

Wells, Kitty, 90

WFBC (Greenville, South Carolina), 23i

"Whatcha Gonna Gimme," 294

"What Shall I Do with Jesus," 294

"What Would You Give in Exchange for Your Soul," 215

"When It's Lamp Lightin' Time in the Valley," 78, 96

"When the Harvest Days Are Over," 169n

INDEX

White, Lasses (Lasses & Honey), 143

White, Percy, 104

Whitfield, Tom, 131-32

"Why Don't You Haul Off and Love Me," 290

playing, 292

Wilby-Kinsey chain, playing, 234, 238

Willett, Bill, 61

Atlanta trip and, 51, 52-53, 54, 55

Williams, Andy, 270,274

Williams, Hank, 81, 141, 234, 271n

on publicity, 175

Williams, Jake, 74-75, 76, 78, 79, 81

Williams, Prater: staying with, 96-97, 98

Williams, Will: hymn singing with, 19, 22

Williams Brothers, 270, 274-75

Wills, Bob, 47, 280, 290

Wilmington, North Carolina: playing in, 223-24, 225

Winchell, Walter, 166

Winston-Salem, North Carolina: playing in, 226-30, 236

WLS (Chicago, Illinois) competition from, 99, 101-2 WSM and, 99n

WLW (Cincinnati, Ohio), 97, 173n, 218n,285

auditioning at, 270-71

working at, 269, 270, 272-84, 286

WMC (Memphis, Tennessee), playing at, 90, 286, 288

WNOX (Knoxville, Tennessee), 196n

Wood, Britt, 109

WPTF (Raleigh, North Carolina), working at, 214,217

WRC (Washington, D.C.), audition for, 239-41

Wright Aircraft, 281

WROL (Knoxville, Tennessee), 196n

WSM (Nashville, Tennessee), 75, 86, 96, 97, 99, 103, 183, 186, 196, 239, 269, 272, 275

Grand Ole Opry and, 82

leaving, 214, 218n

minstrel show on, 143

personal appearances and, 105

personalities at, 118-30

playing at, x, xi, 174

start up of, 82n

WLS and, 99n

XERF (Del Rio, Texas), playing on, 292

Young, Jess, 60n

Zinkan, Joe, 218n, 237

deep sea fishing and, 250-52